The Confession of Dorothy Danner

for Dana

. . . each life harbors a mystery. Our motives are hidden, even from ourselves. Our dreams and our impulses surprise us. And with every action we are capable of surpassing what we already are. Our future is unpredictable, the past indefinite. There is no way to map the boundaries of the soul and no system for calculating its contents.

Abraham Heschel, *Who Is Man?,* as paraphrased in L. Langness and G. Frank, *Lives: An Anthropological Approach*

Contents

Acknowledgments

I want to thank the College of Arts and Science of Vanderbilt University, and especially former Dean Jacque Voegeli, for providing resources and moral support for my Mobile project. I appreciate, too, my year as Fellow at the Robert Penn Warren Center for the Humanities among colleagues who also studied aspects of the American South; the Center was a safe haven for my emerging thoughts about culture and political life.

Many friends and acquaintances read and made helpful comments on the text of Dorothy's life in one of its many manifestations. Two of my colleagues, Phyllis Frus and Nancy Walker, offered especially valuable and timely critical support and commentary. I thank them all.

Some of Dorothy's family and friends were interviewed along the way, making known to me their own stories as much as hers, and I appreciate their cooperation.

Most of all, I wish to thank Dorothy for sharing the story of her life with me.

Introduction

THE

ENCOUNTER

Dorothy was waiting for me.

Not literally me, it is true, but she did want someone to hear her story, to bear witness to the triumphs and tragedies of her life, just as each of us who has reached a certain age waits for someone who will listen attentively as we seek to establish meaning in the life we have lived.

Dorothy may have gotten more than she expected.

She wanted to be noticed and, in some small way, to be celebrated. But as we talked, over the years, I came to feel that she was attempting a kind of confession, to what crime or sin I did not know, and that I was there as prosecutor or priest, as much as witness. I have tried to set down reliably what she told me, but I know I have myself entered into the story in a variety of ways. I brought my own issues and perspectives to the relationship and, surely, to the telling.

Before Dorothy lays out her story and we hear the accusations made against her, you must know something of the context. Only then can you, as reader, do your part.

In 1986, I was in Mobile doing research on school desegregation and, more broadly, on racial politics. I had published a book on the politics of busing for racial balance in Nashville and wanted to do something similar on Mobile. It was supposed to be journeyman's work for an established scholar.

The general outline of recent Southern history was well-known to me, but I wanted to discover what had happened in Mobile particularly. Unlike Montgomery, Selma, Birmingham, and seemingly all other Alabama cities, Mobile had not been in the headlines during the Civil Rights movement. Martin Luther King, Jr., had not brought his forces to bear on the city. I wanted to know if this had been because Mobile had been too tough for the movement to challenge or because it had acceded to change readily, making strident protest unnecessary.

I began to use the clipping files at the *Mobile Press Register* for my research, and the editor of that newspaper published a little story concerning my purpose there that summer. It was the kind of story easily passed by, but Dorothy noticed it and sought me out.

When I returned her telephone call, Dorothy explained that she had been the first person to try to desegregate the public schools in Mobile; she had done so through her Negro foster-daughter, Caroline. Would I not like to hear her story? Yes, I said, I was interested, and I became more so when I mentioned her name to one of the librarians at the *Press Register*, who offered vaguely that Dorothy was a notable person from a prominent old Mobile family.

Dorothy had explained where she lived, and I went there the next day. I drove south from the shaded covering of huge live oak trees and old mansions along Government Street into a black neighborhood of well-kept single family residences. The house on South Washington Street to which I was directed was a neat, flower-bordered, white frame structure sitting next to the Dollie Temple Church of Christ in God. Dorothy met me on the porch in a sleeveless cotton summer dress, escorted me into her sitting room, put her little dog in the kitchen out of the way, and brought out ice water for us both. She was gracious, sure of herself, and comfortable among her fine old furnishings. She sat erect and attentive in her chair facing me, but I remember most of all that she was respectful—respectful of me as an author and professor in a way that quite reversed the social hierarchy I was prepared to accept as her younger, male guest.

We exchanged pleasantries, and she told me what she had done in 1956. She wanted to be sure that her story was part of my book on school desegregation.

Introduction

Caroline
(née Carrie Mae), 1956

She had, she said, taken the child of her black maid into her home in 1950, when Carrie Mae was six. The child, who grew up to call herself Caroline, had lived with her, had in fact been raised in elegant surroundings, had been taken to Europe for two years to get away from segregation, and had been put into the finest private schools there. Then, in 1956, just after Alabama passed the Pupil Placement Law, they returned to Mobile, where Dorothy had tried to enroll Carrie Mae in the white school to which she ought to have been assigned because of her intelligence and accomplishment. Dorothy reminded me that the Pupil Placement Law provided that children should be placed in schools depending on their interests, aptitudes, and available space.

She said she was not altogether surprised when the school board had turned her down. Then, she said, the Ku Klux Klan had burned a cross in her driveway.[1] A second cross was burned. Reporters had called her from all over.

In response to my questions, she told me how she had felt: excited but outcast. Her father had gone off to Mississippi to get away from the embarrassment.

As she sat there, so erect and proud, I came to sense the courage and moral strength it must have taken for her to stand up in those days for what she believed was right.

I asked her about Caroline. She said she may have been *using* Caroline to challenge the system, but that thought had come to her only recently. *Ebony* magazine had done an article on black children raised in the white world; I could look there to see what Caroline had thought.[2] I got the impression that what Caroline had said there had been hurtful.

When I pressed, she deflected the question. Trying to desegregate the schools was not the only way she had attempted to work for racial justice, she said. She had done other things earlier, before the Civil Rights movement had really gotten started. For example, in the

1. *Mobile Press Register*, Sept. 18, 1956.
2. *Ebony*, June, 1974, pp. 84–94.

late 1940s she had paid for a lawyer to come all the way from Birmingham to help a young black woman seek justice in court.[3] Again in the 1940s, she had started the Mobile Inter-racial League, whose members tried to desegregate some white churches by attending services on Sunday morning in the company of blacks. They had not been very successful.

Dorothy said more, mainly it seemed to me, to show how deeply her commitment had run: her black friend, Major Madison, had used her car to carry people to register to vote when that was still a provocative act. Constance Diane Madison, his daughter, was her godchild; Dorothy had bought her clothes when she was preparing to go away to college. Dorothy and her friends, Mildred and Frances Laurendine, had led a successful letter-writing campaign to get the death sentence of a black man convicted of raping a white Mobile girl commuted to life in prison.

Questions formed themselves in my mind: Why had she done these things? Why had this well-to-do Southern woman defied the expectations of her culture and class so egregiously? Did this have anything to do with why she now lived in a black area of town? Did she live on South Warren out of idealistic commitment or symbolic ostracism? What had her family thought? What had become of the child? What had been the price of protest?

During the next hour or so she told me pieces of her life story, generally moving backwards from 1956, until I grasped enough of it to insist that we start at the beginning. As I look back now, I am struck by how confident and factual she was in the first excited telling of the story, certainly more so than later.

I was attracted by Dorothy's commitment. At a time when so many people nakedly pursued their own immediate gratification at the expense of long-term community well-being, Dorothy seemed to be the prototype of the *good citizen*, someone who could see the common good and sacrifice her own interest for that good. She had a moral vision, and she lived it out fully and consistently despite the

3. *Mobile Press Register,* Nov. 19, 1948, and May 10, 1949.

burden it placed on herself and her family and friends. It seemed to me exactly the model of good citizenship that many more of us will have to emulate if we are ever to face the great issues which so divide our country.

I wanted to find out why Dorothy had been moved to protest when so many had not, to discover if the energy she spent living out her principles had been recognized and appreciated, or denigrated and ignored.

Dorothy told me she had three causes which were central to her life: racial justice, pacifism, and animal rights. When I asked her where these convictions had come from, she said only that somehow certain ideas had caught on. "I might have gotten religion," she observed, "but instead I got these."

She said she had done many things because of her convictions about simple justice. Her protests had caused her some pain and had certainly separated her from her family and others of her social class, but she had "never felt authentic in that life anyway."

Pacifism was her first cause, she said. It had begun during World War II, and her stand had confused and angered her first husband and her father. Only in the Fellowship of Reconciliation, the international pacifist organization, had she found people with whom she could share ideas and whose inspiration gave her strength and support. There was no local chapter of FOR, but over the years she had gone to many conferences. In the early 1950s she had refused to pay that portion of her income taxes that would go for military purposes, as part of a pacifist protest, but her father had betrayed her stand. He put money in the bank in her name, so that the IRS could seize it in lieu of her taxes and penalties. This angered her, and she resented it deeply.

Her protests continued in other forms for decades, though. On July 4, 1977, while attending a War Resisters League conference, she was arrested with many others for protesting against nuclear weaponry at the Trident submarine base in Washington state. She spent eleven days in jail when, in further protest, she refused to pay her fine. Among those arrested, she was the last to give in. On April

10, 1982, she was arrested in Beatty, Nevada, for protesting nuclear bomb tests in the desert. She had broken through the government's barrier with Daniel Ellsberg and others.

Dorothy went on, unprompted, to list her protests, in the way that war veterans speak of their military campaigns. She had had strong feelings about the suffering of animals before she heard of the animal rights movement. Even as a young child she remembered how she hated to see worms put on hooks. Somehow animal rights were tied to the other two issues. Perhaps, she said, she identified with the victim. In any case, she had now become very active in the movement. In April 1985, she had picketed Mobile city hall protesting the practice of selling dogs from the city pound to medical schools for research purposes. In October she was arrested five times for obstructing the operation of the dog pound, and was finally forced to spend thirty days in jail and pay $3500 in fines.

Why had she done these things? Was she part of a determined cadre of local reformers, or did she act alone? Did she do any good?

Over the months, as I reflected, queries such as these directed at Dorothy, were supplanted by other, more analytical questions, aimed at myself: Was she a determined heroine of the New South? Was she a con woman trying to mislead a gullible professor? Or was she perhaps just a crazy old lady who had lost her sense of proportion and propriety? How could I know what was true in her story? What was there about my own life that drew me so forcefully into the story she was unfolding? Ultimately, how do we come to judge a human life?

This book is the result of an impulse to know more about this interesting woman, and about her time and place. Periodically, over the next six years, I interviewed Dorothy whenever I went to Mobile to work on my larger research project. I always found her an eager participant, even when her already breathy, weak voice began to fade. (She had inadequate lungs, she said, and because of misguided surgery, damaged vocal chords.) I visited with her in her homes, first on South Warren and later on Kilmarnock Street in another refurbished wood-frame house in a racially mixed part of Mobile.

Her family affectionately called her "Boots," but I always addressed her as Dorothy, just as she said I should. Over time I came to know her as a person as well as a character in her own story. Her frugality, for example: when she invited me out to lunch, she took me to the hospital cafeteria on one occasion and to her church on another, regular haunts both, because one got the best value for money there. Her estrangement from her family: her cousin Mary Bacon would invite her over to her house on Dorothy's birthday just to be nice, although they were otherwise estranged, and the others kept their distance. Her feelings about Caroline: the disappointment she felt, mixed with guilt and caring. Her heroes: rugged, brave men, now almost all dead and gone. Other things.

What follows is the confession that Dorothy made to me over the years. It moves by fits and starts, my questions prompting her easy recollections or sometimes obstinate deflections. The story proceeds chronologically, since that was the way I asked her to tell it, but there are the inevitable, revealing lapses and digressions. I always had the feeling Dorothy wanted her story made known—I did not have to tear it from her. It is as if this book is her testimony, the justification for a life lived on the edge of change, still seeking triumph but perhaps ending sadly.

This is Dorothy's story, but I am always there. An attentive reader will note my presence throughout the narrative. Occasionally, though, there are particular reminders, indicated by parentheses and brackets. Parentheses show comments made by Dorothy during her storytelling that are out of time or context and signal something of contemporary significance. These comments are like basting stitches in sewing; they tie the present and past together in loose but useful ways. Brackets serve another purpose, signaling Dorothy's immediate emotional reaction to her own story, especially in response to something I may have asked or said.

After Dorothy tells her story, four other witnesses are called on to offer their own testimonies on parts of Dorothy's life: her foster-daughter, Caroline; that daughter's ex-husband, Ralph; her first-cousin, Mary Bacon. Although long dead, Dorothy's father, Paul, is clearly the most important person in her life, and he will speak to us through his many letters.

Paul Danner (left),
with Dorothy's grandfather
(Capt. Albert Carey Danner),
two of Paul's sisters,
and his nephew

In the 1860s, Dorothy's grandfather, Albert Carey Danner, was posted to Mobile, Alabama, by the Confederate Army. He remained there after the war, built a fortune, and became a leading citizen. His son Paul Danner, Dorothy's father, carried on the family's businesses in timber, veneers, and coal, even through the hard years of the 1930s. But the Danner firms are all gone now. This branch of the Danner line will end with Dorothy.

Mobile is a place where families are known by their present characters as much as by their past achievements. Yet Dorothy is unique. Listen to her story and see if you too are not fascinated.

Important issues arise from these encounters—issues about the possibilities for truth and about the meaning made of lives when they are told and written and read. The story Dorothy relates to us about her own life is not supported entirely by other witnesses. Whose voice shall we trust? Moreover, it is clear that she remembers and recounts selectively. Are these public recollections the wheat or the chaff of her life?

A palpable tension arises between the present, fractured and partial account of Dorothy's life, told to us in different voices, and everyone's clear desire to have a final and meaning-filled version, a story that lets us know that in the end, life—both hers and ours alike—is not a random walk but a clear pattern. What, then, is the pattern of Dorothy's life? Is it discerned or imposed? Does it matter? These and other issues are taken up later, in the conclusion, after Dorothy's confession and the testimony of others have been given.

This book is about the making of a life story. I am not interested in objective truth so much as I am in reporting the long struggle to fashion a story that reveals and satisfies. I could have written a book different from this one. The epilogue gives a glimpse of how it might have been done, with an impersonal, authoritative narrator interleaving records of public events and private suppositions into one coherent theme. But I believe that book would be less revealing, even if perhaps more dignified, than the one you now have in your hands.

One

THE LIFE

1 Formation

You may call me Dorothy.

I was born in Mobile, Alabama, on February 24, 1916. My earliest recollections: I lived in a big stucco house with a tile roof at 1954 Government Street with my mother and father, my mother's sister, Aunt De De, and a maid from Guatemala. That was our household. I was an only child. It was a conventional family.

I went to birthday parties. I loved birthday parties! I went to Sunday school at the Presbyterian Church, studied the catechism, and read little tiny bits of the Bible that were assigned in children's classes. Once my father heard a story that I brought back from Sunday School. The teacher was reading a book by somebody who had died and gone to heaven. I remember that upset him very much, that such foolishness was being put into my mind. He didn't like it a bit: the idea of someone dying, and going to heaven, and coming back talking about it.

My father's sister's husband died in Quincy, Illinois, and Aunt Venetia bought the lot next door to us and built a house on it. She had three children, one of whom was in the first grade with me. That was Mary Bacon, Mrs. Howard Barney now. We called her Bacon or Bake. We went through school together until my mother died. We looked a lot alike and people would call us each other's names. I'll tell you more about her in a minute.

I was the tallest in my picture at Leinkauf Elementary School, and I've usually been the tallest. Mary Bacon was also tall. Of course, girls

Dorothy,
age four

don't like being tall, they'd rather be a little smaller. I'm five feet eight and a half. Well, that's the average for *men*, so fifty percent of the men are shorter than I, and with high-heels on that makes seventy-five percent shorter. That's a social problem. Actually, though, it's an advantage to be taller; you are able to reach things in cupboards if you have more size physically.

Harriet was one of our friends. Harriet's aunt was the president of the girls' school. It was called Wright's, the girls' preparatory school. It was the sister school to University Military School—UMS—the boys preparatory school. Wright's started when we were in the third grade. We all went over there and stayed together in the same class until eighth grade, when I was sent away because my mother died.

My mother was operated on for a hysterectomy by Dr. McGehee. I've forgotten his given name—we called him Tiny McGehee. Paul McGehee, that's it. He was a general practitioner, and a friend of the family's. I've spoken to a gynecologist who told me a general practitioner is not legally allowed to do hysterectomies anymore. They say Tiny killed three women—of course, it hurt him a great deal—by cutting into the ileum, that's a part of the small intestine. That's why my mother died. On her death certificate is "paralytic ileum," and when you read about it you discover it's usually from surgery, from never recovering. She was only thirty-six.

She didn't need to have a hysterectomy anyway. There was nothing wrong with her womb when it was taken out, but my father read the death certificate wrong because I've taken it to doctors since then. It has "N" and a period, "Cancer," which means negative for cancer. But my father apparently just saw that "cancer," and he always said she died from cancer, as his mother did from breast cancer. He was very upset about my mother's death. He never married again.

Well, I wish he had married. I wanted him to marry. Seems like one or the other of us would have married; neither of us really did. I married, but I didn't stay married. We stayed these two lonely people, with each other mostly. I think Father was a man who found it very difficult to get close to people, and my mother was the opposite. She was able to make him feel really at home in life, with other people, and in marriage.

I wish I could be more like her, but I think I'm more like my father.

I think Father felt a real commitment toward being a parent. Mary Bacon, Bake, has a good many scrapbooks to this day, and she has one her mother kept, and her mother wrote down at the time of my mother's death, "Paul said, 'May God help me,' " or something like that. I think he was unprepared to be a parent, but he took it very seriously.

Aunt De De, my mother's sister, expected, I think, to be called in as a second mother, and would like to have been. After my mother died, she went to New Orleans and worked in a library for the rest of her life. We saw her only at Christmas. She was Dorothea McIntosh, and I was named after her.

In the years before my mother's death I recall some things well. I went away to camp, and I enjoyed swimming, and I became a Junior Red Cross Lifesaver. I was about eight years old when I first went to camp. I went to Camp Merrie Woode, at twelve, in North Carolina, and Camp Nakanawa at thirteen and fourteen in Mayland, Tennessee.

No, I don't think I felt isolated at camp. Bake was outstanding, though. She was a real athlete. She won the diving competition. Everything she did, she did well. She was good at soccer and tennis, too. She played tennis well into her sixties. In fact, I think she just recently stopped playing.

Now, I sort of fell in love with a girl at camp. Her name was Cathy; she was captain of the Valkyries. We were Amazons and Valkyries. Bake was an Amazon. We had meetings at the campfire at night. It was all very idealistic: team sports, you know, and how to be a good loser and care about the group, the team, instead of trying to shine individually. I was on fire with all that idealism! I never got anything like that at Gulf Park in high school. At Gulf Park—the idea of talking about civil rights, pacifism or anti-vivisection—nobody had heard of anything like that. I guess we didn't talk like that in Tennessee either, but we were idealistic. Our social grouping, you know, was meant to be on this high plain of sportsmanship.

Cathy. I was in love with her. I came back and told my mother: Cathy this, and Cathy that. One should be falling in love with a boy at this age. Mother saw that, but I don't know if that was more serious than I want to think it was or less. I went back the next year, and Cathy and I were friends, and she sent me an invitation to her wedding, and things like that. I guess she lives in Knoxville to this day. I think it was serious, yet I know from my later, mature experiences that I can respond to the male. I mean it hasn't... one or two experiences... I have not been with females, but that was a very real feeling.

When I was young my parents left me once or twice. They went on a trip to Jamaica, and I stayed with Harriet's family; they had a boarding house. They said I cried every day for my mother.

Another time they were going to Europe, in September 1928, when I was at Camp Merrie Woode. I was supposed to be sent back to Mobile. I guess I would have gone to Harriet's house again. I'm not sure. But I waved to my mother—they went off by boat, from the camp boating dock—and my mother said for days after that she kept seeing me waving to them, and she couldn't stand it. In New York she had Father send for me, and got me a ticket, bought clothes and everything at the last minute, and I went with them. My mother just gave in to emotional weakness. I would have been perfectly all right at camp and in Mobile with the family, but I did appreciate it when she let me go along.

Nineteen-twenty-eight. I have a scrapbook of it. I think Father didn't really want me on that trip. Well, he wanted me to eat in the children's dining room instead of up in the big grand room with Mother and him, and I resented that. There were other locally prominent people with them. The president of the bank, Mr. Barry Lyons, and Mr. Francis Inge, whose picture was taken with my mother on the boat going over. Mr. Lyon's wife met us over there. I think Father just wanted to have a more sophisticated time instead of a child-caring type of trip.

I loved it. Well, we had money. You know, it was the last time I

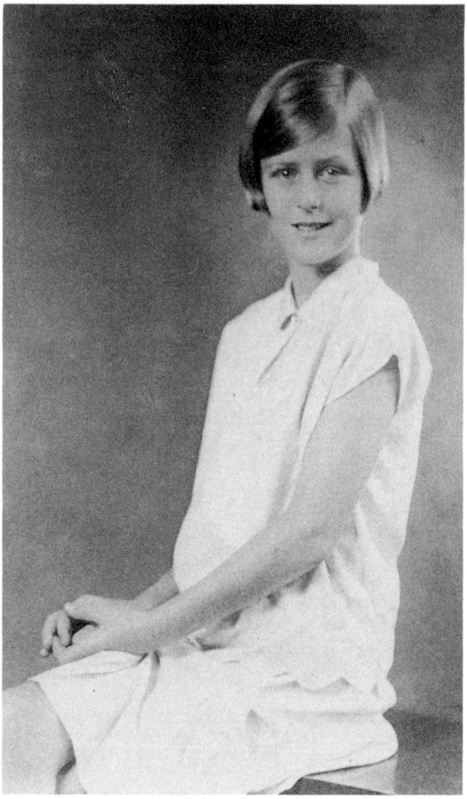

Dorothy,
1927

had money until after my father's death. Things were a lot of fun in 1928. That was when they were doing the Charleston. I was Charlestoning. Mother was Charlestoning. Everybody was doing the Charleston. And the music and the jazz and the women cutting their hair short and smoking cigarettes! Americans were just everything in Paris!

Then, I got very sick over there. We were at one of the famous art galleries, and I was sitting out on those cold marble stairs, and I felt like shivering. I'd been looking at the picture of Joan of Arc where these lights come down to her like angels. We also had the statue of Joan of Arc on a horse in front of our hotel, which was the St. James D'Albany. Anyway, I got a fever and developed pneumonia and pleurisy. I know that wasn't fun for Father. That wasn't the trip he had planned. I had fever of 106 degrees for six days. There wasn't any penicillin to bring it down, and they were talking about cupping, you know putting those little hot things on my skin, but they didn't do it. So, after that I was very thin, about seventy-eight pounds, and I was very weak. I had a cough and a wheeze. It may have damaged my lungs. It may be coming back on me today.

Oh, yes, when I was so sick, I remember the cracks. The wallpaper had too much design on it. That's not good for delirium. I saw these little figures playing violins, moving around. That's what they looked like to me. Then—this was delirium, but I thought it was real—a man tried to get on a street car, and he didn't have any eyes. It was just all skin growing over him. The streetcar conductor tried to kick him out, and I took a knife and put it down on the street car conductor's skull and murdered him—horrible—and I thought I was going to hell. I believed in hell (which I don't anymore), and I told my mother I was going to Hell. She said that wasn't true, that it was just a dream. But those things, those delirious perceptions, stayed with me for years.

I remember I was still talking about it at Holton Arms when I was nineteen. Those hallucinations: I was on a trip, a fever trip. Since then, I have experimented with drugs—I've taken LSD and other things—and I have found out that you're not always sick when you have hallucinations, and that they can be pleasant. But, I've never gone too deeply into it. I'm really not a drug addict or anything.

We missed a couple of months of school, and Mother had someone help me when we got back from Europe. Her name was Frances Whiting (she's from a prominent family, too), and I soon caught up in school. Just about a year later, my mother died. But I was so different a year later; from twelve to thirteen I'd gotten to be huge, and all my hair fell out from the pneumonia. People would hold my hair at school, and I would move away, and they'd have a handful. Well, it grew in curly, but it's not curly now. (This is a permanent. It doesn't last.) But at thirteen I had this new crop of curly hair, and I gained all of my height and weight. I looked like a grown person.

I got very little affection. Very little. Father was just too untouchable.

From my mother, yes. I would crawl in bed with Mother. She had great big breasts. I would move them over so I could get closer to her. She didn't have any type of inhibitions. She bathed in front of me and everything. When I first menstruated, which was before she died, I was thrilled to death, and I ran and told her. I wasn't like some girls, scared and hiding it and everything.

When my mother died, I didn't react with as much sorrow at the time as I have felt all through the years until this day. I miss her. [Dorothy chokes back feeling here.] But at the time, I hate to admit it, I thought that because she had died I could get a new dress that I wanted, one that she wouldn't let me have. I thought I could do what I wanted to do. I guess I have, too, pretty much. But, that's a horrible thing to admit to you. Do you think I should be that honest?

No, I didn't grieve much at the time for my mother. And my Aunt Venetia, Father's sister, who lived next door, didn't approach the death right. She doesn't ever. She always made light of this: She took me over to her house to play with Bacon, and I was jumping on the bed or something silly like that, and she didn't like it. She scolded me. And, I didn't get to see my mother. The visitation was at home, and Father didn't take me to see the casket. I didn't see the service. I guess he was protecting me. But, we did go to the cemetery, and all my school class was there. Two people did the right thing. My friend Harriet came over to see me, and she burst into tears, and also a woman from a prominent family connected with Wright's Girls' School. She's deceased now. She cried, and that was the right feeling. I appreciated that. And that Eva, our Guatemalan maid, she put her arms around me, and she said, "poor little girl, she's lost her mother." I could cry today [chokes back tears] just thinking of it.

Mother died in '29. That was when the crash happened, I believe, right after that trip to Europe when we had money. After that, we didn't have any. Well, Father was an astute businessman, and even though he owed the bank a lot of money, because he bought timber land with a loan, they didn't ever foreclose. They carried his loan without question, even when he couldn't pay it back. I think he closed down the house and moved to an apartment. No, no, he didn't. Not right away.

At thirteen, I went away to Gulf Park High School and College. Father decided to send me there. I think he was probably congratulating himself that he had $800, which I believe was about what the tuition was, and was able to send me there. I didn't want to go. I just have to guess at the reasons he sent me away; I don't really know.

Gulf Park had a beautiful campus. I had my own horse, and rode in horse shows. Father had his horse and came down and rode in shows with me. The school is only about seventy miles from here. It took two hours to get there by car.

They put me a year behind when I went to Gulf Park, which was really bad. It happens frequently. I let the same thing happen to Caroline. Parents shouldn't let it happen. When Wright's closed down, everyone in my class moved to the public schools again. They went into Murphy High School as sophomores, and I went in as a freshman at Gulf Park.

Father wouldn't send me to Murphy High School here in Mobile. He said he was afraid that I'd be a "drugstore cowboy." What we would do is drive cars after school and park at Five Points, which is up here on Ann Street and St. Stevens Road, at a drugstore for curb service, and we'd all get Cokes. We'd hope some boys would come park alongside and talk to us. Father worried about the trouble I'd get into.

Harriet and Mary Bacon went to Murphy. I was the only one to go from Wright's to Gulf Park from my class, and I lost a year. Even to this day I resent it. Oh yeah, and then I lost another year later, through my father, too. I don't think Father realized it, and I didn't either at the time. Two grades. To lose two grades—it's a big thing. That's about as bad as it gets if you are mentally retarded. They never hold people back more than two grades. Anyway, at the time I didn't think about only being a freshman, and their being sophomores. I just thought that I wanted to be at home.

Gulf Park was a nice enough place, if I hadn't been so awful. I hate myself, the way I acted. I was just furious that I was down there. I just went around pouting for three years and not cooperating. I can show you a picture of me pouting. Just acting awful, exactly the way my foster-grandson Alfred acts, the way children should never be allowed to act, but they do. Sometimes nobody knows how to make them stop acting that way.

Gulf Park was a beautiful school. There were about four hundred students in the whole school. My class, the freshmen in high school, only had about eight or ten people in it. I'm guessing. It was a small school. All girls. I think it throws you into a different atmosphere. And Mr. Richard G. Cox, who ran it, ran it for profit. (I was sure he was a Jew, but actually he was Presbyterian, both him and his wife.) He controlled us just as strictly as a whorehouse madam would. There was too much emphasis on how strictly we had to behave with boys and all. It kept us from any unselfconscious types of relationships or any academic or political relationships with boys. We never saw them except at a dance or something, those boys from Gulf Coast Military Academy. But, of course, those were the years of sexual awareness which I don't think we better get into too deeply, because if you break down that barrier, it's hard to know where to stop.

Anyway, at Gulf Park all we ever talked about was boys. There was the purity test. You know, a list of questions about what you'd done sexually, and we'd talk about so and so who failed the purity test, and things like that. I don't know anyone that ever really took it. It may just have been a figment of our imagination. This was ninth, tenth, and eleventh grades.

Miss Cox would measure our evening dresses. They could only be six inches low, from the collar bone I guess, and she would have little pieces of a handkerchief or something that she would pin in if it was more than six inches. Oh, this is absolutely true! She didn't want us to wear much lipstick. I can remember one of the teachers running her finger across my mouth to wipe the lipstick off. That was Cox's mentality. I don't think he was the kind of man who was looking on us as interesting people who would have interesting thoughts at all. He just thought of us as something that men would be after, and that was his main duty to the parents, to keep us locked up.

Cox was in it for money. He admitted it. He wanted a money-making school. It was a beautiful campus; it looked like some big hotel in Miami. Gorgeous grass and everything. We would go swimming the day before the Christmas holidays. That was a big selling point in his catalog, that we could swim that day.

The girls were mostly from the North, Chicago and places like that. They would see these beautiful pictures, and the parents would want to get them into a warmer climate. I didn't feel that they were superior people. Later, when I was at Holton Arms, I did feel that.

I didn't make close friends at Gulf Park. My friends were still here in Mobile. I think I came home every two weeks. I had special permission.

My mother had fixed up Father's house just before the Depression—beautiful new living room furniture and rug and everything. He really allowed us too much freedom to entertain in that room. I don't mean there was any immorality, but I mean, we just didn't need it. We needed more structured types of entertainments with some mothers around, more visible.

We'd have a party, but nobody really gave the parties because it was just the same crowd of people I'd known all along. The boys were hanging around, but we weren't dating. Certainly not in freshman year. I don't know about later. You know, a crowd would meet, a crowd without any engagement ahead of time. You'd sit around and wait for somebody to do something.

If mothers had been there, I think there would have been more little games played, maybe, or a linen table cloth with a bridge set or some pretty things brought in to eat.

I wasn't so very happy, but it was a glorious place to meet. I was angry at my father for making me go to Gulf Park, and I don't know how he could stand it. He said I put up with it nicely, in those letters he wrote to me—that I didn't want to go, but that I never complained—but I thought I complained a lot. I had no idea of any way to approach him to get my own way.

When I came back to Mobile, though, we kids had a good time. Once, I remember, we were left alone, and the boys started a crap game, and they were all around our big hall shooting craps. That's what our get-together had degenerated into. I don't remember the money, I just remember the girls were not part of the entertainment. I think we were sitting on the floor behind that ring of boys. The boys were just enjoying themselves, and Father came in. I think Father was very afraid that I would get into trouble. Go out with some boys and go further than I should, or something. We never talked about that. All that was an unmentionable. Except, I have one letter in here, when I was nineteen, saying, "There are a lot of mistakes that can be made, and I hope you will make as few as possible." That's about as close as he'd come.

Then, we started having dances. We had sororities in high school. I belonged to the Beta sorority at Murphy even though I went to Gulf Park. I think I was the only person that ever did that. Anyway, I had a hard time finding anybody to call out for the dance.

A call out? Well, the girl calls out a boy when a girl's sorority is giving the dance. You're in the grand march when you call out a boy. There's a big tableau. These are very elaborate things. They're gorgeous. I think they were at the Battle House Hotel in those days, now they're in the auditorium. Oh, yes. Mobile has an elaborate social life.

[*Pride:* Would you like to break and have some water?
Danner: No. I'm having too much fun.
Pride: I'm having fun listening.]

I was a sorority "rat" for longer than I should have been. You know, being a rat in any sorority meant you had to take orders and do all sorts of crazy things to humiliate yourself. I could only count the time I was at home from Gulf Park.

Let me tell you about our dance. There's always a theme to a dance, and I don't think we dressed in costumes like we do for the Mardi Gras balls, and I don't remember the theme then, but the president or someone will have a great big bunch of roses. We might all have had them. We would come out with a big band playing, and we would march down the steps from the tableau and our call-out would meet us from somewhere, I don't know from where, he was hidden, and take our arm, and we'd promenade around, and then we'd give them the favors that we had brought along for them. Later, they would have special dances for the call-outs. We didn't have all-program dances.

There were many girls in my sorority, maybe forty. I'm sure it's still the best sorority in Mobile. And, it was very important to belong. I was in because I was well-born, and all my relatives had been Betas. I don't think it would've mattered how good I looked if I hadn't been born into the situation I was and gone to Wright's School.

I never have felt like I was attractive. Well, I know I'm not really homely, and maybe it was my father's stiff attitude about any sexual contact that made me really standoffish or something. Anyway, I just wasn't relaxed around men. The other girls were. Harriet was tremendously popular.

I suppose my mother was attractive. She married at nineteen. If my mother had lived, I think I would have learned her ways, and copied her, the way you do being around somebody, instead of learning Father's aloofness. I think he was a difficult personality. An absolutely honest businessman. Beyond reproach. I mean he was scrupulous, but he was not a person who was ever relaxed.

He was not a handsome man. No, he was ugly. He had a great big nose and an awful small face. Nobody has ever said my father was handsome.

After three years of being exiled to Gulf Park, which was the way I felt about it, I got to go to Murphy my senior year. I begged for it. Or, I don't know if I really begged for it, but I kept on pestering until I prevailed. And when I walked through that entrance to Murphy High School, I just had a mystical feeling. I was so thrilled. I was just so happy to be there. That was just exactly where I wanted to be!

I was included in everything. But I always had to beat the bushes to find somebody to call out for a dance. I didn't have a boyfriend. I just didn't take up with anybody. Or rather, no one took up with me.

Oh, Harriet Little had her choice of everybody. They were just nuts about her. She was voted the most beautiful girl at Murphy. And, she was very sweet, too, and very feminine. People just adored her. And, I did too. So maybe that's sort of homosexual, but I don't think enough to make a big thing out of it. I have a doll upstairs that was bought in 1928 when I had pneumonia, and I have the original shop ticket. It was $50, which was a lot of money back then. Father didn't buy it when I first saw it and wanted it, but then when I got this fever, he went back to that store and bought it, and it was by my bed through all my illness. I was delirious, and I remember my delirium, and I said if I die, give my doll to Harriet. I've still got that doll upstairs.

For years that delirium haunted me. There were some cracks in the ceiling, and I thought these were sort of unattractive, sort of obscene. I thought these were people with distended abdomens who couldn't eliminate—those cracks, that's what they looked like to me.

Where were we? Oh. I know, we were talking about the Beta sorority at Murphy and how happy I was that year at Murphy. But, I had no boyfriend. Oh, we all had dates, but I had no one special. Then, we didn't meet and go with groups anymore; we rotated, and had these elaborate parties with evening dress tuxedos and everything. There were other social circles, lesser than the Beta's, and some of them were just about as good, too. Today, I think they've got them all over the place. Black sororities, too. Probably following the same pattern.

Father closed our house on Government Street that year. I guess he was afraid to have me on his own, so I lived with his sister Mary Donna Frazer, whose son is a president of the bank, at her grandfather's home on Government Street. Father stayed in the St. Charles apartments right across the street. I think that went on for six years, because I believe he was there all during the time I was at Vassar, and he didn't open up the house again until after I graduated from college.

I graduated from Murphy with three stars; four was, I think, the highest number you can get. That's still not really much at Murphy. It was not competitive. But I remember being in a long dress for graduation, and I guess Father was there, but I went alone in my car, I do know that, which is kind of lonely. I don't know why. Father ran for president of the school board that year, and he won it easily. Maybe that's why. I remember what happened afterwards, though—drinking.

I was drinking at that time. We began drinking in Prohibition just like people started smoking dope nowadays. Bootleggers and all: that was part of the scene. It was part of sophistication, the drinking life. I feel that if my mother had been alive I just wouldn't have done those things. Or else, if I'd had a more religious background, because I stopped going to church just about when I went away to school. I would have responded to a religious background.

I don't think I went to any wild parties, but I went to bootleggers. Some of the boys would go to bootleggers to buy whiskey. They drank after their football games, things like that, and we girls wanted to go with them. We wanted to see what it would be like, because there was a lot of talk about bootlegging during Prohibition. We drank this home-made whiskey, you know, dangerous stuff.

I enjoyed it at the time. I just wanted to do it. I didn't really want the whiskey, but that was my idea of an adventure that needed to be lived. A place that needed to be discovered. A state of mind: I wanted to see how your consciousness would change with the alcohol. I thought there was something great to be learned, that being intoxicated would be a great feeling.

I remember one time it wasn't, though. I was fifteen. I must have been a freshman, and my aunt was giving a debut party for Grace Bestor, who's now Ms. Frank Ladd Duvall. She's still alive. She married my cousin who's president of another bank; I have two bank presidents in the family—more than that, my grandfather was one, too. Anyway, I was serving the punch. The boys—this was customary—spiked it. The parents would have this nice punch, and the boys'd come pour this awful whiskey in it. And, I drank it on purpose. I knew it was spiked. I wanted to drink it, and I got deathly ill behind that punch bowl. I mean I was pale and fainting and vomiting. A big boy named Billy Moss and my father had to carry me home and put me to bed. I was ashamed of that. That wasn't fun.

I don't remember smoking, but at Gulf Park they were very strict against it, and they would use spy glasses and everything to see if we were smoking when we went walking on the sea wall. Yes, they did. It was a big thing at Gulf Park to try and smoke. I never got into the habit of smoking until after my father's death. That late. But earlier I smoked a little bit, as a symbol.

Vassar was just the most outstanding school. To me it was.

I didn't think of applying until very late in the year, when we had to be thinking about colleges. There were no guidance counselors back then. Most of the girls in my crowd didn't go very far. Well, one of them went to Randolph Macon. Bake, my cousin Mary Bacon, went to Sweet Briar and didn't like it.

I just told Father I wanted to go to Vassar. I had read something, it might have been in *Time* magazine, that at Vassar you could smoke and drink and have men in your rooms, which was so different from Gulf Park. I resented being locked up, and I think that's why I wanted to go to Vassar. It still has this super-liberal reputation, and I believe that's what drew me there.

Bake went to Sweet Briar and then to Holton Arms. She did not like Sweet Briar. She felt it was just like high school—the classes or something. One reason I went to Vassar was, and this isn't a good reason either, I had a feeling that I gave people the impression of being slightly unstable and wild.

I told you about drinking, for instance. I was the one that wanted to drink. It was important to me symbolically, and I just did it. There was a lot of whiskey around.

I remember a time with Wythe Whiting. His mother was a friend of my father's, and I wish she had married him. Wythe was in First National Bank later, too. He became a prominent man. He's still alive. Anyway, for Christmas one year I think he got about five big gallon jugs of whiskey for his Christmas present, and he was sitting in the middle of them all, practically wanted his picture taken. He was just showing off: it had a lot of status in a way.

For me it wasn't exactly rebellion, it was kind of following an idea. I don't think I was ever publicly drunk—yes, I was, once or twice. But not often. This was after at the Bit and Spur—that's an occasion to do with horse shows—and all of us, twice, we all got drunk. A bunch of boys and girls.

I wanted to be very bright and smart and intelligent, and I'm really not. I still want this. I know now that I fooled a few people, but in the long run they'll find out. I mean I can make the grade, but I have been with these really good minds, and I know that I couldn't master three or four languages or all those philosophical concepts and ideas the way some people I've been close to can do. It wasn't in my genes, I don't think.

I thought if I went to Vassar, people would think I was smart. I don't think I'm very smart really. I mean just average. Not superior. I had a hard time with Latin at Gulf Park, and after I took it two years there, I asked my father to let me change to French, and he did. I took French again at Murphy—I was smart at Murphy High School, after Gulf Park. Murphy was very easy compared to private schools. Lower standards, I think.

Anyway, I had two years of Latin and two years of French. Well, then, I decided that I wanted to go to Vassar, which was foolish. I didn't have any counseling.

My friend Sarah Harris went to the University of Alabama. We had a feeling that was . . . well, if you were in the right sorority, it was alright, but you wouldn't want to associate with the general student body, New York Jews. Something like that. Also, there was a lot of drinking going on there in the sororities and fraternities. I liked that, but I don't think my father would have sent me to the University of Alabama. I didn't ask to go though. I didn't particularly want to go.

Here's how I went to Holton Arms, and this is where I lost my second year. I had two years of Latin and two years of French in high school, and you had to have three years of one language and two of another in those days to get into Vassar. I couldn't get in without another year of language. I went to Holton Arms to get it, and I didn't even realize that I was in high school again.

Mary Bake didn't like Sweet Briar so I think she went to Holton the same year I came back from Gulf Park, maybe before Christmas. Her mother found it. (Jacqueline Kennedy has been there, Susan Ford also.) It's a school where prominent people go. It's not just social, it's intellectual, too. I really loved it. It's very small, but I think it's bigger now that it's moved to Bethesda, Maryland. Anyway, I went up there. It was very hard—I studied all the time—and Mrs. Holton called me in and asked me to study late less. She said I needed to go out in the afternoon for a couple of hours and that I mustn't study the whole time.

I loved it in spite of studying all the time, because it was challenging. I got into the thrill of knowledge, of intellectual pursuits. Now Bake just took French and typing, or something. She was just as competent, or more so than I, but she didn't have the urge to do all these things that I did.

I don't know where that came from. But I hardly made a C+ average at Holton, which you might say was repeating a grade, but I did pass the Regents college entrance exams in four subjects for Vassar. Vassar was my goal.

I was at Holton for one year. But, I was two years older entering Vassar. Nineteen. I should have been seventeen.

Bake came back to Mobile and was queen of the Mardi Gras and got married and had four children. I can't help but think that that's a pattern that's more satisfactory to follow. Lib married very early. (I'm talking about my friend Elizabeth Radcliff, Joe Bailey's wife.) I was at about seven weddings, all of them gorgeous, bridesmaids all dressed alike, and I wanted one of those weddings too. I got married three times, but I never had one of those gorgeous weddings. Well anyway...

At Holton we had tea with Mrs. Roosevelt. We went to the White House. About twenty of us. I don't even remember the reason we went. But I met Mrs. Roosevelt. Oh, I never knew her personally, but I saw her more than once because she came to Vassar too. And then I saw her on the platform with Mr. Roosevelt and the Queen and King of England at Hyde Park. Everybody you ever heard of comes to Vassar. Vassar just gives you incredible experiences.

That's where I wanted to be, but I really think I was over my head. I had to drop chemistry. I honestly couldn't pass it. I couldn't make any sense out of it. And then I needed glasses, and I didn't find it out until my freshman year. I couldn't read those formulae on the board in chemistry. But I would have failed it anyway. I didn't fail, though. I dropped it with a D and took something else. I was on probation all my freshman year, which meant that I had a lower C average. But, finally, I pulled it up; gradually I got through it. But, I never minded the work, being there was so thrilling.

I did not make very good friends at Vassar, and I should have too, because about seven of us went up from Holton that year. It seems like I would have roomed with them or something, but I didn't.

I don't know, I think it's something congenital that makes me stay alone. I inherited it from my father, I'm pretty sure. I think I choose to be alone. I don't think I fail to make the connection. I turn them off. I don't know why. I've come to terms with it, but I think it is a fault, either of character or personality.

Much later, when I was taking graduate courses at the University of Southern Mississippi, there was a professor, I think his name was Dr. MacNinch but I'm not sure, he saw an aloofness in me right away, and he wouldn't take it. He said he would never hire me or anybody else as a teacher who didn't come in and teach the classes *and* socialize with the others, and I didn't do that. That's the flaw he saw in me.

And when I was at this recent conference, it was very flattering to be talked to by Tom Regan[1] and his wife. Well, I know why they did it, because I'm talking about giving this big donation. But, I liked her very much. I don't know whether I'm afraid people will think I'm imposing on them or not. I sort of left her in the crowd. We spoke to each other later, but I could have stuck with her the whole conference, I think.

And when I went to this new church. (I just joined the Methodist Church on Government Street three years ago. Old Danner was a prominent member there. It's called the "beehive church" because it was the active center of the community.) Anyway, there was a man named Mac in our Sunday school class. His wife had died three years ago, and right away he just came up like a shot and sat beside me. He said he wanted to keep me company, and all. He phoned me. I just backed away from him so quickly.

I don't know why, because I really would like to have a man in bed again, to sleep with, to wake up with, to share the intimacy of bathrobes and breakfast, to share your whole life with. He married again, too. He was looking for somebody.

I have just made up my mind that I can't understand it. It's something I'm not going to struggle to overcome—I just lead this lonely life, and I still get a lot of pleasure out of it, and can relate to people in a certain way if I feel like I've got enough control.

1. Tom Regan wrote *The Case for Animal Rights* (1983) and is widely regarded as the intellectual leader of the movement.

2 Awakening

I became politically aware at Vassar, and of course Father didn't like any of my ideas. Father and many other people blame all of my political stands on Vassar, but Vassar has produced a lot of prominent social people who are conventional.

Before I went up to Vassar, I did an idealistic thing. When I was nineteen, between Holton Arms and Vassar, I joined the Frontier Nursing Service in Windover, Kentucky. Another girl whom I knew later at Vassar did it too.

Mrs. Mary Breckinridge came to Holton to get people to join.[1] The FNS were English nurse-midwives who came over to try to lower the infant mortality in the mountains of Kentucky. They visited the pregnant women and delivered them, or got them to a hospital if they needed to. The nurses felt that they could deliver the majority of them at home, though. They rode on horseback to places where there were no roads, way up in the mountains.

Well, Penelope Kirkham, the Vassar girl, and I were couriers. We took care of the horses—remember, I had been horsey. If working for the Frontier Nursing Service that summer wasn't poverty, it was pretty close to it. Of course it was only socially prominent girls Mrs.

1. Mary Breckinridge was born in 1881 into an established Kentucky family. After the death of her two children and divorce from her husband she trained as a nurse and established the Frontier Nursing Service in 1925 to serve the rural poor. In 1965, after 40 years of service, FNS had delivered 15,000 babies and treated more than 57,000 patients in southeastern Kentucky.

Breckinridge got to do it. We had to take care of the horses: curry them and water them and feed them, and go get them out of the pasture. And, I remember getting three or four horses out of the pasture, and riding on one, and the others would sort of bite the rump of the one you were on, and he'd kick, and it was real scary! And then, we had to rub down all this leather harness with saddle soap. Then, we had to serve tea to these English nurses, who were used to having tea. We'd have to get cleaned up from all this smelly work—all this stink from horses—and go fix the tea and biscuits, and then they'd all have tea together.

The Frontier Nursing Service did a wonderful job, though. I think there are a lot of good statistics about it. That summer I saw suffering everywhere. I didn't see the actual deliveries of the babies, but there was a clinic, and these poor people would come in, all of them really needing medical attention. I felt there was nothing but suffering in the world.

There was a mule pulling some logs up one of these mountains. I don't know what sort of construction was going on, but I hated to see him have to pull so hard. He just dropped dead one day.

Anyway, Penelope and I were living in this miserable little log cabin, and there was a slop jar there that somebody had filled up. It was never emptied the whole time we were there, six weeks or something. I didn't know how to empty it. I couldn't have picked it up even if I had wanted to; it was too heavy.

The place got very dark at night, the mountains were all around. I woke up one night (twice I've had something like this happen, once was years later), and I didn't know whether I was up or down or where my body was in relation to anything in the world. It was a horrible feeling in that black room. It was darker than other darks. I was panic-stricken in that place, and for a long time afterwards I was afraid to sleep without a flashlight or something.

I had different sorts of experiences at Vassar. I remember that we burned our stockings as a boycott of Japan. I love things like that!

They were silk, and we decided not to wear silk because of Japan's invasion of Manchuria.

Vassar, like Holton, had wonderful, wonderful teachers. Those teachers made the strongest impression on me of any. A black man came to speak to us once. Well, you know I never had heard a black man speak about politics. I think he was talking more or less like the labor movement. The Communist leader spoke to us. Vassar was supposed to have been pink. Mable Newcomer, my economics teacher, was supposed to have been tainted with Communism. Elizabeth Bentley went there, and she was a Communist. A. J. Muste was a Communist for a while. He became one of my idols in the pacifist movement later, in the Fellowship for Reconciliation. I loved all those things. I just had a real appetite for it! Just all of it! It was like breaking out of an eggshell! I just adored it!

I never really was a Communist—but I've been called one. I never even knew anybody who was one except Earl Browder[2] himself, and if Miss Mable Newcomer was a Communist, I didn't know it. She made us think—like we had to figure out what a girl working in a ten cents store could buy on her wages. We would list all her requirements for clothing and food and rent. The question was: How could she make it on her income? Well, I never heard things like that discussed before. Then, I went to a conference of social workers in New York City connected with one of my courses. Very thrilling! Those things just thrilled me! And we saw a tenement reproduced as a display: a room, I don't know if it had any windows, but it didn't have any hot water, if it had water at all, and they told us how many people lived in that room. Well, that was hard to visualize.

Academically, I just struggled. I don't think I knew how to study. Holton was the only place that taught me. Murphy High School was just a joy ride, and Gulf Park was mostly all deportment and dress.

2. Earl Browder (b.1891, d.1973) was born into a poor family in Wichita, Kansas, and moved from populism to socialism to communism during his early decades. His leadership of the Communist Party during the 1930s supported the United Front position. He was expelled from the party in 1946.

Dorothy,
Vassar graduate,
1939

They did have competent teachers, but nobody ever set you on fire; they didn't have any intention of doing so.

I got only two good notices at Vassar. One was my paper in philosophy, I think I was a freshman, and they put "very good," and "Dr. Geiger would like for you to consider majoring in this field." That was thrilling, and I should have. I would have been good at it, I think. Instead, I majored in sociology in the economics department. My degree is in economics.

I felt this pull. I had this conscience or feeling, like I was meant to do something. Something noble, something unselfish. That didn't let me even consider a major in philosophy. It made me feel like I had to major in something to help people.

I don't know where that comes from, but at the end of each year Ms. Holton, the founder of Holton Arms, made very personal remarks about every girl who graduated, and her remark about me was that she had never met a student before who questioned her own right to happiness so much because of the suffering of others. Holton had depths of feeling and understanding that Gulf Park would never have thought of.

My conscience? Well, one time when she was still living with us, my Aunt De De told me a story about a little frog that said, "Don't pin me to a board." That was an antivivisectionist story. She was really just telling it, because I don't think there would have been such a story to be read from a book. Then, there was a little black girl, kind of like Carrie Mae was later, in the same place in a log cabin on the river (and I wish I could remember her name). Sarah McIntosh, one of my cousins, eleven years younger than I, was going to have a birthday party, and I think the little girl was about that age, and I wanted her to come, but my mother said no she couldn't come to the party. Well, that wasn't a very big deal but I remember it slightly. Then, I remember when I visited Sarah Harris at Tuscaloosa there was almost a lynching, and that was horrible. Oh, it might have been '35, '36, or '37 maybe. People were happy over it. You know the boys wanted to go to it. This was the same drinking crowd I told you about. This rumor that was just passing around, "They're gonna lynch a nigger." And that was the most horrible feeling I had. They didn't kill anybody that time, but those things were going on, lynchings, and I remember I was having a date with a boy named Ross Little (his sister married my cousin), and they had just lynched two men in Mississippi, the Blowtorch Murders (you might have read about them).[3] They tied those men to pine trees and killed them. That was haunting us on that date. The pictures were in the paper. We talked about it. Much later, I remember Ross telling me about how in the army they'd have a Japanese prisoner in the boat with them. I think what he said was that that Japanese knew he wasn't going to get away from them alive, and I don't think he did.

Alright, let's go on back to Vassar. Endless gray days. You never saw the sun there. In my senior year my father took my friend and me to Bermuda just to get to a nice sunny climate. When we got back after spring break it was still gray April in New York.

Was I happy? Things are too complex to be really happy. I was involved, intellectually stimulated, and that meant more to me than boyfriends. I remember I went to seven dances in seven nights in Mobile during Christmas vacation. And, I had evening dresses. I remember I could drink a straight jigger of bourbon, and I was proud of being able to drink that much straight. I don't drink or smoke anything now. I once went to West Point with a boy who graduated from Murphy with me. No, that must have been Annapolis. He went to Annapolis. I went to West Point too, but I can't remember with whom. At the Junior Prom at Vassar I didn't have anybody to ask. The same ole situation that I'd always been in at Murphy. I invited a

3. In April, 1927, two black men accused of murdering a white shopkeeper were taken from the sheriff on the steps of Montgomery County Courthouse by a mob of about 100 whites, and a blowtorch was used to force a confession from one man also implicating his partner. Gasoline was poured on the first, and he was set ablaze. His partner was shot. The sheriff said he recognized none of the unmasked lynchers.

boy from Yale, Gilly Burton, and he couldn't come. This boy that I finally had a date with, I wasn't at home with him. I really didn't enjoy it. But, in my senior year, I did. I was engaged and almost got married, and I should have gotten married. To a Mobilian named Payton Bush. He had a lot of money. My grandfather and his grandfather were in business together in the banks here in Mobile.

I still knew everybody in Mobile, and I came home all summer and Christmas and Spring vacations. Payton was a friend of my cousin Robert Bacon. He was about eight or nine years older than I, eight I guess. He came to New York the last part of my senior year. We had all sorts of privileges, and I felt like I had it made. I had all the academic credits and all the grades and everything else I needed to graduate. I was so happy that I was free.

They still had some restrictions, though. When Payton came up, we were allowed to go to hotels alone, but only special hotels. For instance, the Biltmore. I was allowed to stay there. They kept an eye on me. Payton was allowed in my room, but they knocked on the door if he stayed too long, and he did once or twice. We were being chaperoned at a distance. Well, Payton asked me to marry him, and I got letters from him all the time. I didn't save any of them. He was a heavy drinker. He and my cousin both were. (Both of them are dead now.) It didn't work out. I guess we just fought too much. I thought too much, and was rude, and talked back, and so forth, instead of having a happy love affair. Of course, I was always drinking, too, at all these parties and that doesn't help anyone's disposition. It makes anger much quicker.

Anyway, Payton and I would go out with Grace Bestor and Robert Bacon. (They were a good deal older. They have a little girl who was later made Queen of the Mardi Gras, just like Grace was.) Well, I was talking to Grace one day back in Mobile, and I said, "Yeah, Payton and I are still fighting, but I'll still go out with you all tonight." She said, "Well, I don't think they want to go." That was the end of it. Just that.

I guess I was just spoiled rotten or had a bad temper or something. Or maybe it was lack of sexual fulfillment.

Well, sexually I certainly was not thinking of doing anything and neither was he. I mean we just were *good*. But I'm sure we really both wanted to do it very badly.

At Vassar we didn't have many dates, but now they've got male students on the campus. Right before it became co-ed, the Vassar girls went away every weekend. The campus was vacated, but it wasn't like that when I was there. We just studied all the time, and we talked about things on a little more mature level than we had at Gulf Park. I think almost everybody was a virgin. You couldn't say that now.

I remember Dottie Dodge was a close friend of mine (she was a class ahead of me at Vassar, so I haven't seen her at any reunions, but she came to Mobile and visited with me once), and she would discuss something vaguely sexual, or she did on one occasion. Ann Straus, Dorothy Dodge, and I were once in the same room, and neither Ann nor I even understood what she meant. She would say that when she was kissing this boy, Freddy, after awhile she didn't want him to touch her anymore. That was the end. I don't think Ann or I had ever knowingly had an orgasm and been finished and wanted anything to end. We really didn't follow that. I'm sure I was filled with sexual feelings all those times and maybe had orgasms with kisses, because I can remember romantic embraces. Well, this was with Payton. I think when they were knocking on the door at the Biltmore. The doors weren't meant to be locked when you went in with someone.

What did I want to do with my life? I wanted to do something worthwhile. I felt obligated, that my life belonged to—well, I don't really believe in God, but we'll say God. It's a concept that's useful. At least it's understandable to many people. I didn't feel like I could live just for pleasure. I wanted to do something worthwhile.

That's youthful idealism, I guess, because I didn't mind wearing all these expensive evening clothes. I loved them and the music—I adored that music. Big band parties. Oh, I adored to dance. I learned to dance at Gulf Park with the girls. We played the Victrola after dinner every night in this big hall, and girls would lead girls. I didn't lead, though. I learned to follow.

Well, I came home after Vassar. You see, I had been away nearly ten years, except for coming back at holidays, from age 13 to 23. It never occurred to me that it was a pretty long span not to have had much home life.

Father moved back into our gorgeous house. He thought that I would be a nice person to have around, now that I was educated and twenty-three years old, and would probably work. He never demanded any kind of work from me. We had two servants—a man and a woman—to keep house.

That was 1939. And then, there was the war: Hitler in the daily newspapers. I mean we weren't out of the world like at Gulf Park, when I didn't know what was in the news. But when Neville Chamberlain had his umbrella and said "peace in our time," I was all for it, a hundred percent. I just thought it was marvelous—that it was going be perfect. Then, when Hitler started going into Austria, and everybody was jumping out of the windows and all that, I remember seeing it all in the paper, and then people were talking about, "Suppose we're not going to stand by France and Britain . . . suppose Paris and London get bombed." We would never be able to stay out. Not that war.

The news wasn't discussed, though. I just never heard any political talk at home or with friends. People just didn't talk about important things. The talk was always about your personal life and your social life. Actually, I wasn't very aware of many political issues. I wasn't really aware of the Holocaust until later when I affiliated with the Fellowship of Reconciliation, my pacifist group.

I was becoming sort of a pacifist even in 1939. I wanted to stay out of the war. After Vassar, when I was living in New York, Mary Long Herget and I—(she's a Vassar girl, I was in her wedding, she lives in Jacksonville)—she and I went to hear Lindbergh speak at the America First rally, and I passed out America First pamphlets. Now that was very right-wing, maybe fascist. I was on that side then. I wanted to stay out of the war.

My father was always being invited to millions of parties. Miss Virginia Whiting was one of his steadiest dates. (She was very important to me at the time of Father's death. She was like a mother to me in some ways.) Her son and daughter were in the same group of drinking and partying friends I had. Then, Father fell in love with Miss Delphine Burton, and he told me he was in love with her. And he said, "If you ever hear I'm going to get married, don't believe it, because I'll tell you first. Before I tell anybody else, you'll hear it from me first." Well, I wasn't as sweet to Miss Delphine as I was to Miss Virginia. I went and took sides, and Miss Delphine said, "I don't think Dorothy likes me." Now, I wish that I had pulled very hard for her. She had two men wanting to marry her at the same time, two rich men. The other was Bill Payton, who owned WALA radio, and she chose him. She just died recently at ninety-five.

I think caring about people and caring about animals is part of the same caring. Not that one's against the other.

I cared about the war and the things we started seeing. I remember a horse thrashing about on the newsreel, when Japan was invading Manchuria. And all these horrible things. This wounded horse was in the water and thrashing to get out. Aunt De De cared about that horse, too. And, I didn't have many people in my life; I mean I had friends, peers, but I didn't have any home for ten years, from age thirteen to twenty-three, and I didn't have a sister or brother to care for.

Aunt Venetia had a way of putting people down. Not just me, but other people. Father, too. She didn't build him up. I think she had a lot of fights with her first husband who died early, in his thirties. That's why she moved to Mobile. And the second husband, I think, was an impotent fag, more or less.

He was a musician, a church organist. The man didn't have male friends. I don't think that he gave her any kind of sexual relation. He was not a money-maker. He liked to wear these nice-looking smoking jackets around the house, you know, not like a masculine man. He was a lovely companion for her, though. Nothing wrong with his character. He may not have had any homosexual inclinations, but I think he just wasn't a macho man. She got along well with him, and my other aunt said something about how much better she did in this marriage than the other one.

Once I was back in Mobile, I got this job offer almost right away, in Jasper, Alabama. Sarah Harris probably brought me the application, because she'd been working a few years already—she had gone to the University of Alabama just for a year or so, and by 1939 she'd been out in the working world. Most of my friends didn't go to college but worked and knew about filling out applications and everything.

I got this letter in the mail saying I'd been hired to work for the WPA, and Father gave me very poor advice, I think. He said, "You better go up there right away," you know, without even communicating that you wanted this job. He never gave me a feeling that I was in a position to bargain. So I did go, right away, and I had that job up in Jasper, but I wanted to be back in my big house. I was away from home again, and I loved my Government Street house! Oh, yes, and I loved my Dog River house too! Father provided marvelous housing, and left it all to me.

I think Sarah spent a lot of time in my house, going to the river with us too, because she wasn't married. She was having an affair instead of getting married. He should have married her, too. I mean there was no reason why he shouldn't. They were both young and unmarried. He was in with the Alabama Power people, and all that crowd. Big money. He used to visit her in my house, too. They even got together there when Father and I were home. Father didn't know anything. Sarah told me, but that wasn't very nice.

Anyway, I got the job, and I lived in a boarding house in Jasper, Alabama. This was 1939 still. I mean before the war, before our men left. Of course all of these years were almost Depression, and very few people had anything like my father did. He wasn't rolling in wealth either. He was just a good manager. I got ninety dollars a month. I saved. I took a picture of my first check. I've still got it. And

I interviewed these people, these miners, who were starving because the mines were all closed. They had nothing. No work at all. I could interview twenty people a day—that's what it meant to handle a good load—and they were all starving!

There were some pitiful tales: about how they were going to break into a grocery store to get food for their kids, and then we had to ask them how much flour they used, how much lard? All these terrible, government, intrusive questions. And then, after a certain period, they'd get $30 a month to live on.

Enough? Well, they lived. They didn't starve anymore. Once they qualified, you would see them carrying their little lard can home to make biscuits. People would faint in school once in a while. Children wouldn't have anything to eat.

How did I feel about these people with these sad stories? Oh, I thought it was terrible. I cared about them. I didn't have any ideological framework. I didn't know any political answer, at least none that I could latch on to: I didn't want to go to war, and the war is what stopped the poverty. I didn't have a political group to join until I found the Fellowship of Reconciliation. So I didn't know how to channel my political thinking. It was just sensation. I didn't have any idea what to do about it.

The other girls? The girls I lived with were just Alabama girls. Working girls. We worked for the government, but we didn't talk politics. We might have talked over the technicalities of the cases, but they were all very similar. We knew why they were there, because there was no work in the mines.

I paid $30 a month for my room and board, and I saved $30 a month, and I had $30 a month mad-money, and I felt like a millionaire. I was as happy as a lark, financially.

I had a date there. We went out to drink. Same ole thing, sitting in the car drinking bourbon whiskey. I don't know where this man came from. I just remember sitting in the car drinking. That was a familiar place to be. I never kissed him, though, and my going out with him was sort of frowned on at the boarding house. It was his reputation. I don't know, I guess those girls were just not as sophisticated as Mobile people, and so I had to meet their standards.

I wasn't sexually active at this time. Never. Not until I was twenty-five. I guess it's a perversion of sexuality to never have intercourse but to have necking and drinking and things. But anyway, it does prevent pregnancy.

I just think if I could have fallen in love with some appropriate person, biology and social expectations would have naturally led to marriage. But I'm sort of glad Father made me so strict because otherwise I could have done all that drinking and really become dissolute.

I was there in Jasper just a few months. I got transferred to Mobile and was in the WPA office here. People got more money in Mobile: $39 a month, I think. Nearly everything was closed here, too, but Mobile wasn't a one-trade city like Jasper, which had nothing but coal mines.

We worked in an old house. The Lowenstein house was converted into an office, and I would go down to that house and climb those funny stairs round back to a little office, and I would envy my father's servants staying behind in the beautiful house with nothing to do all day. I wanted to be there instead of working.

My father had his office in the bank, and he had his mill making veneer. That kept him busy all that time. Well, he never worked very hard, though. He just made good business decisions and kept his mind on it. He was extremely prompt and handled things well, but he never put in long hours.

Most of my friends were married, and that year I went to a lot of Carnival parties for the Mardi Gras Queen. Just dates and dances and everything. In Mobile everybody keeps on doing those things until they die.

I think I could have been Queen of Mardi Gras—I think it was 1938—I've got letters in there from my aunt which said that I ought to make the debut. I don't think Father thought it was of much importance. It was a big waste of money, and I don't think he thought

Dorothy,
Southern belle

it mattered to me. I didn't put any pressure on him for it, but I resented it later because so many other people from Mobile were debutantes in my family. But then, anybody who allows themselves to feel resentful, which is a very bad thing to feel, that trait of character, can find plenty to inflame them in any situation.

Anyway, I quit the job. I shouldn't have.

I'd been back probably a year or less. I think Father was very disappointed with me, because he was happy that I was working.

Sarah and I went to New York, to live together in Greenwich Village. It was my idea. I persuaded her to go. We drove up in the car that I had, probably one that belonged to Father, or to the mill. A lot of Vassar girls, of course, went ahead of me. Certainly the ones that are at Vassar now think that they can choose their own career. No, I didn't go to New York with the idea of choosing a career. I guess I went for sexual experience. To freedom.

Adventure and sexual experience—it was calling me. Oh yes, I knew it. I told you I could have gotten married, but I didn't. I told you I never had a real boyfriend, exactly, that was really mine. I somehow didn't develop right. All my friends married, they all stayed married, they didn't divorce. They all had families, they were all prominent, and I don't think there was one of them that wasn't a virgin when she married. Except Sarah. Sarah was kind of old, we both were. I was twenty-three when I went to Jasper, and I was twenty-four when I went to New York. I had my twenty-fifth birthday there.

We drove to New York, settled in a boarding house on 12th Avenue, and then we tried to get jobs, and I knew we couldn't get anything very good.

Let's see, we sublet apartments for the summer. I think we had one or two of those. I went to school and took speed writing—instead of regular Gregg shorthand—and typing. Sarah already knew how to type. I got a job as a typist at a real estate agency on West 8th Street, and that's why we got sublet apartments.

My job was very hard. It seemed hard to me. I think the people in the office were Jews. I was at their beck and call, and I'd run upstairs and back down, and just do exactly what they wanted me to do. It would make me feel very tense. I got $18 a week.

We paid $45 a month for the apartment we found. Had to walk up two flights of stairs, and it looked out onto a fire escape and courtyard. All these apartments were grimy with soot because of the air in New York. And no air-conditioning. This one had three rooms. The bathroom was off of the living room, and it had a shower, a round shower curtain over a leg tub. The kitchen was a two-burner gas plate, with a refrigerator and a little sink. Sarah put her cot back in those closets behind the kitchen. There was a porch off the living room. I put bookshelves in front of it and that was my bedroom. It was partially furnished, somebody had left some furniture.

Sarah had a million dates. I had not so many.

She didn't know people. She was just attractive. I don't know whether I really feel like telling you about my, uh, losing my virginity or not. Do you want me to?

We went to the Village Barn to drink. We went around drinking, but not much because we didn't have enough money. Father sent me $200 a month. Sarah's family didn't give her anything.

We met another Southerner. He had an Alabama license. We kept leaving him notes on the windshield because he was from Alabama, and he took us to his room or apartment or something. He had "Strange Fruit," that record. Have you ever heard it? Well, it isn't about homosexuality. It's about a lynching. "Strange Fruit." We played that record over and over. I can still sing it. At least if I had a voice I could sing it.

> Southern trees bear strange fruit
> Blood on the leaves and blood at the root
> Black bodies swinging in the Southern breeze
> Strange fruit hanging from the poplar trees
> Pastoral scene of the gallant South
> Those bulging eyes and twisted mouth
> Scent of magnolias sweet and fresh
> And the sudden smell of burning flesh
> Here's a strange and bitter crop

Erskine, I think was his name, I've forgotten, and all of these people, they were so much fun. So funny and different, you know. Greenwich Village was partly Italian. Well, we'd meet these Italians in many places, in all the restaurants, waiting on us, and beauty parlors, doormen and such, and then we'd meet Southerners. Entirely different types, too. And Sarah could get along with people and relate to them very quickly, easily. Which I don't think I could.

Anyway, before we went to New York, we were in New Orleans together. We were in the bar at the Roosevelt Hotel, and we talked to two men, and they drove back to Mobile with us, I think, and stayed overnight in my father's house. One of them was named Howard Fish. Same name as Hamilton Fish, who was a politician or something. They were selling hospital equipment. They were upstairs from my room, and I was getting ready to go to bed. I didn't know them, and didn't care about anything else. I just decided I would. Sarah said, "Dorothy, don't give yourself to that man." I guess she had a lot more sense than I did. But, anyway, I guess we didn't. I don't know what they were doing in my house. I mean we shouldn't have done all those things. That was about as bad as I'd ever been. I think he left some of his suspenders, or else they were my fathers and I thought they were his, and I hid them. I was very nervous over it.

But we kept up with those two men, and they met us in New York. We went out with them and other people. I had decided—this was pretty silly, to make a decision like this, but I did it—that I wasn't going to be an old maid. I thought you're an old maid at twenty-five. So, I went to Commodore Hotel with Howard Fish to lose my virginity on purpose the day before my twenty-fifth birthday. It wasn't as romantic as being swept away in the moonlight passion or something. He was eighteen years older than I, so I guess he's dead now. Of course people like that are always married. He had a number of children and a wife, and it made me nervous.

This other friend of his, whose name I can't remember, came over to get me while I was typing, a little bit before I got off, and he was sitting there in the office. I just got more and more nervous. I think it was the night after I'd been with Howard, but I was feeling very sexual in this office taking that dictation. All of it just made me nervous. I mean I couldn't relate to the man giving me the dictation. I was just a very, very nervous young woman. Well, I told my boss I was going to leave for another real estate agency, where I could be a regular agent, and this Jewish man said, "Well, I think you'll do fine, if you do as well for them as you've done for us." I had no idea that I was doing even passably well.

Anyway, let's see. I worked for several other people. One: M. W. Kellog Company as an expediter. Then, I worked for Eastern Airlines. I took reservations. I lost that job, too. They let me go when they re-organized. Anyway, we had this other friend from Mobile named Elizabeth Gaines, and she and I drove back to Mobile for Christmas. Sarah stayed up there. The day we arrived in Mobile was December 7, 1941, the day Pearl Harbor was bombed, so we heard it all then.

Oh, I forgot to tell you, in New York, the reason I was so poor was because I was spending all of father's money—$200 a month—on going to a psychoanalyst. Dr. George Eaton Daniels. 129 East 69th Street. I drove up there every day, five days a week, and talked to him for an hour. It was a complete waste of time and money. He was a true Freudian. He didn't give you any advice or counseling. You just lay down, and you had this stupid stream of consciousness. I saw him about a year and a half. As long as I stayed there, more or less. I terminated it. I think it was really completely useless.

I had decided at Vassar from what I read that analysis would be a good thing to do. You'd read this case history or something, and the book would end up saying, "The only suggestion for this situation would be complete psychoanalysis," or something like that. Well, I believed in it like I was interested in drinking or these other things. I thought there was really something to it, that it would really reveal a lot to me. Well, I asked Dr. Daniels once, "What do you think my greatest problem is?" And he said, "Your failure to get married." So that made me feel awful.

I worked at the Mobile Public Library for awhile. My aunt, Dorothy McIntosh, had worked there. They put me in the reference room. That was a nice place to be, but I kept complaining about something. Father told me it was something I shouldn't be talking about. I just think I was bad. Just like I was complaining about Gulf Park, I was complaining about my jobs now. Somebody needed to say: "Be cheerful, straighten up, act nice, enjoy yourself." Because, it's just plain bad to be a complainer, a sourpuss, as opposed to being competent, fitting in, and getting along. I was always finding fault in something.

The war came, and then everything was different. We had these ration books, and all these shipyard workers moved into Mobile. There was a tremendous demand for housing for them, and I rented out every place in my house. My father let me. The attic and everything else. I had three girls in the attic.

Father let me do that. He may even have moved out to the Dog River house. It's not far. It's eight miles from the court house. Surprising isn't it? Well, I just felt like a millionaire. I didn't get very much money from them, five dollars a week apiece, but it added up to about five hundred dollars a month or so.

These were shipyard workers; I had no friends among them. They were people who came in to work for the war. Most of them just had rooms. Later on, I had a few boarders—that was after I was a widow—after my first husband had died. That happened in 1944. I was twenty-eight. Before him, in 1943, there was somebody else.

There was a dance being given at the Elks Club downtown—not at one of the gorgeous places—for the Free French Fleet. They were stranded. They couldn't go back to France, and they had been on the island of Martinique for a long time. Then, they came to Mobile: all these French sailors. The Red Cross probably put on this dance; it did a lot of things like that. I was invited because I spoke French. Anyway, I went down there, and girls came who couldn't speak a word of French. All they could say was "he's a loup." *Il est un lupe.* A "wolf" was all they could think of to say, but they all enjoyed those sailors.

There were three of us who met some of them again. I think all of us had affairs with French sailors. I know I did. I was crazy about Camille. Camille Piquot was his name. From Bordeaux. I had his picture in that cute little thing with the pom-pom on it. And he gave me a flag that he used in Martinique, and all sorts of souvenirs.

It was a love affair. He had a wife—he didn't tell me about his wife until later. He wrote me about her and sent me a picture. But, while he was here he pretended to be an eligible sailor, and he wanted me to take it up with my father—to talk about marriage. He thought he could figure out his other one later, I guess, if he could get a serious intention from my father. Well, I'm sure Father found out. With all the souvenirs around and everything, he had a pretty good idea. He didn't like it anyway.

The fleet sailed after a few months.

Now a friend of mine got pregnant and had an abortion. Well, you couldn't have abortions. She went to a gynecologist, my cousin worked for him, and he said this was happening to a lot of people. He twisted her uterus with his hands to induce an abortion, and then let her go on home. Well, I was with her when she started hemorrhaging, and her mother came over, and she had to be taken in an ambulance to the Protestant Infirmary. She was still pretending that she wasn't pregnant. They had Catholic nurses there, and she said those nurses just watched that bedpan; they just looked at it so carefully. She was scared herself, because of the huge amount of blood she lost.

Anyway, not too long after that, I was introduced. My father and I went to a party at the Admiral Semmes Hotel for the Crown Prince of Norway. I think he was a single man; I don't remember anyone being with him. And there I was introduced by Marion McPhearson, a sort of prominent woman, to Memto Nicolo DaPonte, a Dutchman. He was forty-four, and I was twenty-eight.

Nicki was divorced and had three children. They were all in Holland; he sent them alimony every month. He had always worked for the Royal Netherlands Steamship Company. He had an office in Merchant's Bank and wanted to stay in this country. He handled their business efficiently. He was a drinker, too.

Yeah, drinking's a bad thing. It's just a bad thing that happens to people. I didn't know any other kind. Father was a very moderate drinker. He wasn't a problem drinker. Too rigid a character to let himself go, even to relax too much. He always served whiskey, though.

Oh, I could have been an alcoholic easily. I was drinking heavily. I would go to bed dizzy and wake up with an awful taste in my mouth, and I think I would have been, if I hadn't discovered the Fellowship of Reconciliation and my political causes. Because that was about all that I was exposed to: this drinking life.

Alright, I had this affair with Piquot, that's what I called him. That was his last name. I was still thinking about him when his ship left, and he wrote and sent me a picture of his wife. I guess we had a good relationship, except he was cheating on me by not telling me he was married.

There are just a few people who would be absolutely honest, I guess.

I was bad to Nicki, too, worse than Camille was to me. I met Nicki in these glamorous circumstances. I had on my best dress. They were serving champagne and scotch, and I think I was drinking a little of both of them. I met two people that night, but I kept on seeing only Nicki. He was an immediate and persistent suitor, but I didn't find him attractive because he was old, forty-four looked old to me, his teeth didn't look right, he had sort of a big stomach, and was a little bald-headed. Nicki and I spoke a lot of French. My French had really gotten tuned up with Piquot, that other boyfriend. And that was one thing I loved about Nicki, speaking a different language.

Anyway, this was the worst thing I did. Nicki and I got married in three weeks, and we didn't have a real wedding. But the very worst thing I did, and I think this was really bad, on our wedding night at the Buena Vista Hotel in Gulf Port, Mississippi, I wrote a letter to

Piquot in French telling him I was married to Nicki. That was an awful thing to do. Nicki didn't make too much of it, but he did refer to it, saying you hurt me on our wedding night. That was the main reason I married Nicki: because I found out Piquot was married. I found somebody else who spoke French, and I got married. It wasn't a good reason.

I didn't have a proper wedding at all. I didn't have any family. I did tell my father before. I said, "Mr. DaPonte has asked me to marry him, and I've said 'yes'." Father didn't say, "No" or anything. We drove down to Biloxi where you could get married without a three-day waiting period.

One reason I wanted to marry was because he had a house. It was a cute house. It's still there. I've seen it recently. The steamship company furnished him with this house, and I wanted to get away from home. Well, I just guess I wanted to get away from Father or from being a daughter. I did love the house that Nicki had—I liked it better than a big house—and I liked it that he was foreign half the time to me. In fact, he spoke everything, which is very impressive. And, he could be very charming. He had aristocratic manners and could entertain people, but then he would get drunk, and have a blood look in his eye, and be very abusive—to me or anybody else whom he wasn't afraid of, I guess.

We drank all the time. We drank every day of the week. He'd come home from work, and we'd fix these big Old Fashioneds. He'd make all these pretty drinks; I might as well have been swallowing whiskey down whole, the way I used to. And then, let me see what else . . . it got hotter and hotter. We married March 11, 1944. Well, in June or July, it became terribly hot. There wasn't any air-conditioning. We wanted to go to Dog River where it was cool, and so we moved down there. We stayed at the Dog River cabin. Father thought that was a mistake for Nicki to move into my house. Besides, Father could hear us fussing and fighting. He was in another house down there. The guest house. And Nicki would call me a whore and things like that, because of that French boyfriend I had.

Let's see . . . before we moved down there, I sent out announcements. Every time we came home from town, we had gotten all these wedding presents. Just opening them every day. We had all that stuff to put in the cabin, and I think Nicki was enjoying it.

I think Father was happy to see me married. I remember one time, we were shut up in the bedroom, when Father came in the house, and I thought well, can this be possible? Can I be this grown up that my father can be in my house, and I can be in the bedroom with some man?

That year I did a lot of work for the Red Cross even though I was against the war effort. I worked in the canteen, serving gumbo, and I was working one day a week, eight hours, as Nurses Aid for the Red Cross.

Something bad happened. I can't remember what we were fighting over. He had brought me a big bouquet of red roses, he used to do things like that. I'd come back from Junior League meeting or something. Anyway, he was mad, and I don't remember why, but he hit me. He had hit me before, once, in the face.

I remember that time. We were going down to Ingalls Shipbuilding, and I was to act real nice and all that. We were going to see Robert Ingalls himself, the old man who built it all. I was trying to be what I was meant to be, but by the time we got there all I could think of was that slap in the face, and how we were talking so nice when I had just gotten slapped.

Well, this other time, we decided to have a big Christmas, and we had a maid to help us. I had two big turkeys stuffed and bought these red apple candles for the mantle piece, and had all the extended family in. We used all the china and stuff that had been given to us as wedding presents by my family and friends. My Aunt De De was staying in the house with us for Christmas. We had a huge party. I don't know how many people, maybe thirty or something. And afterwards, when they'd all gone, there wasn't room for the two big turkey carcasses to be stuffed in the ice box. (I guess nowadays I'd know how to keep house better.) I should have cut them up or thrown most of it away. But, I left one out, and that's what ends up causing the whole death and tragedy.

The turkey had oyster dressing, and I ate some of it after it got bad, and I got very sick. I couldn't get over it. I didn't just vomit and get over it, like when you'd been drinking. It stayed with me; I kept on being sick. It was bubbling when I ate it. I don't know how I could have done it. And De De was there, too, and I would try and go on the sleeping porch and lie down, but I couldn't be comfortable wherever I went. It was getting on Nicki's nerves, because what company was I? I was a drag on everybody. And he was saying, "If you've got to go to bed, go to bed and stay there." By then nobody was there but me and De De and Nicki. He was yelling at me to get to bed if I was sick instead of walking around, but I didn't want to go to bed. I wanted to feel better. I'd have to lie down every once in a while, but then I'd get back up. De De went back to New Orleans, and I can't remember what the circumstances were, but it all happened because of my being so sick. I was sick for two days.

I can't remember everything. Oh! My father gave Nicki a gun for Christmas, and they would shoot out the electric light down by the water, the two of them. I don't know how they went and put it back up because it seems like you could only do that once. I knew how to shoot, too. Father taught me. But, anyway, Nicki started chasing me around the house with that gun—a long rifle, not a hand gun.

He was scaring me. He was making me think he was going to shoot me. I've almost forgotten. . . . So, I locked him out. Then, he put his hand through the glass, and it cut him, and I wanted to telephone. I crawled along. This must have been before he got in. He couldn't see me crawling to the phone. I've forgotten all of this episode.

I don't know how I got to town, but I got up to Father's house some way or other.

I remember he threw those roses down and stamped on them. It seemed like night—after a meeting. Yeah. And he was mad at me for some reason, stamped on his own roses.

I don't think I ever saw him again after he chased me with the gun. Anyway, I ended up at Father's house.

I was scared to death. I thought I was in fear of losing my life. I don't know whether Nicki was drinking or not, but I shouldn't think so. He didn't drink in the day, and he didn't hide his drinking. I think it was in the day. But I don't remember. Maybe, if I could make myself read things. . . .

But the next thing I remember, I was at Father's house and my friend, the one that had the abortion, she knew Nicki, too, and she was talking to me about it, and Nicki was phoning every minute, just ringing the phone off. This went on for two or three days.

That is something I should have considered: a reconciliation. That's what I wonder: because I did the same thing with Arthur, my last husband. I just let the marriage go like that, without ever thinking about it.

Why don't I have more sense? I don't know. But I should have thought about the fact that Nicki was trying to be reconciled. Well, I wouldn't have anything to do with him. I wouldn't talk to him. There was a maid, and I don't know whether she answered, or whether I heard his voice and hung up. At the time, we still had the maid down at the Dog River house, so in a day or two, I've forgotten what time of year it was, but it wasn't over two days or three days, the maid phoned from Dog River and said, "Mr. Nicki done shot himself." His body was lying there in front of her. It's a log house, and there's still blood on those logs. He shot himself in the temple, and it left a stain on the logs, from his head.

My father and Uncle Mel and I went down. The two men took over and shut me out of this important event in my life. They were protecting me, but people don't like to be protected.

We had a funeral. I stayed with his body at Higgins Mortuary for three days. I felt that that's where I wanted to be.

Nicki had three sons, and Tom's the one who visited me recently. And when Tom was sitting here, I saw the same bald spot, and Tom is sixty-three now, I think. Nicki was only forty-four. Tom is more slight in his build, but he did a number of things that were like his father, even though he hadn't seen him since he was about seventeen. Tom was a cheerful sort of character, and Nicki was cheerful, too, and he put his foot up like that. Nicki used to dance like that, a kick in the back, sort of cute, a little sign of happiness or something. And when Tom was here all sorts of happy things came back to me, and I thought I had forgotten all of those good things I'd had with Nicki. Yeah, I had a lot of good times. A lot of fun and conversation, and talking French and discussing many things.

Nicki left an interesting suicide note which I have since destroyed. He said, "Tonight you made your final decision, and I've made mine. You could never understand the tumult in my soul." Then he wrote something about the two other children and one little boy of nine starved to death. (Well, that little boy was not starved, he's living today. He's had three wives or something.) And, then, Nicki made some dramatic statement at the end of the note, "without you I cannot live." Well, we would never use that construction. That's a foreign-language-translation type of construction. I kept that note, but then I destroyed it later in another, almost-marriage love affair. I was sorry I didn't have it here for his son.

Why did Nicki kill himself? Well, I think his first marriage had gone on the rocks, and he was afraid it would look real bad to his company, his job and all, to be getting a divorce a second time. He'd have to move back to that house, maybe it was rented or something. I guess he was drunk, probably, when he killed himself. His mother had a prayer book in Dutch. I've still got it. He had that open, and he had some kind of little sexual advice book open. He was in a desperate situation and looking for counsel and guidance, I guess.

No, I've never had an impotent husband. They've always been competent. But the second one was best. I was not really very attracted to Nicki. I was with the Frenchman though, but there was a lot of unreality with him. I mean it was such a fantasy. I wasn't very sexually responsive or orgasmic—I was just beginning, maybe, to learn my own responses. Nicki wasn't a thrilling lover, but he was there and ready for it any time. I can't accuse him of any sort of impotence at all. But you know somebody with a slightly large stomach, and sort of ugly teeth, looking old and all doesn't thrill you when you're in your twenties. I'm sure I showed that too. When you're with a man sixteen years older, you kind of feel like you have the upper hand, in a way.

After Nicki's death, I wore mourning clothes, which was very foolish. Very dramatic and unnecessary. It was not customary at all. I kept on wearing black stockings, black dresses. All my friends came to see me, and after that I started working for the Mobile public library. I was twenty-eight.

I was back in Father's house again, though I didn't want to be. I wanted to go back to Dog River and live there alone, because as well as the sexual urge, I had a strong desire to have my own place. Even though Father's house was gorgeous, it wasn't my own little place that I could fix up. In fact, it was too massive. But, Father wouldn't let me go back down there. He had all the windows boarded up. That made me furious.

He was always there to. . . . I'm sure all that was a lot of trouble for him. Of course, I think he paid for the funeral, I have no idea what it cost. Nicki was buried out by my mother.

Pretty soon after Nicki's death his son Charles came to see me. Charles was just eight years younger than I. He was a very good looking boy. He joined the Marines, which trained in North Carolina, just to get over here to see his father. And he was just adorable. He'd call me "mom," and I should have kept up with him. It could have really filled up my life. He has five wonderful children now. He fell in love with a girl named Caroline Blackledge from here in Mobile, but he had to go back up to that training camp. He was ready to marry Caroline. He would have made anybody a good husband. Very steady. Anyway, she wrote him a letter of good-bye, and he finally married a darling girl named Frances in Holland, and they sent me a picture of their first child, and they named it three names for its three grandmothers: Johanna, Frances, and Dorothy. I thought that was very sweet.

During World War II? Everything was closed. They didn't have the Strikers International Ball, that's the biggest one. I don't know about high school dances, but the big mystic societies did not have their usual dances. They've multiplied enormously now. New people have started their own. I think there were about a half dozen then.

The war ended in '45. I resigned my membership in the Spinsters, the only one of which I was a member. You were still a member after you married, but you were no longer an active member. But I resigned altogether; I just wanted out of it. I resigned my membership in the Junior League, too. The Junior League was demanding. They wanted you to do a certain amount of volunteer work, and they would check up on my Red Cross activities (those counted as Junior League hours). I just didn't want them bossing me around, seeing how many hours I was working. And after Red Cross work stopped, with the war's end, I had to take up something else. I just didn't feel like bothering with it. I didn't see the larger picture, and the advantage of it. I resigned from the Presbyterian Church. I don't think that I really did anything very consciously or with much forethought. I did it all impulsively.

I think that's a weakness of character. It's foolish to do things impulsively. It possibly is due to the fact that I didn't have. . . . Well, my father did the best he could. But most people have more than one distant authority figure. They've got a whole bunch of people.

So there I was, drifting, feeling like there was no point to life. You go through all this training, and these stages, those endless schools, to get nowhere. Well, I already told you about the time I saw the psychiatrist, and about how he said my biggest problem was my failure to get married. So, I'm thirty years old with nothing. No husband and no children. I remember my thirtieth birthday. Father said, "Thirty's a nice age to be." He didn't understand.

3 Causes

I've got three causes: pacifism and race relations and antivivisection. Beginning in 1944. Vassar was the intellectual stirrings, just slightly, but I didn't find any real political orientation. I always wanted to be married. You just haven't got status unless you're married. You're nothing, if you're not married. Then, I really wanted children, too. I wanted them physically. I had a real physical need for pregnancy. I was happy being married with Nicki, I would have been with anybody almost, I was so happy with wedding dresses and the state of being married.

This may have contributed to Nicki's suicide: The war worried me a lot all along, and I read an article given me by my Aunt Venetia. She got these things because she went to church a lot. She went to Episcopal church on Government Street—All Saints. She started to teach Sunday school. Her husband was the church organist. I think he also played downtown at Christ Church. He may have played at many places. He also taught music. Father thought he was a nice husband. I guess he was, but the children didn't respect him, any of them. They were cruel to him, I think. He just lacked that manly quality.

But this is what I was going to say: they were more liberal than anyone else in my family. Aunt Venetia brought me an article by Vera

Brittain on the bombing of Berlin.[1] And it was terrible. I think I've still got it. I kept it. It was horrible: the saturation bombing of Berlin. Many nations condemned saturation bombing, and I think Hitler even hesitated before he bombed London which wasn't bombed as severely as what is meant by "completely saturated." All this was just horrible to me, and Father and Nicki just didn't think anything of it. It was just horrible talking about people in the air raids going into the subways for shelter, and still being turned into cinders.

Then, Aunt Venetia got me in touch, some way or other, with the Fellowship of Reconciliation.

Nicki didn't like any of that. Neither did Father. My attitude was contributing to Nicki's mental unrest: my being against the war, when he's got his flesh and blood over in Holland, to whom he's giving half his money every month to help out.

I also met this lady named Miss Erma Appleby.[2] I know Aunt Venetia knew her, but I don't know whether she introduced me to her or not. She was a remarkable woman. She had an effect on a lot of people in Mobile. She was a member of the Fellowship of Reconciliation and some kind of director of the YWCA.

Later, Miss Appleby ran for Congress, against George Wallace, I believe. We stuffed envelopes for her, and I made a radio speech for her.

Anyway, Miss Appleby and I, and Miss E. Lura Moore, my English teacher at Murphy High, all took a trip together to a Fellowship of Reconciliation Conference in Nashville, Tennessee. And, then, I became really, really excited over the FOR. Tremendously!

Well, I think it was the fact of these boys: it was very masculine,

1. Vera Mary Brittain (1893-1970) was an English feminist, pacifist, and writer. She won a scholarship to Oxford University in 1914 and served with the armed forces in World War I. She lost her brother, fiancé, and friends in the carnage of trench warfare. Her writing and lectures won her fame as a trans-Atlantic intellectual.

2. Erma Appleby (d. 1971) graduated from Grinnell College in 1908 and spent her life employed by the Young Women's Christian Association in a variety of positions across the country. She spent the last decade of her professional life in Mobile serving as director of the local YWCA, from which post she retired in 1946.

and it was a strong group. They had been to jail, and they'd been carried off by police in labor protests. And, they let me in. The Fellowship of Reconciliation was the parent group of CORE and Amnesty International. A. J. Muste[3] was quite a figure in those days, and Bayard Rustin[4], John Swomley[5], and George Houser[6]: those people just were very impressive to me.

Miss Appleby said she wanted Mildred and Frances Laurendine to meet me, which was very flattering. They were girls who'd had no help; their father left their mother with four children, without any money or anything. They had a hard time. They had to live with relatives and walk to Murphy High School from a place way down at

3. A. J. Muste (1885-1967) was a prominent leader in the non-Communist Left. He was an ordained minister of the Reformed Church of America and a 1912 graduate of Union Theological Seminary. During World War I he preached pacifism, and he joined the Fellowship of Reconciliation. During the 1920s he was active in the labor movement and helped to form the Amalgamated Textile Workers union. He wrote and edited a variety of labor magazines. He helped to found the American Worker's Party in 1933 and disavowed Marxism-Leninism in 1936. Muste became FOR executive director in 1940, and simultaneously he accepted a post on the executive committee of the War Resisters League. After WWII, Muste was accused by FBI Director J. Edgar Hoover of working in support of Communist front organizations. Muste persisted in his anti-war activities into the Viet Nam war years.

4. Bayard Rustin (1910-1992) was a lifelong behind-the-scenes activist leader in support of civil rights and racial justice. Rustin joined the Young Communist League in 1936. He reversed himself in June, 1941, when the American Communist Party supported the Soviet Union rather than political principle. Rustin joined the staff of the Fellowship of Reconciliation and for twelve years ranged across the South to encourage and support non-violent protest against racial discrimination. In 1953 he became executive secretary of the War Resisters League. Throughout the civil rights movement Rustin was directly involved as advisor to Martin Luther King, Jr., and others.

5. John Swomley (1915-), an ordained Methodist minister, served as associate secretary of the Fellowship of Reconciliation from 1940-44. He was executive secretary of the National Council Against Conscription (1944-52) before taking the post of executive secretary for the Fellowship of Reconciliation (1953-60).

6. George Houser (b. 1916) attended Union Theological Seminary and was imprisoned during 1940-41 when he refused to register for the draft. He was a Methodist minister and served on the staff of the Fellowship of Reconciliation from 1941-1955, and was executive secretary of the Congress of Racial Equality (CORE) from 1945-55.

Dog River. They adored their father, though. He divorced their mother, and just married somebody else, and they never would speak to her or even let people know he was married again. They were strong Catholics. Still, everybody adored him in that family because he read to them in a wonderful voice from William Cowper Brand's *The Iconoclast*, and other things like that. He was a lawyer and apparently just a great personality, rather than being someone extremely reliable and responsible like my father.

They're an old family, though. Their people had been here before everything. Old Laurendine land tracts go back to the beginning of civilization here. The family didn't make any impression commercially on the city, though; they didn't start any businesses or anything.

Mildred and Frances were both single then. Mildred's a year and a half younger than I. Frances is about three years younger.

Then, later on, (I know I'm not being very chronological), Mildred and Frances and I and a fellow named Barney Camp something, (I don't know Barney's name, he wasn't a pacifist, he was just going for the ride), well anyway, we were all going to the Fellowship Conference. We went way up to Estes Park, Colorado, in my car, and it was so thrilling. That view was so exciting up on that plateau. Have you ever been there? That's when I found religion again, because these people believed in religion without bothering with myths and the supernatural. It was an ethic for them, an antiwar ethic, and it all made sense to me. We'd sing the regular old Protestant hymns, only they would mean war resistance, and we'd hold hands and sing things like "This Little Light of Mine," with these really tough men who had been in jail. They were serious men.

I went to another meeting soon after, in North Carolina, at Kings Mountain—sometimes I went yearly. Maybe more often.

Mildred and Frances did not join the Fellowship of Reconciliation. Mildred nearly lost her job at Brookley Airfield when she was investigated after having been to this conference. They suspected her of un-American activities, I guess. They had a Russian there, a real live

Russian called Kosokevitch, and remember this happened when some people thought Russians were very dangerous.

This was about 1947. But in the meantime we had this racial incident which you read about. Marie Gayle, this colored woman, was beaten up on the city bus in Mobile. Let me tell you about that.

We started something called the Mobile Inter-racial League, Mildred and Frances and I, in 1947. We three were the only whites. I was the president; they were the secretary and treasurer. We were elected. Maybe we numbered ten or twelve altogether. We met at black churches and black YMCA's. Mildred, Frances, and myself: we had a nice program started.

Anyway, one day I was phoned by Miss Effie Gude, a black woman—well, she's not black, but politically we called her that, she's barely colored—and was told about this incident.

Marie Gayle was twenty-eight years old, a black woman. Here's what she said in court: She got on the bus down at Bienville Square, across from the Athelston Club, and she had a lot of packages, so she sat in the vacant front seats. They were not occupied, so she sat. In those days black people could fill up from the back of the bus and sit in those seats. There might have been a white person in front of her, but she wasn't in front of any of them. And the bus driver told her to move back, and she said . . . well, she demurred anyway. She said she had all those packages, and they were empty seats, why did she have to move back. They said she fought like a tiger. Who knows. I doubt it. Anyway, the bus driver and two other men kicked her all over her body on the street in downtown Mobile. They had to take her to the hospital, and her head was all bound up like that, and then she was thrown in jail directly from the hospital, with all those bindings on. She was charged with participating in an affray, and the black community was very stirred up. The bus situation was the worst problem, the most volatile problem, we had. We could have had it here just like Montgomery did with Martin Luther King, if I'd been enough of a leader.

Well, Marie Gayle thought I would do something about it.

Anyway, I went around to a lot of lawyers in Mobile, they wouldn't touch it. So Marie herself said, "Get Betos, get Betos." Well, his name wasn't Betos; it was Beto without an *s* on it, in Birmingham. So I got him, and he said his fee would be $1200. I said I'd pay him, and so he came down here to have a trial. The jury decided that no more force was used than necessary, and that was the end of my $1200.

I remember the Inter-racial League being involved in another civil rights case. This boy was named Samuel Taylor, and he was accused of raping a white girl named Katie May Dukes at Vigor High School. He had been sentenced to death and had his execution reprieved seventeen times. Big Jim Folsom was governor. I guess that's one good criticism of the death penalty: people hesitate to enforce it, and that just seemed like such torture. Well, one time, Eddie, my brother-in-law was reading my scrapbooks, and he said, "Would you do the same today—defend a rapist like that?" Well, at that time I wasn't too sure that it had really been a rape. I don't remember ever seeing any medical documents about her examination. She was trembling and frightened whenever she reported it to somebody close to the school. But anyway, she wasn't dead, and she wasn't unable to marry, or maybe it was traumatic, but it didn't seem so bad to me. I felt that there might have been some doubt about his identity, but I no longer feel any particular doubt.

Anyway, Mildred and Frances and I dived into that case. We went to see Katie's teachers, and we went to see her parents, and we went to see Samuel Taylor up in Montgomery, in prison, and we almost went to see the governor, Big Jim Folsom. But we didn't. We came back, and I started a writing campaign using the people from The Fellowship of Reconciliation, who responded well. Somebody at the *Press Register* said, "I guess you want to pin a medal on him" or something like that. Anyway, our efforts did succeed in his sentence being commuted to life in prison instead of the death penalty. I checked with Mildred's nephew, who is a lawyer, in 1980 or 1981, and got him to check up on the case, and he found that Taylor had been released about that time. I'm not sure of the date. He's living again out in Prichard. I've never seen him. I don't know what happened to her.

Voter registration was a big part of our effort, too. And, we did a kneel-in at the Church of Christ. We went in with members of our group: Gilcrease was another one of them, and Major Madison, he's the one who is still very active in politics (his son's a lawyer now), and Mildred and I. I don't know who else. We tried to go into that worship service, and the people there gathered around us and wouldn't let us in. I don't know what the preacher was doing, but someone tried to get the people back in church and off the sidewalks.

It was just our individual acts, Mildred and Frances and I, and it was all based on non-violent tactics, which I'd learned through Fellowship of Reconciliation conferences. We did go in. After the congregation went in, we went in too. And, that resulted in all sorts of telephone calls. Critical phone calls. I wasn't threatened with death. It wasn't all that bad, but I remember my beauty parlor operator was a member of the Church of Christ. She asked me why I did it. Many people challenged me on it. I can't remember at all what answer I gave.

I still know all these black people, the ones who were in the Mobile Inter-racial League. One of them is Jerry Rushing, and Dorothy Rushing his wife. They now have three grown children. I think they married about that time, 1947. Jay LeFlore was one of the main ones in the group, and you've heard of him, I know. He was the leader of the NAACP here. One of them was Alex Herman, I know his daughter-in-law is now a friend of Caroline's. One was Major Madison: I loaned him my car for voter registration, too, and all this was getting folks upset. You know the white people didn't like any of it: a black man riding around in my car and all the rest. All of those individuals are people that Miss Appleby knew about and made us aware of.

We went to Montgomery to talk to the legislature about the Boswell Act, which restricted black voting. It said that people had to be able to read and interpret the Constitution in order to vote, and the white registrars of voters used that to keep blacks from registering. The day we were getting ready to go to the legislative committees, we read in the newspaper about Judge Richard Rives, and we got in touch with him right away. He was an ally. It was like a miracle finding him.[7] That was very exciting. He told us how to approach the committee and how to do things for best effect. Joe Langhan, our state senator, later defeated the Boswell Act.

My life changed very much in 1947, 1948, and 1949, when I met Mildred and Frances. They read voluminously, and had all their lives. I liked that. We were very congenial. They just fit in with all of my interests of going to conferences and things, even though they really shouldn't have been going to a pacifist conference and working for the War Department at the same time. And, then, we all became interested in civil rights together.

I was living on Government Street, after Nicki died, when I met them. The house was very pretty and impressive. And, Mildred, I think, is definitely a masculine type of woman, if you want to say that's the other type, but she'd never used a word like that nor has her sister ever used one about her or showed any recognition or indication that she wasn't like the rest of us. But Mildred certainly lives a life that would even be approved by the Catholic Church. She has never had any sexual experiences at all, with men or women, I guess. So, what more can be asked: if you're born so that you're not attracted to the opposite sex and you're living as celibate as the Pope?

Frances is a lot more feminine. But, Mildred has a certain amount of male aggressiveness in her. When Miss Appleby introduced us, Mildred came to see me right away. You know, we were just strangers, and she has pursued me relentlessly throughout the rest of my life, and still is. It's not all bad, but I don't think I would have encouraged her friendship, as much as I did originally, if I had found it so clinging to me. I feel certain in my mind that that is a romantic, sexual attachment, but she doesn't see any of that. She won't discuss

7. Richard Taylor Rives (1895–1982) was admitted to the Alabama bar at nineteen and served as its president in 1939. He practiced law in Montgomery and was appointed to the U.S. Fifth Circuit Court of Appeals in 1951.

things like that, and I don't think Frances would like it if she ever knew I mentioned it. I don't think it ever crosses Frances's mind. But Mildred's been a big person in my life and it's not been altogether happy, but she's occupied a lot of my time.

The Fellowship has got a lot of religion in it. I found religion through them, and they did a lot of fasting, and one time I fasted all of Easter Week. I think Mildred did it with me—just to have liquids all week and then on Saturday—or maybe Friday and Saturday—nothing, not even water. Anyway, whenever it was, Mildred did it; she was really carrying on. That last day, she cut up about it, like it was something terrible, like she was going to die. We were following the lead of a bunch of people, A. J. Muste and others, who took themselves off to a separate place, and all lived together, and had a nurse and a supervisor for their fasting. We just did the end of it with them.

We knew about all of this through the Fellowship of Reconciliation. Just the magazine. Like the animal rights movement, there's no local chapter here in Mobile. I just go to conferences and read their literature. That's all the guidance I have.

And then, I took Caroline in 1950. She was just five when I first met her so that would have to be '49. Her mother, Hazel Thomas, came to work. I hired her for my father. Then Carrie Mae, Caroline, showed up in the backyard. Her mother brought her little daughter to work with her.

She had her sixth birthday at Dog River, July 4, 1950. I played around with her a lot that summer. I spent a lot of time with this cute little girl. And then Hazel left us. I don't know what the conditions were, but they were friendly, she just didn't work for us anymore. They lived not too far from here. I went to see Carrie Mae, and she was living in such bad conditions, so I asked Hazel. . . . This was done. . . .

I think all of the things in my life could have been so much more satisfactory and productive if I had given them more thought ahead of time. If I tried to see what the consequences would be in the future. I just said, "I want to take her back home." I didn't do any planning at all. I just wanted to clean her up. I really didn't give any thought to it, and millions of problems are still involved because of it.

Well, people didn't pay much attention to it. It wasn't noticeable. It wasn't public, and who cares what you're doing on forty acres of piney woods. I mean you've got black people around you all the time.

I was living at Dog River. Carrie Mae, Caroline, was living with me in the cabin, and I was remodeling the house. So, I started taking her to school a long ways from Dog River. Then, I changed her school to the one where the bus picked up black children. That was in 1950.

Later, I bought my house at 203 South Warren, a pretty ante-bellum house. We moved in that house together, and she stayed there until she was ten. She walked to school and was doing very, very well. I just felt like she was a genius. Which she isn't. Still, I was just thrilled to death to teach her reading and all those other things.

Of course I didn't give it any thought. I wasn't looking around for a child. She just fell into the picture. I think it had elements of political principle in it. I was president of an Inter-racial League and everything, and had been active in this bus case.

I guess Father thought it would be something I'd tire of, that I'd give her back again. Just keep her a little while probably.

Well, even on South Warren Street people didn't pay much attention to it. She could have been living on the place, working for me. The neighborhood did become black, though. The person owning the house next door wasn't afraid to sell to blacks because I had this black child. I could just guess that.

We went around mostly with the black people in the neighborhood, so I quickly had a position which I feel Christian missionaries almost always have, whether they want it or not, it doesn't matter, of superiority with this group that's less developed, if you want to put it in a charitable way. So, I had a position of leadership in the blocks, and all the children would come there, and I would have birthday parties and teach them a little, reading a book or putting on little plays on the back porch. All sorts of little elementary-type activities.

Yes, absolutely. I was playing "mother." I was just delighted to be. Caroline called me Boots, which is what Father, Mother, and the McIntosh family called me, and I went down and bought her clothes and did everything mothers do.

I remember I would perspire in the stores when I was shopping with her. I mean it made me very nervous to take my black foster daughter in for clothes, and to have people ask me why I didn't get a white one, if I wanted a child. I would really perspire. I found out what situations made me sweat. Nobody noticed her in my house, that was a place that was already integrated. I don't know whether the black people could try on clothes in shops then or not, I think they could, but I didn't enjoy it. It was something I would have to get up my nerve to do.

Restaurants? I don't think we ever tried. We'd go to curb service somewhere. Mildred and Frances and I took Caroline to drive-in theaters, and the proprietor stopped us once and said she couldn't go in unless she had a uniform on. She was still a baby, but she had to be dressed like a maid if she went in. I can't think of all the boundaries that we explored.

When Caroline got to be ten, in 1954, we went to Pendle Hill, a Quaker place in Media, Pennsylvania. We went just for a few weeks, for a course I wanted to take. We drove up.

I could have written up a nice little article about interracial traveling based on our trip, but I didn't. I was sort of doing it in my mind, though, because we had to carry a chamber pot and a sterno stove and sleep in the car. She couldn't get into a hotel or motel anywhere on the trip, or in any rest room, even at a filling station. It didn't matter that she was a child. It was pretty interesting to see how black people had to stay with relatives when they traveled. They had to know somebody.

We camped out but we didn't have a tent, we just used the car. Yeah, just the two of us. I remember the pretty places along the way even now.

When I got up there, I had the chance to get married again. Elias

Tamara. (I've got his name written in my album. He gave a little Bible to Caroline—I've still got it.) He was an Arab whom the Quakers had brought over from Palestine. He lost his house when the Jews came in. We were all going to these lectures together, and well, he proposed to me. I got a real proposal of marriage.

So, that was a real possibility, but none of these people were really suitable you know. Suppose I'd married that Arab or that French sailor? Even the people I did marry weren't so very suitable either.

Caroline didn't like Elias and me seeing each other. She'd run and bust us apart, if the three of us were on the train or something. We took a trip to New York once. She was fussing against him, and she told me later that she was sorry, when she was older. But I didn't want to marry Elias particularly. I guess I should have, whether I wanted to or not, if I wanted children. Even though he was in an intellectual place, where everyone talked about pacifism, and all these theories and political things that I loved, he was not political. He was not a reader. He was a very different type. He had, oh, maybe twenty-five tailored suits, hand-tailored suits, even though he was an Arab refugee. That was the type of thing his family thought he needed to be outfitted with instead of knowledge of theories. He wasn't at all intellectual.

We were in Pennsylvania maybe four weeks or six weeks, and that's when we decided to go to Europe and stay with Madame André Trocmé. We decided that quickly, too. I thought Caroline would have more opportunity over there, and would learn to speak French. At first, we were just thinking only of France.

We came back to Mobile and got our passports and all that kind of thing. Then we went to Europe. We left from New Orleans. The boat was leaving from Mobile, a Holland American Line freighter, twelve passengers, but you couldn't board until the last port of disembarkation, whatever that is, and that was New Orleans. We had a problem again of spending a night. A Quaker family took us in there. I don't know how we got their names, but they offered us hospitality. Mildred drove to New Orleans, and we spent the night with them. It took three weeks to get overseas to Europe.

I had a wonderful opportunity that I turned down. I wrote the *Pittsburgh Courier*, a black newspaper, and asked them if I could write up these interracial travel experiences. They offered me 5 cents a word, but I didn't take it. I was scared to. I was too timid about coming out with my own beliefs. In Mobile, people didn't pay much attention. I hadn't really done anything that was very noticeable. Well, this was something I regret having done. I think it was very foolish. I wrote them back and asked for ten cents a word, which was ridiculous. Why should I get that? Five cents was tremendous, and it would have been tax free if I stayed over there a certain length of time. It would have been good.

We'd been written up in the *Courier* before, and they knew us. Mildred and Frances and I had a picture in there called "Crusaders for Democracy."

We got to Versailles, and it was a horribly low standard of living, and I was so miserable. The whole house was unheated and damp. I went to Europe on impulse because Mrs. Trocmé invited us. We were to live with her for $150 a month including board. Which was cheap. They weren't even ready for us when we came. We had to stay in a hotel or something for a few days. Then, when they did let us into the room for two, it was all taken up with the bed. There really wasn't any room for anything else. The old wardrobe had somebody else's clothes in it. The food was very poor, and Mrs. Trocmé entertained German tourists, which was part of the Fellowship's ideal. Most of the other French people wouldn't do so, they wouldn't speak to them, and the Fellowship takes up with the enemy so to speak. It doesn't take the sides that the war does. Madame Trocmé served the Germans and us pumpkin soup for about two solid days. Well, who wants it in the first place? That was about all we had, it seemed to me, pumpkin soup. And then, I would have to get up and fix Caroline's breakfast. There was this big ole piece of French bread. You had to cut it with a guillotine type of thing. And, there wouldn't be anything else offered to me. Madame Trocmé would give me a little piece of cheese wrapped up in silver paper, or something like that. I wanted food in ice boxes. I felt like I was starving and freezing.

Caroline walked a long way to the French school with Mrs. Trocmé's children. The school complained over her drinking too much water. They served wine to the French children. Little carafes. The children's dining room looked like something out of a Dickens novel: this dark place with these natural wood tables and the little wine jugs on the tables. Caroline was picking up French, but of course she didn't know which grade to be in or anything. I took her out of that school. She wasn't unhappy. She was having a good time.

Everywhere she went, she was such a novelty to people. They might have seen an adult Nigra, but they hadn't seen one quite like her. We could go everywhere. We did run into a little bit of discrimination, but nothing like Alabama.

Then, we moved into the Hotel Denise on the Left Bank in Paris, and there I almost got pneumonia again, like I did before. The climate was terrible. And I knew I was sick, and there was no heat in the place. So I went to a doctor, and he said I had a big fever, but didn't tell me how high. I wouldn't have known how to interpret it from the centigrade thermometer, anyway. I was supposed to take penicillin. He gave me the prescription, and I was to go buy the needles and shoot them myself or something. I couldn't take that. So I didn't take anything. Just went back to the hotel, and they turned the heat on for me, and I stayed there until I felt like I didn't have fever.

Caroline was put into the American School, and it was adorable. They loved her there. I really don't know whether that was the name of it or not, but it was a cute school. They were made to curtsy there. They said you have got to have all these different kind of manners. They thought Caroline was adorable, but we just couldn't make it back and forth to that school with the transportation on the subways and everything.

We were in Paris a couple of months. We went to the American church, and they sent her an invitation to a birthday party in the American community. It would have been nice if I could have settled and stayed there, but I was too uncomfortable. I searched for twenty-two months in Europe for a life with minimum standard of living, and I never found it. This was right after the war, and there wasn't any housing available in France. Things were very expensive.

When I moved around Europe, I was looking for a place that had heat and a refrigerator and a stove, where I could cook and be comfortable. Even a small place. I never found one. Never.

I don't guess I thought about how long I'd be gone. I thought I would investigate. I was looking into the Quakers, they are pacifists, and I felt like I would belong to that group. But, I never could make their stand; I couldn't take the sacrificial poverty of their life. The simple life, they called it. It was worse than soldiers' barracks.

I can name just a few places here and there where we went, but I can't remember when. There was Majorca. There are many beautiful things to remember about Majorca. Then, we were in Toromolino, Spain. I think we stayed about two months everywhere, because we'd have to spend a good bit of money to get a lease on an apartment by the month. We had the most gorgeous house in Spain. Incredible. With servants included with the house. It belonged to an English lady who allowed this servant to approve the people who leased it. It wasn't anything like American standards, but we had good food cooked for us there by Trimadia, the maid, whose garden was in the back. The garden had sprinklers and all, the house had huge doors which opened onto patios, but the toilet wouldn't flush right, and the water wouldn't run right in the tubs, and it wasn't hot, and there was no heat at all in the house. You were supposed to put these little coals in braziers to break the chill. Well, I'd just as soon be outdoors. It was just hopeless. But the atmosphere was fascinating. There were these boys running down the streets after cows and things like that. There was this music, this flamenco dancing. This must have been the heart of flamenco in Spain; it was going on all night long in the fisherman's bar. It just permeated our consciousness. One time, the little boys came and serenaded Caroline as she stood on the balcony. She was just thrilled with all these experiences.

Every place we went we took Berlitz—the first course. We bought the Berlitz first course, and they were the same words pretty much. Before long these street noises started being words that I could hear

Dorothy and Caroline, playing at dress-up for a Christmas card, Holland, 1954

and understand. Caroline picked up all of the languages.

I paid my way over there, and I was thinking of money, and I didn't want to do it twice. I wanted to get my money's worth.

We went to Holland to see Nicki's family, and we met his first wife. She was about a year older than he, and we got our pictures made together there. She told me how Nicki would get drunk and all with her, too. I don't think he ever hit her in the face, but she divorced him. I don't know the answers to other questions. It would just be surmise.

We swam in the North Sea, and Caroline had all these ideas about the barbarians coming down from the North, and she picked up all these historical facts. People thought she was brilliant. Well, she was not brilliant, but she had lots of exposure to things other people didn't have, and these things would just come out from her, and they were interesting concepts for a ten- or eleven-year-old child to be expressing. I think she enjoyed it all. I didn't enjoy it.

We were traveling alone. Just the two of us. Then, Caroline was in Switzerland in a boarding school and in England in a boarding school. I traveled: to Yugoslavia, because she didn't go there; to Sardinia, a place most people haven't gone. It's nothing but a big ole rock. Some of these places can get very dreary: the little ole hotels with nothing, just nothing at all to see or do, except the scenery.

I kept a map all the time. I would unfold it and study it. I was just on a travel binge. I would feel that these places were just calling me, and I'd go to the next place. I even started to come home around the world, which would have been a good idea.

I stayed a long time. If I had been totally unhappy in Europe after six months, I could have come home. I think I should have. Father suggested leaving Caroline over there and coming home. I didn't want to do that. It made me angry. Anyway, in Yugoslavia I had a traveling companion, a male, but it was not a love affair at all. He was just somebody to talk to. He was a son of a prominent political figure in Egypt. His father was famous. He was dark, but he wasn't brown. He was a reddish color with beautiful skin. We just happened to go to the same cities once or twice.

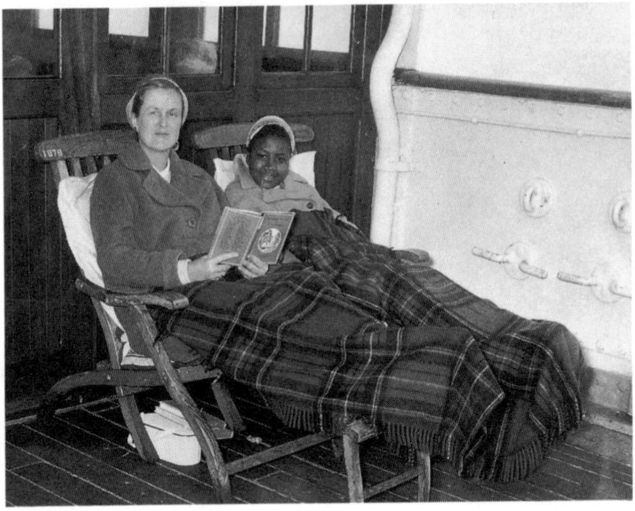

Dorothy and Caroline,
returning from Europe, reading
Treasure Island, 1956

The train rides were interesting. I'd meet people everywhere. I met two English women in Yugoslavia. They were taking their holiday. Two teachers. Caroline wasn't with me, but we looked them up in London and went to their schools and homes and wrote to them for awhile. I made these casual friendships everywhere, so I was really never alone. There was always somebody to talk to. The list of the places I went covers almost every place you can think of.

I went to Istanbul, Turkey, alone. Oh, I went to the Blue Mosque, of course, right away. That's a most spiritual place, because of the architecture. It just makes such an impact on you. I just wanted to fall on my knees. Arab women don't go there to pray. It's all men on those little rugs, praying. I guess they let the tourists in, because they let me.

I dressed up once like an Arab woman in one of these countries, and the police came and told me to take it all off. They said I wasn't acting the way an Arab woman would act. The things I was doing, hanging around, looking at the children, the stores: it wasn't the way they would be doing. It was alright for an American tourist to act that way, but only if she looked like one. It was just some foolish sense of adventure that made me do that. Somebody suggested it or something. I don't remember where I got the clothes.

Do I regard myself as adventurous spirited? Well, I think that remarks we make about ourselves, and evaluations of ourselves, usually don't sound good. It's better to let other people judge you by what your acts have been. But to answer you: I think the search for adventure or novelty or change is part of the human spirit.

Actually, though, I think mine was a foolish life without a lick of sense. Biologically, I think, I should have been married at fifteen, but that's far too young to assume the obligations of marriage. But, by twenty or twenty-one you should have had about six or seven children and been happy.

I think that's what would have made me happy. I would have been too busy. As I've said, I don't think happiness is really the goal, or really possible, but a certain balance of energies and happenings in your life is fulfillment enough.

You say: If your female colleagues were sitting here with us today, they would look at me and perhaps say things like, "You know, you were an early feminist. You lived a life . . . you traveled to learn, to have adventures, you weren't tied down to a family, and you should be proud of your achievements."

That is a nice way to look at it. And when you asked the question last night about which generation I would rather have been in? Well, it's really just which one I would rather have been young in, because I've *been* in both of them. People born later have just been in one. I've been in Southern society, but I've been in the sexual revolution and the drug culture and the hippies—all that—just as much as the young people were, and it affected my behavior too. Only I was in my forties and fifties instead of twenties and thirties.

I don't know what I was looking for in any of my life, or what I'm looking for today. I don't know that anyone of us is fortunate enough to have a sense of what's motivating him. I had no real goal.

Oh, I've got to go back again in time. Before I left for Europe I had an almost-marriage with a Dutchman named Jan Heidema, who's living over in Holland now. He had come to the States with his wife. He was sent over by some company, like Nicki. I think his job was buying or making cross-ties for railroads, and anyway his wife didn't like it here and went back to Holland with their two daughters. He stayed, and he rented a room from Miss Virginia Whiting, whom my father frequently went out to dinner with. She introduced Jan to me. We really fell for each other. And, I feel exploited by Jan because of the very strong sexual feelings that he aroused in me. We talked mostly: you know, this sexual brinkmanship, with very little physical contact. I imagine he went home and masturbated, but I didn't. I couldn't think of anything but Jan, he was just racing through my mind all the time.

We weren't talking about marriage. He was still married. He really had no legal right to propose to anybody. Father kept reminding me that he was married.

I wasn't paying my income tax, I was taking the tax refusal stand of a pacifist, and Jan wanted me to give up. He said, "Pay it, pay it all." That was very upsetting to him, the idea that he would get in on anything like that. And then, he said about Caroline, she will have to go away to a school. He would have been an excellent parent, making firm decisions, very thoughtful, instead of impulsive. But those issues, pacifism and my race relations, were a handicap to a conventional marriage, and I wouldn't give them up. I felt like that was the will of God or some silly thing like that. My will was to give them up, but the *right* thing was not to, and I didn't.

Then, the company gave him leave to go back home, at Christmas, to join his family: his wife had said something to someone in the company. I think she burst into tears and said, "I don't think he wants to come home, he's got a girlfriend in America." Ms. Laurendine, Mildred's mother said, "Don't let him go back to her." Well, I wish I had tried not to let him go back. That was my last chance to have children. I was about thirty-six then, or thirty-eight. I've forgotten.

After he went away, I would cry and throw myself over the bed and weep these terrible racking sobs. Caroline saw all this, and she sympathized with me, I think. I bought sleeping pills and started to take them. I had a mental picture going through my mind exactly how I would turn on the radiants in a gas stove, if I decided to. . . . I guess I was close to suicide, but I didn't attempt it. I was very depressed, and my friend Mildred was not at all sympathetic.

He went over there, and decided to stay married to her. They did divorce later, though. They didn't get along with each other, they really didn't.

So, while I was in Europe, Father wrote one of his letters and said, "I hope you don't try to see Jan over there." He was always so impractical and unkind. That was one reason I was so at loose ends: I thought I was going to get this family situation, which everybody aspired to, and which our society seems to set as such a goal, and I didn't get it.

I was crying a lot. I cried a lot after Jan went back. That was Christmas of 1953, because we went to Europe in September 1954. Oh! At the time I was going with Jan, Frances started going with a boy at Brookley Field named Ralph McLaney, and so we all met and went out together. She married Ralph, and she had three children. Her first one was born the day Caroline and I got back from Europe. There's a little birth announcement in my album. Her two daughters are lawyers now. Her son's married. So, she made it, and I didn't.

I guess that was why I was wandering around Europe. I really didn't know what to do with myself. My ideals didn't employ me fully enough. Pacifism wasn't enough. I wasn't at a place where I could go to my "pacifist job" every day and let that take my time. When we came back from Europe, it was the Ku Klux Klan scene.

I didn't go to Europe to look up Jan, if that's what you think. I never tried to, even though I was in Holland. I didn't even know how to. I don't even think I even knew which city he was in. Tom DaPonte could look him up now for me and probably find him, but I don't see any point in it. He did remarry finally. In about 1958 or so, which was just about the time that I married my second husband, who was wildly unsuitable.

Jan and I didn't write, not after he went back to his wife: that was the end. I had a lot of impulses to do things like. . . . Things that happen in Mobile all the time—these murders of love—mostly black people just killing one another all over the place. I had murderous instincts toward him going through my mind, you know, cruel things to do to him, but I didn't do anything. In fact, what happened was sort of my decision because I didn't give in to his demands. I would have had a strong man who would have made good decisions and would have taken into account my beliefs and thoughts. Father either ignored them or acted like they didn't exist, or was quiet and wouldn't discuss them. Pacifism and race relations were important to me.

If my mother had lived, I think I would have been more conventional, and probably my life wouldn't have been as interesting.

4 Consequences

After coming back from Europe, I decided to enroll Caroline in the nearest school, which was Azalea Middle School, a traditionally white school close to Dauphin Parkway. I went there alone the day of registration because she had pink-eye. I shouldn't have told the ladies that she was black, but I did. That was silly of me. I should have just gotten her registered and gone home, but I told the woman that she was a Negro child, and they wouldn't let me register her there.

I don't remember exactly when after that that the Klan burned the cross, but we had an eight-foot fiery cross burned in my father's driveway. A band of men in robes and hoods did it. After that, we had many, many phone calls from all sorts of people: racists and the press mostly. My friends didn't call. We were on the front page of *Mobile Press* and *Register* day after day. We kept making headlines, even though we hadn't done anything different from before.

I wrote to the school board and pointed out that Caroline met the specifications of the Alabama Pupil Placement Law. But they didn't really attempt to put that law in place. They offered me other schools, other black schools, to choose between, but I kept her at home, and said I was going to tutor her, and they said I could.

I wanted to test the Pupil Placement Law. When we were in Germany, we were aware of the Autherine Lucy case. She was a black girl who tried to get into the University of Alabama. We went to a place called America House, while we were over there in Germany, and I

Caroline at a dance
at Oak Grove School,
in Maine, 1957

asked people to write the president of the University of Alabama about that case, but I never thought about Caroline doing anything like that until I became aware of the Pupil Placement Law which just fitted her so well.

Did I think about whether the Klan would react? No, I didn't think about it. I didn't think whatsoever. I never anticipated the cross being burned. I didn't think there would be any reaction at all. This was the first time in many years that the Klan had burned a cross in Mobile. But after that incident, there were a rash of cross burnings. And this Bernard character, I've forgotten his name, he was a gunsmith in Mobile and a Klan member, ran for political office shortly afterwards because of this "favorable" publicity. He got it from the Klan burning crosses and making trouble.

I think I sent Caroline to Emerson School for the rest of the school year, which was a black school at the time. Then, I applied for this teaching position at Oak Grove School in Vassalboro, Maine, and we went there the next year. That was when she was in eighth grade twice. That was very foolish, I did the same thing my father did. She had a perfectly good eighth-grade report card, and then I went and made her get another eighth-grade report card. She was not further advanced toward graduating that year. It was very foolish of me to let Miss Owing put her back at Oak Grove.

I left the school at Christmas. I stopped teaching there because I got tired of it. I didn't want to work there. There was not enough interesting companionship. It was too lonely.

Caroline finished the year. I think she liked it. I gained a lot of weight in Europe. It's the only time that I've ever been very much overweight, and I lost it at Oak Grove School because all the girls were dieting. I lost thirty pounds there, and I came home and lost ten more pounds. So, that was when I married my second husband, when I had lost all that weight. And that too was a very impulsive, foolish marriage, to an unsuitable partner, fourteen years younger than I, who not only drank but really mainlined drugs.

Larry Gene Patrick. A laborer. I met him when he was putting a roof on my Warren Street house. I had him paint my kitchen, too. I approached him sexually. I was forty-two when I met him. I married him about a year later. We went down to Florida for our honeymoon. Anyway, he was a very bad character. He had been in the penitentiary in Florida. I've forgotten the name of it. He was a violent, dangerous criminal.

Did I know about that? I knew enough to know to. . . . I don't know how to answer questions like that. Of course I should have had better sense. I don't know how to answer it! [She is distressed, on the verge of tears]. I mean I had my eyes open! [Now angry.] I could see. You know a lot about anybody if you've got any sense, when you've known him five minutes much less about a year! Maybe I didn't know everything, but I knew enough!

The physical attraction of a young man—that's what moved me. He was only twenty-eight years old. I was forty-two when I met him. I think I married him when I was forty-three, and we stayed married a couple of years, I guess. We divorced in April 1961, the same year Caroline had Alfred.

I still correspond with Larry's sister and have been to see her. She's in Dallas now. She's been to see me. I talked to him on his death bed which was, I think, in 1986. He died of lung cancer at age fifty-five. His was an utterly wasted life. His father was still hanging around with him most of the time, they were a pair of bums. They were both horrible drunkards. The father didn't shoot dope. Larry would buy it, cook it down, and then shoot it in his arm, and then he'd look real dreamy-eyed. Just off in another world with that dope. Absolutely useless to anybody for any reason. He certainly couldn't be a husband when he was full of that. He was passed-out almost. He didn't work. Not often. Sometimes he got a job for seventy-five cents an hour from some construction place or other.

Larry hit me, and beat me up, and left a big scar. He shot at me once, and I guess that was when my cousin's husband, the lawyer who lived next door at Dog River, asked me about my black and blue face. He probably told Father, and Father and he decided I had to have a divorce. They made that decision, and Father told me that

Larry would never stop shooting dope. It was hard enough to stop smoking; it was hopeless with something that was that strong a habit. So, they got me into the courtroom and were preparing me to testify; all I had to do was bring a witness to the physical assault. But, I said some mean remark to my cousin's husband, so he walked out. He wouldn't take the case. I didn't want to divorce Larry anyway.

Later, I got another lawyer myself, and then I was more in control of the situation. That lawyer tried to get Larry to sign a legal paper which meant he wouldn't contest the divorce. Larry said to the lawyer, "She doesn't want to divorce me." I guess he never thought I would leave him, because there was a great deal of pleasure being married to a young man. I can wake up some mornings now, remembering, wishing I could turn over and see him. Not a gray hair on his head. Curly black hair. A strong laborer with beautiful muscles. I guess he thought I'd never be able to do without him, but I did divorce him. I saw him again after a while, and he phoned every so often and stopped by to see me when he was in Mobile. I sent some money for his mother's tombstone, I think, when she died, and I met his sister and all. I've kept up with the in-laws of all my husbands.

Larry was in the house with Caroline when she was in high school. After Maine, she went to St. Mary's, a Catholic boarding school in New Orleans, and then, she came back to Mobile and went to a Catholic school very close to where she's living now. When Larry came into the house, he was a very bad influence on her and her friends. This man obviously shouldn't have been around at all. It was just a weakness in me, to want a person like that.

I think he attempted to rape Caroline once. I didn't pay much attention to it at the time, but she was kind of torn up, her clothes and things. She had a room of her own upstairs. I don't remember any words. I don't think, no, she didn't use any words or anything that I can recall. I just recall the fact that she looked like she had been the victim of a scuffle of some kind. I remember the way she looked. Probably Katy May Dukes didn't look much worse than that, and the man got the death sentence for it. And, we've learned since then to trust a woman more when she says that she was assaulted, instead of thinking she invited it. I took the old-fashioned way and thought she invited it probably. I didn't do anything about it.

Caroline had many boyfriends of her own at this time and wrote in her diary telling about—a diary that I got hold of—so I had reason to believe that she invited him—she wrote in this diary, "Check Larry out." That was pretty much in her disfavor, I think.

When she was a junior in high school, she got pregnant and got married. Before the marriage, she had some consultations with doctors. One of them said she had a tumor. It was a "pregnant" tumor. He x-rayed her which is bad for the fetus. Alfred had all that abuse as a fetus. It was an awful strain on me, having to deal with all this.

She was pregnant at sixteen. She'd be seventeen in July, and Alfred was born in August. She was married in February, when she was still sixteen, to Lester Foster, Jr., who was a radio announcer. And, it turned out that he had another pregnant wife, or girlfriend, and two little boys, too. At least he furnished Caroline a little house; he bought some furniture on time or something. He was running back and forth, a busy man trying to put chickens in both houses and not let either one know about the other.

Then, when Caroline was very large with her pregnancy, she had two wisdom teeth out. She just had to have them out because they hurt so bad. The dentist gave her some strong drugs which she took afterwards for the pain. Of course, all this was bad for the fetus, too. We didn't think about that. Well, she was under the influence of this dope, like a drunken person, and she was crying about Lester saying, "He doesn't l-l-love me," and all.

Well anyway, I took her back over to her own house. She was bursting into tears, crying and crying. Before I took her, she fell down the steps at that house on Warren Street, head over heels, pregnant. Then, I think she burst into tears over that. And, I just thought I couldn't stand it any more, living in this upset condition. So this is where I made the mistake which kept me from bringing up Alfred. I got on the train with her, and we went up to her grandmother's in Chicago, and the baby was born up there. (The grandmother and I have been in a tug-of-war ever since.) Caroline didn't care a thing about him, right from the beginning. She always said she wasn't pregnant, even when she was this big!

I hadn't ever discussed sex with her. I had done no differently than my father in that respect. Caroline certainly never discussed it with Alfred either, she wouldn't do anything for Alfred.

Her sexuality: well it just exploded. I mean, all of a sudden, there were packs of men outside. Young boys, I guess, not men. You know, it was embarrassing to come to the house and see them all waiting for her. So, what can I tell her? She could give me lessons. It would be ridiculous to think she needs to know the facts of life. It wasn't sex education she lacked, it was the goal of being a respectable member of society. Of getting married and having children, instead of just being a wild woman.

I should have just given Caroline back to her mother right away, and let her take care of all those problems. I can't deal with all these things. I don't know why. [Dorothy struggles for composure.]

Well, Lester was mad that he had fixed that little house and bought some furniture on time, and then I'd gone and taken her away. So he phoned one of these magazines where their wedding had been written up—*Ebony* or *Jet*—and he said she was pregnant when he married her and that I gave him $500 or something to do it. I said, "Get out of the house. Here's $500"—something like that. And that, of course, hurt Caroline's feelings. She felt like she was attractive and didn't need to be treated like . . . that I bribed somebody to marry her.

She said, "Boots, I'm scared," when she got pregnant. I really should have put her out of the house right then. I think I put most everybody out. Everybody that I've come in contact with just about. Anyway, she said she wasn't pregnant. He said she wasn't pregnant. Then, he put that charge in the paper. Maybe they didn't publish it, but we got that news when they called us. Well, that brought Mother

Dorothy with baby Alfred
and Phil, during Mardi Gras
in Mobile, 1963

Dear, that's what they called the grandmother, into the picture with a vengeance. She was so mad with Lester. He stayed here in Mobile after I took Caroline up there.

I left her there for the birth—and Mother Dear took her to a doctor for an examination, but she didn't take her to him when she was having labor pains. Caroline wrote me a long letter—she writes well—describing how awful she felt. She said, "I'm not comfortable even for a minute." Well, she was about to give birth when she was writing the letter, and they didn't get her to the hospital or to the doctor. They called the ambulance and these people delivered the baby without any anesthetic, there at the house. She named him Alpha Omega. I don't know what she was thinking. We called him Alfred.

She stayed up there a little while and then came back to Mobile. She said she didn't have a child. She always just completely denied him. The child stayed up there until November 11, I think. When Mother Dear said I could get him, at three months, I went up and brought him back. I went up alone.

Caroline was back with Lester, and he sent her to Daniel Payne College, a very poor college. She shouldn't have been given the idea that she could continue as if she didn't have a child. That was another mistake. She should have been forced to acknowledge the responsibility in some way and get bonded with the child. I brought the baby back to Mobile. She must have lived at Warren Street for awhile, when I lived with Mildred. This went on for a couple of years.

When Caroline was sixteen, and we still lived together on South Warren, I took another child into my house. Phil was the son of a couple who had a little cottage right across the street from me. He was the youngest of twelve children, but most of his brothers and sisters had grown and gone. I just started caring for him. His family wasn't very good—they were just no good drunkards—and when I asked them if I could take him, they said yes. He was nine. His parents moved over to Birdville, a low-rent housing project, so I kept Phil two or three years, I've forgotten. I still had him when Alfred was born.

Phil was in the second grade at Craighead; he was old for his grade. I taught him to read, and he could read through the fourth-grade reader, which someone at Barton Academy said was very unusual for a boy of his capacity to do. He wasn't very smart. So, I was just thrilled at my ability to teach reading!

Caroline and Phil liked each other. One time while we were driving, Caroline said how much Phil and I looked like each other. But, that was just the color of our skin she saw. Phil said she looked like chocolate candy. It was all for fun. He could be a cut-up, and sometimes a real devil.

Anyway, I gave him back. I can't remember whether it was before or after, but one time I came home and smelled pine smoke in the house. I called the fire department, and they found that a fire had been set in the attic: the fire chief said it was definitely arson. Phil did that, so you can see he was disturbed.

When he got married, he brought his wife by to meet me. That marriage ended, though. Later on, Phil and a girlfriend were found dead in his apartment; they had left the gas ring on. His family asked me if I would pay for the headstone, and I think I may have, but I have no record of it. I remember I went to the funeral.

I sent Caroline to Mexico, to a university, for a summer-school course. Ralph Rich was a student, and he was also the bus driver for this group of students from the University of Wisconsin. So, she seduced him, I guess. I would put it that way. I don't know what happened really.

She stayed with him in Madison, Wisconsin, and enrolled in prelaw courses. They were too much for her intellectual capacity, and at one point she had a sort of psychotic episode when she was spouting out these law cases. Just so and so against so and so: this, that, and the other all running through her head. Not making any sense.

They pretended they were married, and I found it out. I told her I knew the way she was living. She said she was glad I found out, or something like that. Well, I think he was a nice boy from Wisconsin, a white boy, and he decided that he would marry her.

They went to Mother Dear's house. Alfred was with me in Mobile. She got a Baptist minister to marry them. Several ministers refused to, I think. Caroline has a beautiful wedding picture somewhere. She had a pretty bridal outfit on. Ralph married her, and I think he had every intention of being a good husband. They came to Tuskegee, Alabama, together. They both were students at the Institute there. Later, Ralph divorced her for adultery. She was running around with everybody else. She didn't appreciate the good luck she'd had: somebody taking care of her child and sending her to the university, and a loving, sober husband with academic degrees, doing graduate work, and all. He was a nice boy.

At one time when they were students at Tuskegee (Alfred was staying here in Mobile with me), we all went to a conference. This was some sort of black conference on civil rights; I've forgotten which one. It was held in Birmingham; I think it was 1966. Anyway, we rode through Prattville, Alabama, and we tried to get served at a place called Kennedy's Pit Barbecue, and when they saw us. . . . If I'd gone in first, maybe it would have been better, I don't know. Caroline was in the front seat, and I was scrunched with Alfred in the back seat of a little tiny car, and it was hard for me to unfold and get out. Caroline was already there at the door—she always acts in a queenly manner—and they just pushed that door right back at her, animal-like, keeping her out, with white people still sitting at their tables inside, about six o'clock in the evening. Not too late.

So, I went over to the little take-out window, and I said we came to buy some dinner, and he said the place was closed. I said, "Well, when did it close?" He said, "It's closed as of now." Bang! and slapped down that take-out window. So, I went next door to a pay telephone and called the police. Oh, I should have had more sense than to think that there was a law, and that the police would enforce it. It doesn't work that way at all. The police came, but they didn't let us in to get anything to eat. We all went down to the court house, and so did the owner of the restaurant, Kennedy, and he had a lawyer down there. It was an interesting scene. We didn't get anything to eat from the law. Ralph found some other place to get something, I think. But it all resulted in this man Kennedy suing me for $100,000 for false arrest without probable cause. See, I guess I arrested him. I didn't even know what I was doing.

Anyway, that was very traumatic for me, that lawsuit. I had just gotten $100,000, and I never had that much money before. The Bacon-MacMillan Veneer Company had been sold, my father had bought me stock in it long before, and I had just gotten around $100,000, which I thought would have lasted me the rest of my life. It was just the most marvelous thing to think of, and I felt like Kennedy knew about that money and was after it. But he didn't; he couldn't have. Anyway, my father was very, very upset and wanted me to settle it out of court, but I didn't want to do that.

I wanted it to be a big lawsuit, and I got a wonderful lawyer. His name was Donald Jelinek. He was down doing work in Selma for civil rights. He'd been in jail and done all those things that made me have confidence in him. He was from the North, somewhere. I wanted the lawsuit. I wanted the whole trip—the publicity, the write-up, the exposure, the civil rights cause—and I kind of thought I'd get a husband out of it like, I think, Autherine Lucy may have done.

I was prepared enthusiastically to have a big significant lawsuit. Jelinek said it would get big publicity. My father felt just the other way. He wanted nothing of the kind. You know: "Pay him off." "Get rid of him." "All he wants is money." "We can't stand all this." "Prattville's the home of the Ku Klux Klan." "The lawyers and the judge and FBI, everybody there will be sympathetic with the Klan." Well, Father put so much pressure on me until I paid the man, I've forgotten exactly how much—maybe it was just $3,000. I'd been working at Project Head Start and that was all the money I'd made there. I had to pay Kennedy off, and that was the end of our case.

After I did that I was so angry at Father, and so mad with myself for doing it, that I cried for about three days.

The whole thing took a year or two to resolve. (The last lawsuit I had took eight years.) Anyway, I could have killed my father. I hated him because he didn't support my lawsuit. I felt that it was immoral, from my point of view, to pay the man who had shut me out. We confronted that man in the court house hallway, and Alfred said, "You're my enemy." He was five years old, which is kind of cute. And, Kennedy said, "No, I'm not," or something.

Anyway, later we sued him back again, for $100,000 each I believe, the three of us. The three of *them*. I couldn't sue because I'd settled my claim. I sued for Alfred and Caroline and Ralph. We had a lawyer that's well known around Tuskegee, I've forgotten his name now, but the jury decided that Kennedy did serve colored people at his restaurant, even though they had black people on the jury. They said there'd been an instance when he served blacks, but that wasn't actually true. We didn't get a cent.

Well, Ralph and Caroline were divorced by that time, but they still spent a night together in that motel where we were staying during the lawsuit. That was 1966. Alfred was in Head Start, then he was in the first grade that year.

Alfred went back up to Mother Dear's regularly. Sometimes he was in Chicago, sometimes in Mobile. He's got that habit deeply ingrained in him now. When he's tired of one place, he gets restless and moves on.

He was just like a little Southern white boy when he was with me. When he came back from Mother Dear's, he was sick. He had diarrhea and had lost weight and was a broken-hearted, broken-spirited, silent, unresponsive, and abused child. He was two maybe. She thinks to this day she didn't beat him enough. He'd have turned out alright, if she just could have whipped him into shape or something. I've tried to tell Caroline that he was neglected and abused. She wasn't the slightest bit interested in him.

When I started taking my master's degree in elementary education here in Mobile at the University of South Alabama, I left him up there for two or three years, which I shouldn't have done. When he came back that time, it was after my father died in 1968.

When my father died, among other things, I took a trip to New

York, and that's when I met Arthur Trabits. Arthur was the cab driver that drove me back to the Fifth Avenue Hotel from a Broadway show. We stopped, and he started talking to another cab driver that he knew, named Phil Rosenbloom, from one cab to another, about the races. And I said, "Oh, you go to the races? I've never been to the races." So he invited me to go to the race track with him. He and Phil came to see me in a station wagon, not in a cab, and took me to Aqueduct Racetrack the next day.

Things happened from there. Arthur's sister had a daughter who was about to get married in Miami, and Arthur was going down for the wedding. He invited me to the wedding, but I knew he couldn't invite me to somebody else's wedding that I didn't even know. So, I said I couldn't go, but why didn't he stop by and see me on the way back if he's going that far south. He did, and we visited back and forth, by telephone, and we wrote a lot. I wanted to get married just because it's always been a goal, even though I didn't have any possibility of childbirth. Of course, he didn't want to. I don't guess men ever do, but I won that battle somehow. I got him to the altar. I remember: he was a smoker then (he's since given it up), and he kept stepping outside for a cigarette. Jack Shearer, the Methodist minister, knew that I was on pins and needles that Arthur was going to leave every time he stepped outside for a cigarette. He'd go with him to make sure he wasn't stepping out for good.

We had a honeymoon in Mexico and came back to live together in my house, my father's house, at Dog River, and we had to figure out intricate financial arrangements because Arthur was so money-conscious. He's a Hungarian Jew. You know Tony Curtis is, too. They're just sharper and shrewder than anybody else about practical things, about money and all. And, I think he gave me a pretty square deal. I don't think he robbed me, but it was always very difficult; it had to be thought out exactly, you know. We were going to be half and half on everything. We never said mine is yours and yours is mine or anything. I got all sorts of benefits from being his wife that I didn't know I would get. I was going to the University of Southern

Mississippi at the time, and I got these veteran's benefits of $200 and something a month for education as the wife of a veteran. That was very nice.

Anyway, I did my practice teaching while we were married, and I already had a maid that would come in every day from 8:00 'til 2:00 and serve lunch. Arthur really had it made. I was gone practice teaching. It was pretty far away from here. Anyway, he had his meals served by the maid, and I already told her what to cook. He said it couldn't be fairer. That's his idea of having it fair. But I didn't mind. I was proud to have him come around to pick me up once in awhile at school. Most people thought I was lucky. I remember one person said, "I am so glad you've got him, Dorothy." Later, this woman didn't give me a tutoring job; she gave it to somebody who didn't have a husband just because she thought I was advantaged or something.

We were married for about two years. Then, I got mad with him. I locked him out of the house, and I said I threw away the keys. It was a lie. I didn't really throw them away. Wasn't that foolish?

I don't even remember why I did it. He wanted to come back for a long time. I stayed at Mildred's, and it was just like Nicki, repeating the same thing, sort of, only Arthur never hit me, never abused me, and was a cheerful companion. Finally he decided he would sue for divorce, and we got a no-fault divorce. We didn't have any property settlement disputes at all. He stayed around Mobile for awhile, and then he lived in Biloxi a while too.

Arthur didn't like Alfred, didn't want Alfred around, and I wish I'd chosen Alfred instead of Arthur. Arthur was a big joker. He didn't take parenting seriously, molding the child's character, setting him an example. Alfred had been very much against smoking, and Arthur smoked and made him feel like it was alright, and Alfred has that horrible habit today. It will probably kill him. And Arthur taught him a lot of dishonest tricks with money. I gave Alfred some money in the bank as a Christmas present, and I had plans to show him how it would grow. Well, Arthur showed Alfred how to get it out of the bank. Until then, Alfred didn't know how to get it out. I never had any idea that he would. Then, Alfred came back with this money all over the place, and Arthur acted like that was funny. Then one time, Alfred took $100 out of my purse. Arthur was taking him out to a restaurant, and Alfred had a $100 bill, and Arthur didn't say a thing to him about it. He let him get by with that, and Alfred's a thief today.

Alfred was living with Arthur and me, and then I sent him to New York Military Academy. He realized that as a pacifist, I shouldn't be doing that. He made that connection at nine years old. While he was there, he was good at horses, but he wouldn't attend class or study or anything. If I'd left him there, though, he would still have learned a lot of discipline. He was the second lowest in his class rating the first year, and the lowest when he dropped out the next year. And, he's supposed to be of normal intelligence. Before he went there, he could read and write well. Then, I sent him to another school, an entirely different type, where famous people send their kids. It was close to his summer camp in the Adirondack Mountains, where I had been sending him for years. I believe I would have preferred the fascist-type school to this ultra-liberal one. Anyway, Alfred loved it, and most of the children did. They wouldn't let him come back in the end, though. They said he was a bully. The little children were afraid of him, and some of the teachers were afraid of him too.

He was about twelve, I guess, but very big and strong. So, I had him back with me. I put him in a public school. There was a question of who he belonged to, me or Mother Dear. She wanted him back up there. I was taking these courses in Mississippi, and I put them ahead of going up with him to Chicago. He asked me to go up with him. He climbed trees to keep from having to go. He locked himself in a room; we had to take the lock off the door. He went out in a tree over the water to keep from going back up there, and I made him go, and I wish I hadn't, and he'll never forgive me for it. Arthur and his brother drove Alfred back up there.

Later, I just put all my efforts into figuring how to get him away again. But, the courts finally gave him to his mother, Caroline, and she entered him into an orphanage—it was a beautiful orphanage—in Philadelphia, called Presbyterian Children's Village. I visited him up there. He didn't graduate. He wouldn't study or something, but he did well on the stage. He has presence and a wonderful voice. They had good guidance counseling; they had a nice future planned for him: he would have been able to join the Philadelphia Company, and he would earn money and act at the same time. Well, he wouldn't do it. He went back to Chicago and did what a lot of boys do, which is an appropriate thing to do. He got an apartment with some other boys his age and entered a junior college. Well, all that was good, and I should have sent him money. I don't know how he did any of it because he had absolutely no earning capacity. Not one cent. But, I was doing entirely different things at this time. Anyway, he didn't come back down to me until his twenty-first birthday, in 1982, because I told him I wanted to give him a car.

Caroline came down from Philadelphia about the same time, and I rented her an apartment, in the same complex Mildred now lives in. Then, Alfred started bumming and staying with his mother. He pushed her down once. He would bring girls in. He was driving taxis, and he would bring home these girls, and I told him he couldn't do it. He locked me in the room one time. Kept me a prisoner even after my giving him all this. . . . This was in the apartment that I was paying for. He didn't want to keep working.

I've kind of forgotten what happened. He went out to Texas, close to Dallas, where Caroline's got two or three sisters. He stayed out there. He was doing pretty well. They said he had a nice apartment. This was 1985 or 1986. Really, I lost track of him. He had a job out there selling some sort of lingerie in a boutique and working at a video store at night. He left to come over here, and everything's gone from bad to worse. He's just become a criminal.

Caroline was divorced by Ralph Rich in the middle sixties. She never finished her degree at Tuskegee. Oh, she has a diploma from them, but I think she got it after the fact. I think it was after she graduated from Howard University Law School that Tuskegee gave her a diploma.

She left Tuskegee, but I didn't know it at the time. She took the car. I loaned them a little ole car, and she piled all her clothes in it. She never could keep her things up, or never tried to. They were always just junked up together. She abandoned that car with all those clothes in it and disappeared. So we thought she was dead. Mother Dear was phoning me every morning and saying, "They're going to find her body in the piney woods." That was horrible: having those phone calls and having to call the missing persons people I reported it to. Then, I think I phoned *Ebony* and one of their investigative reporters found her enrolled as a student at Howard University.

She didn't tell me where she was. She was struggling to put herself through. She stayed there about seven years, which was unrealistic and very hard. She got through, though. I went to her graduation; I've got her diploma on the wall at my office. Then, she got a government job. This was very impressive to me. It was a GS-11 level, I think. Incredible. Mildred worked for twenty, thirty years to get a GS-11 level.

Caroline really had it made. She had professional status, so that she could come to work late. Well, that was a mistake. She abused it. She said she had seven alarm clocks, but she couldn't get there on time. Well, maybe she didn't have her brain right or something. She couldn't make it. Anyway, she made a lot of money and spent it wildly. I don't know what her salary was, but whatever it was, it was a lot more than nothing, and she'd had nothing before that. Then, she thought she could go into her own business, and she left the government. I think she got severance pay. She started a business—an employment agency. She must have been a salesperson's delight: she bought everything you could conceive of for an office. She'd pay out her money, and buy it all. She had three or four people working for her—and they were robbing her because she didn't come in to work. She expected them to make her money without her supervising them. They were taking the commission and keeping it, and running up big phone bills. So, she went bankrupt. Then, she opened a travel agency, which she knew nothing about. She didn't even have a phone at that time. She got a lot of publicity, which she's good at getting. She had bouquets of flowers on opening day, and everything.

She said, "Sometimes opening day is the best there is." That one went bankrupt, too. She was bankrupt for the second time.

Then, she started something called the Young Entrepreneur Society. She wrote a newsletter, and maybe she was making a lot of money off it, some way or another, but I don't know. Then, she got this old man who's dead now—I'll never know his name because she won't tell it—who hired her to start this naturalist religion and get herself ordained a priest or something, so that they'd have some tax-free status. I guess, he thought she could get something through mail orders or something, some such scheme. But, he paid her. She was making money off doing this writing for him, and she did write the book, and lived that way a while. This happened in a place close to Philadelphia called Phoenixville. Well, finally, she didn't have anything left, and this other white man, Bill Allen, took her in. I went up there and stayed in the apartment with them. He was a very kind man. He was about sixty-nine or something, and she was still thin and attractive looking. Well anyway, she ended up on welfare. This is getting into the '80s, close to the present, 1980 let's say, and she took up with a man named Bill Angry, a black man. They lived together for awhile—he was on SSI. Whether she was on SSI or welfare, I don't know.

Let's see . . . '81. I was in New York in 1981, and she came to see me. Then, when I talked to her on the phone, she could hardly talk. It was pitiful. I went to see her in Phoenixville. I think that she was full of wine when she couldn't talk. Anyway, I told her I was going to pay for her way down here. If I wanted to be really nice, I would have taken a U-Haul trailer and brought all of her furniture down. Well, she was supposed to arrive on a certain plane at night, and she didn't. I couldn't get anything out of her about when she was coming. She just didn't know what she was doing at all, apparently. And finally, I met her on the wrong plane, not the one she was supposed to come in on—she didn't even know who I was. She didn't even recognize me, walking by with this queenly way, with her head in the air, right past me. I took her to this apartment which I fixed for her, and she didn't have much with her. She left all of her things behind. She thought that one of her two girlfriends was going to put them on the

Greyhound bus, collect, and send them as if that were nothing. Well, you can't send things collect by Greyhound. And she hadn't packed them. She'd just put them in these old boxes without even sealing them. Well, one of the girlfriends did collect the things, and washed them, instead of sending them with filthy roaches coming out of them, and sent them to me one by one to me in smaller boxes. Not pre-paid. The other friend said she wanted $1000 for what she was keeping, and Caroline had left behind this scrapbook I had made for her with beautiful pages. That woman has still got them or thrown them away. And Caroline's still furious with the one that sent her the things. Just no sense. She was completely senseless in all the things she did and said. She couldn't talk about anything but her clothes for ages.

Then, I got her this job nursing somebody. She was making money, big money, and before you knew it, she had $1000 and more. I was delighted. Alfred was driving taxis, and she was making money. They were getting their feet on the ground. Then, the lady died. Caroline got another job, and she was fired immediately. And, then, I took her to this psychologist, and he thought she was crazy, and he put her on the seventh floor of the hospital, which is the crazy floor. We were going to send her to the state mental hospital. Alfred got word of it, and he phoned one of his grandmothers or great grandmother. The two of them came and got her out, and I didn't oppose it. They took her to New Orleans. She ended up there in horrible conditions. Men all over the place, again. They might have murdered her in the end, these men, walking in and out. And Alfred was upset by the men, and he brought her back here, and I kept her at the motel. We kept going to the social security office until she got her disability approved. Finally, she got in the nursing home over there. That's the end of her crazy, mixed-up life.

Cerebella ataxia,[1] that's what her disease is. I know what the disease consists of; the cause, I can't say. If she had enough intelligence,

1. Ataxia is a failure of muscular coordination expressed as irregularity or awkwardness of movement, especially of walking but also of upper extremities, the speech mechanisms, or even eye movements. The motor abnormality associated with cere-

in spite of her handicap, she could be trained by the Rotary Clinic and get a job as a handicapped person. Maybe earn a living on the outside. She's free legally. It might be a little better than the $344 disability which she'll get on the outside. Any time she wants to leave, she can get that. But, she hasn't got any kind of a grasp of anything that she is able to do, or any kind of self-discipline, or she doesn't make contacts with people. She just wanders along.

Well, who knows what might have caused it. Drugs, I suppose; I can't prove it. Well, I don't think she actually took any injections of any kind. She just popped the pills, and I think she's had cocaine.

I did some drugs, too. After my father died. In 1968.

Around that time. Let's see, I wanted to take drugs like I wanted to take alcohol in that earlier period, but I hadn't been drinking for a long time. I just wanted to know what they were going to do to me. Everyone was smoking and passing around these marijuanas, and you had to learn how to hold it. (Maybe you've tried. I'm not asking you.) You hold it way down in your lungs for a long time. I think it ruined my lungs which were probably already pretty bad. It taught me to smoke. That's where I learned for the first time. I never had inhaled a cigarette before. So, I started smoking. I smoked a pack every other day and stopped every day in between for about a year. But all that was very bad for my lungs. Then, there was the LSD. You know, you just chew up those little pills and then have a rush. If you haven't had one, well, it's very exciting. It's very terrifying. I mean people can just go into hysterics of terror.

One time, I had a death experience, but most of the time I enjoyed it. It was like riding out a wave. It was fun. I was at Dog River, and all of a sudden the woods and the river around you sort of came alive, and they're all pulsing, and there's this great stuff out there. (You never lose your consciousness completely, you're always sort of aware of your name and where you are.) But, after awhile, I got sort of used to

---

bellar lesions depends on their locale in the cerebellum and whether adjacent neural structures are involved. Midline cerebellar dysfunction results principally from degenerative (nutritional-alcoholic) or neoplastic (medulloblastoma, hemangioblastoma, metastasis) disease.

it, and it wasn't as thrilling, because it's just some kind of a brain wave. You can look at a picture, and it'll dance around and wiggle.

It wasn't all that much fun, but at first it was like a spiritual experience. The first time I took LSD, I saw this sort of arc in the sky, and all these elephants and things going around on it, and there was no pain in the world anymore. Sort of a blessing over everything. Those are the kind of experiences I had. I was still taking LSD when I married Arthur. He didn't like it, and he would've liked me to have stopped, but he was very kind about it. I did stop. I don't remember when, but I lost interest in it completely.

Yeah. Marijuana and LSD together. They were part of the same scene. I think that LSD, as I said, may have affected my central nervous system, and Caroline's, too. Maybe we got the same thing. So, I was not a good example for her, not at all, I'm sorry to say.

It sounds like a novel, doesn't it? *I* think it sounds like a fool's progress: someone who didn't take life seriously enough.

After Arthur divorced me, I was going to lose his social security, and I wanted my social security money as much as anybody. I had to get a job to make my quarters so I could qualify on my own. I had a few, but not enough.

I couldn't get a job teaching. I substituted a lot, but they didn't hire me at any school. So, I answered a job for a live-in nurse-housekeeper. I got it right away at $100 a week. They withheld taxes—so I got only about $86 a week. I wanted them to withhold. That was the point of it. The man was ninety-three, in a wheelchair with arthritis, with an indwelling catheter and a bag on his leg. He was a very nice man. A Presbyterian. His son brought the groceries by every day. It was a nice house, and I lived there. I worked constantly. I didn't have an hour off during the day. There was no time set aside as my own. I did the laundry and the cooking, and I had to dress him, put him in his pajamas, get him out of bed, lift him up and down on the toilet, wash his face, put his eye drops in, give him his hearing aids, get him breakfast, wash the dishes, get him settled at the table, and then his neighbor would come over to play cards with him. I liked to cook, and I was eating meat then, so I could enjoy it, but I was too tired all the time. It was too much work.

I didn't get enough sleep. He wanted to get up immediately when he would wake up in the morning. I should have won that battle, but I didn't. I wanted to say, "I'm not going to start working 'til seven o'-clock. You can just stay in bed. I'll be there at seven." Our beds were close to each other—our rooms. He wouldn't have it that way. When he'd wake up, he was helpless, and he didn't want to stay in bed. I didn't blame him, but I was tired. I wanted to sleep until seven. He said, "If you don't come get me, I'm gonna get up by myself." Well, that meant he would fall. He'd fallen with the last nurse, and she was fired. So I felt trapped—I could have said, "Alright, the first time you get up, I'm leaving." I'll bet I was in a strong enough position to have gotten by with that, but I didn't think of it. He would call out to me, and it was cold and draughty, and I'd have to get up. I quit finally, and he quickly died in a nursing home without all that attention. His son wrote me a nice letter when he died. I only worked there nine months, from early 1979 through Christmas.

I applied for a job at VISTA, and I got it. I thought they were going to take out social security taxes, but they didn't. I taught these little Spanish-speaking children in a day care center the government sponsored. I had many happy moments with them. I picked up a little Spanish from them and satisfied my maternal instincts. They were adorable. Rachel, I think was her name, she was the boss of our unit, and she made a very easy schedule for me. Just from kindness, I guess. She would let me start about 8-8:30 AM, then leave about 1:30 PM instead of staying 'til 3:30. The hardest part of it was preparing the art work for the children. They had lots of toys, though, and they had a schedule of nothingness that filled in the day. But the most important thing they did, the most highly structured, was some kind of paper-pasting and crayola work, and it wasn't fun unless you had it prepared. You could prepare it, if you'd read the book. You could make adorable things, little log cabins for Lincoln's birthday. Little things like that. It took a little homework to have your material ready. But, it was keeping me busy, just that half-day. This was in New Mexico, close to El Paso. I was there thirteen months. I had a nice apartment. They asked me to stay another year, and I stayed another month trying to make up my mind. Alfred and Caroline both came to see me out there. Then, I put my cat and my dog in a U-Haul trailer behind my big ole '73 Cadillac and drove to New York City.

My cat got lost along the way when I was sleeping outdoors one night. Oh, that was sad. The dog was getting very old then, about fourteen, I guess, but we made it together to New York. I had acquaintances there, and I finally got a beautiful apartment at East 56th Street and Sutton Place. It was so different from my 43 West 8th Street place when I was young. I was there for my sixty-fifth birthday just like I was there for my twenty-fifth.

New York: that's where I would like to live. More than any place. Manhattan Island.

I asked Social Security to tell me how many quarters I had, but they thought I was putting in for early payment. They started paying me, which is what I'd been waiting for, so I didn't have to worry about working anymore. I wasn't working for the money anyway; I was working for Medicare.

I enjoyed New York a great deal. Caroline came to see me. And then, I had this big amount of money come to me. I mean really big. You probably wouldn't believe it if I told you how much. The big money was a once-in-a-lifetime thing. I don't know if I should let you in on how large an amount it was or not. I don't remember the amount, but I had to pay about $250,000 in taxes.

My father had timber land which was owned by the bank in trust, and I've had many lawsuits over it. I got newspaper ads against the First National Bank because they were trustees and let the land be used against my wishes. It cost me $750 an ad. They got an oil lease on it and sold timber. All of this development was against the environmentalist position I favored.

I went to a CPA in New York, and had I stayed there as a citizen, I would have state and city taxes amounting to $30,000 and much more probably. So, that was what put me in the U-Haul trailer again, with my dog, to come back. I hated to leave New York. I went to Florida, where they don't have state income tax, and I would come back over to Mobile for my various lawsuits and things. I thought I couldn't afford to live in Mobile. It would have cost me $10,000 a year just for taxes in addition to the apartment rent. Then, I found out Florida had a catch, too. They have tax on intangibles, which is stocks and bonds, on the gross amount you own, not on the income only, so they would have gotten me on that. I lived in Florida about a year, then I moved back to Mobile.

I didn't have a home. I had sold everything, except I had this one Negro rental house that nobody would rent. Nobody would buy it because the hurricane had ruined the roof. So I repaired it. I lived at Mildred's until I got it done, and then, I lived in that little house. It was a much lower standard of living than any other house I've ever owned. It was just a small shotgun house, and I enjoyed it thoroughly. It was fun! It was like a ship. I knew exactly where to sleep and do everything.

That's where I was living when Alfred got his automobile. I bought him an automobile. He wrecked it. Ruined it. Pawned it. I got it out of the pawn shop, because I had a lien on it. He had sold it, but he didn't have the right to sell it. Nothing that I've been able to do for him has seemed to improve his circumstances any.

Well, I think it's mainly because I didn't . . . he didn't stay in one place, with one person to love. He did not learn to really relate with love to me. I hoped what I gave him would be enough, and he would respond in a loving way. Instead, he started responding negatively to anything and anybody. I blame myself. And Arthur, too. His coming into the picture was very bad for Alfred.

My life has been alright, but I don't have the satisfactions which I would have had, had I done things more carefully and more moderately, with better judgment.

I think that I've always been off the track. My whole life has been one of snap decisions and not sticking to one thing—putting people out who should have been my primary relationships. If you don't take the time to visualize things, then you just do it any ole way. It's like flipping a coin. But then, it's all a surprise to you when it comes tumbling down. It shouldn't be.

5 Reflections

At first, I didn't have that much of a philosophy or belief about pacifism. I just couldn't stand the way people were cremated alive in the subways from saturation bombing. It was more of a physical, animal pain than it was any political philosophy. To belong to the Fellowship of Reconciliation, you're supposed to accept some simple little statement, and I really couldn't accept that exactly. I wasn't sure that I could live up to it, or that I could apply it in my life.[1] I wondered if I could really believe it. So I didn't become a member. I don't think I've ever been a full-fledged member.

I spoke to A. J. Muste once, and he said that I was one of those people who didn't think I was good enough to be a member. I guess that was what it was. I didn't think I could apply all those principles in all circumstances. I was a member of the Presbyterian Church, and I got out of the church, too, and I wish I hadn't ever gotten out. I had a long conversation with the minister and didn't accept everything he said, and so I just broke a generation of contact with that church.

1. The Fellowship of Reconciliation asks applicants for membership to sign a pledge stating that they will strive to make its vision a reality in one's own life and in the world. FOR members are to identify with those in all nations who are victims of injustice and exploitation; to refuse to participate in any war or to sanction military preparations; to strive to build a social order that will use resources of human ingenuity and wisdom for the benefit of all; to advocate fair and compassionate methods of dealing with offenders against society; to show respect for personality and reverence for all creation; and to maintain the spirit of self-giving love while engaged in the effort to achieve FOR's purposes.

Later, I started going to church all the time with Mildred and Frances—the Catholic Church. I loved it! Oh, I really could have been a good Catholic! But I didn't—I don't—believe in any of it. I mean I don't believe we have any life after death, so what are you being saved from? And I don't believe in miracles or supernatural things—*any* of all that. But I do believe in these things that religion appeals to in us, and it's a very important social force. I just don't know what we can do about the fact that you're essentially swearing to a lie when you're asked to accept all those other things.

Do I have higher principles than anybody else? Well, my cousin Mary Bacon could have given you some light on that. She said—way back there when we were much younger—she criticized me, rightly I think, along those lines. She said I always thought I was better than other people. She meant morally, not socially. She meant that I had an idea that I was on a morally superior plane, and that it just may be a false idea. I was, though, in a way.

Miss Holton, in the graduation speech, said that I questioned my right to happiness—I told you that before—because of the suffering of others. And, I do feel that I'm compelled to asceticism and self-denial in a certain way, though I've never done it as much as the Fellowship people and radical Communists did. I've never gotten down to the dirt poverty that I find in most causes.

Last night, I spent my night alone, which is generally the case, and I thought "Well, now, why do I have to live such a lonely life?" You and I could have gone out without any offense of propriety. We could have gone out and had dinner. I could have eaten fish; you could have eaten meat. In the old days I would have eaten meat and would have drunk alcoholic beverages too. And, we could have even danced, if we'd been in a place that had an orchestra. Well, that's fun, I guess. I don't have that kind of fun, and I'm hardly even aware that I'm missing it, but I am—because somebody told me once that I was dead, and, I guess, in a way I am. You can just lock the door yourself—I might as well be in prison. Jail was easier for me than it was for some people.

Pacifism, race relations, and animal rights. Yes, they were all connected with each other. We took Ethel Taylor, my maid, with us to the pacifists' convention in 1948, to Greensboro, North Carolina. I was thirty-two, she was sixty-four, I think. Ethel looked different, but you weren't quite sure why she did. Anyway, somebody was talking to Mildred and said, "Is that woman a Negro?" Mildred said, "No, I don't think she is. . . ." I'd have lied, too. I won't say I've never lied. Then, Mildred came back to us and told us what she'd done; so then, instead of leaving it like that—with a lie—because Ethel was going to be living in the same dormitory with us, I went and told Tartt Bell, who is today an outstanding leader. He is in Washington, a Quaker, a leader of the American Friends Service Committee, a very high position. Well, he was there in Greensboro, and I went to him—I think he must have had some authoritative position in the conference—and told him that Ethel was a Negro, and he—I think he said she'd have to move over to a nearby Negro college. So, we said *we* would all go there, too. We all went to the dormitory over there at Greensboro College.

Ethel was a very close friend of mine. Oh, she was very, very good to me. She loved my mother and talked about her a lot. And, she seems to be the only person whose friendship I welcomed—I had Father and Mildred and Aunt De De—but I accepted Ethel's more than theirs. I always fought off other people who seemed to love me a whole lot—but I appreciated Ethel's.

Anyway, that was a political move on our part, which made us stars. We were stars of the convention right away, doing that glorious thing. So, instead of being outside the conference, these Indians and others—even the Russian—came over to our place for little meetings in that college. Oh, it was so much fun! I wish I were alive again at that conference! And, I don't know whether we met Corbett Bishop[2] there or later, but, oh, pacifism was so much fun!

I received three overtures from that episode which could have changed my life if I had accepted them. I don't know why, when op-

2. Corbett Bishop was an independent pacifist and absolutist conscientious objector. Imprisoned three times, he would not eat or walk to aid his jailors and was expelled.

portunity knocks, I shut the door. First of all, Tartt Bell asked me if I would like to be a member, said that he would like to recruit me as a member of the American Friends Service Committee. That should have been my life. Why I didn't do it, I don't know. Then, Muriel Lester said she would like to take me with her, at my own expense, on a trip to Africa that was coming up. I should have done it. I don't know why I didn't. I think I was going to and just didn't. The third one was Robert Frazier, the mayor of Greensboro. He decided that he wanted to see more of me. He came to Mobile. He was introduced to everybody. He was seriously interested, but I wasn't interested in him. Oh, I should have been, I should have been. He sent me Christmas cards for a year or two. Once, I phoned him when I was there, but I've never seen him again. I'm sort of jealous of his wife now. I went back to see Tartt Bell, once, but he was not interested. He was too involved in other things. Muriel Lester's dead now. But that conference was just the turning-on-of-life to me, so much more than anything else. It seemed to me the churches in Mobile didn't speak to issues like that, and the social life in Mobile wasn't exciting like that conference was to me.

All of these things I did, like sitting on top of that car in front of the animal shelter, were all modeled on acts of other people. I mean I didn't think about tactics. Passive resistance was not originated by me. Attending the FOR conferences: that was like a light switch for me. The ideas and the people excited me.

I think I found Christianity through them again on top of this mountain top in Estes Park, Colorado. How gorgeous they looked! We were holding hands in the circle and blessing everybody. All this was just regular ole Sunday school stuff, only we'd bring politics in—"you gonna give us Greece for Uncle Joe" (Stalin, that was), and a lot of cute little political jokes like that. Then, we simulated nominating and electing American presidents; this was 1948, and somebody got up and acted like one presidential nominee, and someone popped up and did another one. So, then, I stood up in the crowd and spoke. This one time I got up and copied a speech of Sam Johnson's that I had heard in Bienville Square here in Mobile. I said I was a Strom

Thurmond Dixiecrat: "Do you want your children to go to school with nigger children? Do you want your wife to be safe in her home?" Just exactly like he had said it. They laughed and cried at that.

I went to many conferences. Evanston, Indiana—the Peacemakers—that's a group, even more radical than FOR. I subscribed to the Fellowship magazine, but later on I couldn't stand to look at it, during the Vietnamese War, because I remember I saw one issue with this Chinese person just suffering so. I don't know whether there was a dead baby on it. I couldn't look at it; it made me too sick.

Corbett Bishop came to Mobile to see me. I think he stayed with me—well, not at the same house, we had two houses. He had a beard. He looked a beatnik before it was popular to look like one. Father came over, and he spoke to him some, and then later on Corbett said, "Your father asked me if I was here to try to get some money." And, Corbett just gave me his book collection, all the books he had. I had a lot of them for years, and I sold some of them. They were interesting. Some of them were these old Quaker diaries put together in book form. A lot of Quaker stuff. He wasn't a Quaker, though, he was Church of Christ.

I have a strong inclination to go up to Hamilton and see his grave or something. He said his mother would rather see him dead than a pacifist. He was far out! Real radical! That was what was fun—these characters! I just never thought life could be that much fun. I guess that's why I chose to go to Vassar, too. I had an inkling of its radicalism.

Also, I've meant to tell you that I knew David Dillinger,[3] the one with Abbie Hoffman[4]—all those people—and Bayard Rustin—I knew a lot of them. Actually, I didn't know Abbie Hoffman, but I did

3. David Dellinger (b. 1915) was an editor of leftist and pacifist publications (*Direct Action* and *Liberation*), a radical activist in politics, and a leading member of the Chicago Seven, whose landmark trial occurred following the street riots connected with the 1968 Democratic National Convention.

4. Abbie Hoffman (1936–1989) was a cultural revolutionary noted for his attempts to transform the antiauthoritarian sentiments of many young people in the 1960s counterculture into a political force. During the trial of the Chicago Seven, he demonstrated his talent for guerrilla theater by mocking the judge and standard courtroom decorum.

know George Houser, who was a racial cause célèbre himself. See, I was meeting Negroes among the pacifists, too. Not many, but for the first time sitting down and talking to them and *hearing* things about civil rights. Then, Bayard himself was black; and, oh, he was most thrilling as a speaker! George Houser asked how could I feel so strongly for racial justice, because like a good Communist, he thought people were formed by their environment. Well, I had a very foolish answer at that time, because I don't believe in it now. I said, "God is everywhere." I felt it: that God was on the other side of a barrier but that you could always have intimations of His presence in any culture.

That seems to be the main point of interest in me: to have violated my Southern belle heritage. Why did I want to do that? Why didn't I continue like Bake? That's not that interesting! Mildred and Frances are not "society": so their story wouldn't be interesting? All right. Maybe if my mother had lived, I would have made my debut and gotten married.

Most of the time, I was away from home. So, I had to get my life from what I was exposed to, and this is the one exposure that clicked.

The Fellowship of Reconciliation was Christian, but it now involves Jews as well as Christians. It may have Buddhists, too. I've been with Buddhist monks at Fellowship conferences. That's the fun of it to me: how else would I ever meet a Buddhist monk, watching him banging on those little gongs and spinning prayer wheels? That was at the World March for Peace. We took a certain part of northern Alabama, then other people would do the same in other places. Anyway, the Fellowship was too Christian for some of these anarchists. They didn't want to believe in any of the Christian doctrine. The War Resisters League is atheistic. You can really see the difference, the coarseness. Of course, a lot of these things were thrilling to me as a woman, too, because these are very masculine organizations, and I met a lot of attractive men, but I never had affairs with any of them.

I never went to the War Resisters League's meetings. Well, I only went to one, in Seattle. See, I was in jail up there.

Oh, I just loved the Seattle jail! We had ice cream, chop suey, chow mein—good food.

I was put into jail because I paddled a little tiny canoe-like boat into the naval base that had those big Trident missile submarines. It was July 4, 1977. Exactly. I got my picture taken in that boat, too, because I've seen it on a slide. We were doing just what the Chinese students were doing in Tiananmen Square—political protest—only our government didn't hurt us. It's just playing a game in America.

I found out about the Trident action through the Fellowship magazine. They have a yearly conference, and I used to go every year. I've been going to the annual meeting of the Humane Society of the United States for several years, and I would be at the National Alliance for Animal Legislation and Education Fund in Washington this year if it didn't conflict with my Vassar reunion. I'd like to go to all of them. I'd like to go to four or five conferences a year.

The Seattle protest was planned very well, run just like the army. We lived in these little tents that they had rented in some kind of campgrounds. We drilled just like soldiers. Shelley Douglas (he and his wife are important in the War Resisters League) was out there marching us back and forth, maybe a hundred or two hundred of us. It was a big crowd, not just a straggly few. And, you know, we practiced lying down or whatever else. No, we didn't have to lie down on this one, we had to climb a cliff and row a boat. One girl swam over, but that was not the year I did it. The Fellowship of Reconciliation had made this protest action for several years. The Trident submarine base was used to protesters; I imagine they practiced too.

The rationale for the action was that we were reclaiming the missile base for the peaceful use of the population. We were going to have a Fourth of July picnic. We all carried our little picnic baskets. There was no way to keep us out if we came by water. Now that was fun: this tiny little ole boat with three of us in it—it wasn't safe at all—in very cold water. Greenpeace's ship, the *Rainbow Warrior*, was there supporting us. There were helicopters hovering above us with bullhorns telling us to, "Get back—do not proceed." Well, if it had been in China, they could have just machine-gunned us. So, America is kind of like play-acting. But we influenced those Chinese students. It was the same idea.

So we got there. Those of us who came by boat had to climb up the bluff, and I had a hard time climbing even then, in 1977. They had little pills for me, for my breathlessness. They were supplied by Pan Am. That's what I love: these protest people have so much *knowledge* of how things work or who's who. The government men had their helmets and their long riot sticks. They could have beaten us down, and we couldn't have gotten up that hill. But, of course, they helped me—being in America, they worried about my breathing—so they sat us down nicely in a car. Usually you do get handcuffed to each other, but not this time. I have been handcuffed more than once, and these were plastic string handcuffs, not the metal kind, and they're always too tight. It's not comfortable, being handcuffed. Then they took us to the jail and sat us all down in a huge room for processing. They estimated that two hundred climbed the fence and arrived by water. And three thousand were outside the fences. It's easy to get your courage up in a crowd like that.

At first we were in jail in Tacoma for several nights. I remember a lot about that jail, being in there with the tough girls. That's a different experience from being with the pacifists. Those girls were more hostile than lots of people. Then, we moved to Seattle, and I don't know whether I was in Seattle eleven days or whether it was all a total of eleven days. But I could have gone on and stayed in until the trial, and I wish I had. I was adjusting to the life. I had this cute little upper berth, and they had this well-designed table, like library steps, two triangles, to step up to it. In the Mobile jail, the top bunk is too high to crawl up on, and there's nothing to step on, and the girl underneath, if she's mean, won't let you step on her bed, and it's hard to get up there if you're old. But this time it was easy, and those little tables were useful. We could eat on them as well as step. It was a beautifully-designed jail. I could have stayed there forever. Besides, I was making points with the pacifists, because I was in there longer than anybody else.

Most of the protesters stayed outside the fence. Nothing happened to them. The others got arrested, fingerprinted, and then out of jail right away. I stayed in longer than everybody else, but the pacifists kept offering me hospitality. And, finally, I decided to take it. I wish I hadn't. Very soon I wanted that jail cell again so bad. With the pacifists, I was out in this old place, with a bathtub that needed scrubbing out, no reading light, an uncomfortable bed. I was *miserably* uncomfortable.

I met a boy on one of the ferries around Seattle, and he was a real tough, Communist-type fellow. You know there are Communists in these groups. Of course, some people think everybody who wants change is a Communist, but there are various degrees of radicalism, and you're getting closer to that kind of thing in the War Resisters than in the Fellowship. Anyway, he told about how he'd been shackled with leg-irons and everything. He was tough, and that's always been a thrill to me, to be with all those tough characters, and to have found political awareness among them. A. J. Muste once said, "Anarchy is a defensible position." Well, it's just so exciting—but I don't know what he's talking about. So, why did I fall in with them? I don't know why I did it. It was just thrilling to me. I did what I wanted to do; and, also, I felt morally alive. My feelings of what was right and wrong supported the feeling of fun, so together that was irresistible.

I never was a pacifist completely, and I've not been a complete vegetarian, nor completely interracial, in my life. When you push anything far enough—reductionism, I think it's called—there comes a point where you can't support it. It's true in all of these things.

I can't conceive of a pacifist world. You know they really do get deeply into these things at conferences. They have lots of programs, and people will tell how they raised their children, and whether or not they spanked them, and they'd go into it in detail. They think it out quite clearly: whether they should use any force. I'm not that deep or committed.

Animal rights? It's just like the Fellowship of Reconciliation. Until I found FOR, I didn't know that pacifism was more than a word. I had feelings, but no place for them. I was horrified by WW II, but I didn't know anybody else felt that way. I discovered the pacifists. I just ran into people that felt the same way. Then, I discovered other people were horrified by the war, too.

I had feelings for animals all along, but there wasn't any animal rights movement to speak of. That just happened recently. I did have my feelings, but I didn't know anybody else that had them. I did pursue them to some degree. I went to the National Antivivisection Society in Chicago, and I didn't like it all. There had been a picture of a dissected frog on the front of *Life* magazine—the women I talked to were talking about it. I said, "Do they really do that?" She said, "Yes," and sort of smiled. I thought, "She's a sadist." I was turned off by that organization.

I remember I wrote a letter to the newspaper about animal research for heart trouble. I spoke to a group of people about animal abuse at a conference. I had a picture with me which said, "Formed by God, Deformed by Man"—a little fox terrier with his legs sticking out like that. Scientists had put it that way on purpose, and I stood up in front of this group at a FOR conference and started saying things, and they didn't like it. I spoke to A. J. Muste about eating meat. I was eating meat then, but he gave me the usual line. He wasn't receptive to it, or else I didn't present it well. I didn't find "it," whatever "it" is, with the Fellowship, but I was looking for it. And it should be there.

It was only recently that I found the animal rights organization, exactly like I found the Fellowship. I had the feelings but didn't know there were others who felt so strongly. I found the animal rights movement, and it's only recently exploded.

Well, there was this lady—she was my mother's age—named Lola Belle Jackson. She was the head of the Society for the Prevention of Cruelty to Animals here—but she also liked to drink bourbon whiskey, and so did I. We went out with the French sailors together, even though she was twenty years older than I. We were kinda buddies. Anyway, she was aware of the pound, but didn't do much about it. The shelter didn't have any roof; it was just a fence with different runs. I would worry about those animals at night in the *cold*, and I took Mildred out there—and I think Mildred's mother, maybe—and we just talked to them, just talked to the dogs, whistled to them.

Later I heard this radio announcement about the suffering and devastation done by the steel-jaw trap and about the need to outlaw it. Well, I was just thrilled to death to hear that, so I found out who put it on the air. It was Margaret Barnes. I was just thrilled that somebody knew that much, knew how to put it on, knew the politics behind it all. I didn't know anything. So I met her, and she told me to get in touch with the Humane Society of the United States. That's the big one, but its a foot-dragger now; it's not on the cutting edge. It's overweight with money and conservatism. It still has a few things to recommend it, and I've been to a number of its conferences. But, I went to the first one back then, with Margaret Barnes. We all stayed at the Y. Now, I have a passionate commitment to animal rights, and I go to many conferences.

I have done some direct action things for the animal rights movement. Let's see: first, I went to the Mobile city commissioners. They didn't have a city council back then; the council form of government began four years ago. I went to the three men—Margaret calls them "The Three Stooges"—they were Arthur Outlaw and Robert Doyle and Lambert Mimms—the commissioners. I could speak a little better then, but still not well. I don't know whether I had a handout for them or not, but that's one thing about the University of Southern Mississippi I'm grateful for—teaching me always to back up speeches with printed matter—so I may have had. And I remember I was saying, "Will you vote to stop pound seizure?" They'd never heard the term. I remember Outlaw saying, "What?" And I said, "Stop pound seizure!" and told them what it meant.

They could have stopped it, those three men, right then and there. They were just about to do it, without even giving it much thought. Then, I think they said they'd have to consult the S.P.C.A. and Mr. Marchand, who ran the pound. Well, I went to the S.P.C.A.

president, and she said she was going to say to stop it. Her name was Joan Richardson. And this is where I made a big mistake. (I've made lots of them.) She said, "Don't go to see Marchand, let me go to see him." Well, I went ahead anyway, and I made him angry. It shouldn't have done so because I had known him way back. I mean I'd known Marchand back before WW II. But when Joan felt like she should speak to him instead of me, I didn't listen. I went and spoke to him. She understood his psychology or something. I think she could have gotten him to say yes. Well, he said he had to hear from the University. So, the University of South Alabama got alerted, and that's what ruined it. They came in and said how they had to have dogs for research. They persuaded the commissioners not to end pound seizure.

We had been so close to winning it until then, and it was really just burning me up. I was really involved in it. I knew they were taking the dogs for research every week. They wouldn't tell us which day, though. Well, Margaret Barnes and Beryl Rebert and I, and my secretary, and maybe some others, we picketed around the pound. I didn't even organize that first picketing; others did. It was the day that animals were being taken out for research, and this action broke the news to everybody, especially the people who would come in bringing dogs. We were urging them not to leave them at the pound. That was good—it got newspaper coverage.

There is a horror book of pictures taken by a man, Swedish, I think, who is very active in the movement. Horrible pictures. I had pictures photocopied by my secretary, and I gave them to the city commissioners. It was on my mind that these things were happening right here in Mobile, and I could hardly live with the knowledge that those animals were being taken. So, I felt that I had to go block the entrance to the pound myself.

I had to do it by myself. I didn't discuss it with a group. I woke up, and I felt like I had to do it. But, of course, it had been going through my mind for quite a while. All the protest acts are there to be done. I knew how big my car was. I wanted to stop it the day the dogs were going out. I just went there, and I think it was open—and I blocked it. I don't even know if I had a picket sign. I guess I did. Bernadette,

(photograph by Victor Calhoun, courtesy of the *Mobile Press Register*)

Dorothy being arrested at Mobile dog pound protest, 1985

my secretary, was watching, so I wasn't exactly alone. She notified the media. I learned all these points from the Fellowship—it knows how to use the media. We consider that a legitimate tactic, too.

So, she notified Channel 10, and then Mr. Marchand said, "Hey, you got to move that car." Well, I've known him forever and like him, kind of. I said, "I'm not going to do it." Then, I went and sat on top of it. He went in, I guess, to call the police; that's what usually happens. You just about know all the steps of it, unless you're in China.

So, they called the police, and they took my picture, and they handcuffed me, and I sat down, I think, and I couldn't get up, because I don't have enough strength in my legs without pushing up on something. They had to carry me to the police car.

These things have been done so many times. We rehearsed them at War Resisters League and all. We rehearsed lying down. Everybody knows what you do. Police know it, too. One of the police said, "O.K., Bootsie, lie down now." Anyway, that was a good picture, with my handcuffs on.

I loved it! That was a great moment! I was thrilled! I was smiling my head off, and they handcuffed me and stuck me in the car and pushed my head down. They are kind of rough on people in that car, but they have to push your head down to keep it from bumping. And then all that stuff inside the court house: booking and fingerprinting—it's a pain—especially that ink all over your hands. Well, it seemed they wouldn't keep me in jail. They didn't want the publicity. But I wanted them to. I wanted to be arrested.

Then, they took me in to the judge. You're in jail as soon as you're booked usually; you're locked up. But, they took me to the judge right away. Mr. Marchand had taken a picture of me on top of that car. He came to court and the helpers at the pound, too—all of them. It was really fast, fast justice. Marchand was going to show the picture, and they thought I was going deny it, that I was going to say that I wasn't blocking it, and that I wasn't guilty. So, I let him tell his story. I said, "Yep, that's the way it happened." And so, the judge said, "I'll fine you $500." I said, "I don't want the $500—I want to go to jail."

I don't remember how they could make me pay instead of putting me in jail—I've forgotten that part—because I didn't have $500, and they won't let you write checks. I don't remember all that part. But, obviously, it would have been better politically to go to jail. That's what happened the first time I did it.

I did it five times. Yeah, as soon as I got out, I'd do it again. All this was in 1985. I did it until I finally got sentenced to thirty days in jail. And, I had these little signs prepared that Mildred, my friend, and Bernadette, my secretary, were supposed to use for picketing the jail which said, "Let Dot Out!" and "Stop Pound Seizure!" They didn't do it, though.

I fasted for a while. I didn't eat meat, and this was before I had really stopped eating meat. I said I wasn't going to eat meat until they stopped pound seizure. And, at one point in jail I stopped eating altogether. I wouldn't eat at all. I did lose a lot of weight, and I've never gained it back.

I served the entire thirty days, but they let me out on weekends.

Major Madison, Jr., was my lawyer then, and I was out of jail on a weekend once, and he told me I ought to stay out—not go back to jail—but go to the city council, and then they'd arrest me there. I should have done it. That would have been a good tactic, but I didn't. I gave him a few thousand—it was all very expensive—for his lawyer's fees.

It may have been that weekend—I guess it was—I went to Universal Hardware, and I bought the biggest chain you've ever seen, the biggest one they had, and I took it over there to the pound. First, I went back in the night, and there was a car parked there, some kind of guard. Well, I went back again, and there wasn't any guard outside. I chained up one of the entrances and put this big ole padlock on it, which is just another symbolic act of not letting them take the animals—all kind of silly really. It's just a game.

I picketed the University of South Alabama Medical Center, too. I picketed out there, and one of the men kicked one of my signs, one of the doctors. And, I talked to a lot of medical students. This girl from Pensacola picketed with me out there. Then, Dr. Christian Abee, he's a professor of comparative medicine in the College of Medicine, he showed me the animals that were going to be vivisected. These animals in huge cages—about four of them would take up this room—very big. The dogs were not closely confined. And they had *huge* dogs in them. One of them had already been operated on. One of them was growling—I thought he had some sense. The others were like most dogs, slobbering all over you, just happy. There were two people who worked there; they were happy to see me, friends of Connie's. They said they had never seen any cruelty. Dr. Abee took me in all these other parts of the University, to see all the rabbits and mice, they had all these beautiful little animals.

I got a lot of television coverage. I was on almost every night for a while. And lawsuits—we had lawsuits against them—they were televised. Dr. Abee and I (or Mildred sometimes) were debating each other on television a lot. Yes, right down there at Channel 10. Then, see, we thought when they got the new city council installed, one elected by districts rather than at-large, that we'd get them all to be antivivisectionists. And, I went to the polling places to agitate: "Elect no vivisectionists." Sometimes Bernadette would go with me. I was paying her $45 a day, which is $5 an hour. So she got picked up once, too, and I had to pay for her lawyer. We went to the voting polls with our signs and petitions and got people to sign them. I never did anything with those petitions. I think I've got them over in the office, and I might be able to use them in this coming campaign. I may put a horror picture up against Arthur Outlaw and say, "A vote for Outlaw is a vote for this," because he didn't stop the traffic in dogs. I might use it against *all* of those city commissioners, the incumbents.

I did all sorts of politicking. I carried a little ole can. People would give me money, I don't know why. Then, the new council members were elected and went in, and they didn't vote for us—not a one of them stood up against pound seizure.

They stopped sending dogs to L.S.U., Tulane, and Auburn, but they still send them to the University of South Alabama Medical

Center. They stopped selling them to the middle man, that's all. Then, they went back on that arrangement with a subterfuge, and we discovered it. We took it down to the city council. They stopped that, too. I'm proud of that. And for the rest, I guess I am just de-sensitized to it all now. I didn't know what other action to take.

I could start again in politics. I have had a lot of fun.

Two

THE TESTIMONY OF OTHERS

Dorothy's father,
Paul Danner,
in his youth

6 Paul Danner

Paul Danner died in 1968. Virtually all that remains of him, beyond personal recollections, is contained in the scrapbooks, photographs, letters, and other memorabilia that Dorothy has carefully saved throughout her life. Among the letters that Dorothy allowed me to examine, I found two sets of correspondence that shed light on important transitions in Dorothy's youth: (1) her years as a student at Gulf Park College, 1930 to 1932, after her mother's death; and (2) the transition period from Holton Arms to Vassar in 1935. Those were times of obvious stress and readjustment for Dorothy, and these letters permanently if incompletely open to our gaze the intimate relationship that existed between father and daughter in those critical years.

The voices that are carried through these pages to us decades later suggest a Paul Danner generally more open, affectionate, supportive, and responsive than Dorothy's recently told story might suggest. Paul Danner may have been a reticent, formal Southern businessman, but he seems also to have been an attentive and sometimes indulgent father. Notice: When he sends her to camp in Tennessee he invites her to "write me about anything you want to, no matter how personal or confidential it may be." At Gulfport College he tells her not to worry about getting A's on her report card; B's are all he wants. He is careful with money but is willing to buy expensive frocks when he is asked. He guides and shelters her, and prays, "Don't ever let anything destroy our delightful spirit of frankness and comrade-ship."

There is a puzzle here. Which is true: old letters or old memories? Was Paul Danner cold and aloof, a controlling father with little sense of his daughter's real needs; or warm and gentle, a prudent guide doing the best he could for his only child?

Paul Danner
Merchants National Bank Bldg.
Mobile, Alabama
Tuesday, July 1, 1930

My Dear Boots:

As I am leaving today for a trip to Louisville I can only drop you a short letter and there really isn't much to say.

All of us are well and I am sure you are going to keep well. Don't fail to write me about anything you want to, no matter how personal, or confidential it may be. You can trust me absolutely to keep anything in confidence always.

Have a good time and try to get all you can out of camp.

Lots and lots of love,

Father.

To: Miss Dorothy Danner
Senior Camp Nakanawa
Mayland, Tenn.

Paul Danner, President
Jas. E. Kane, Sec'y-Treas.
MOBILE COAL COMPANY
(Incorporated in the Year 1884)
Main Offices
1101–1702 Merchants National Bank Bldg.
Mobile, Ala., U. S. A.

Friday, Dec. 12, 1930

Dear Darling:

Was so glad to get your letter. I know that it is hard to find time for writing, especially so near the Holidays.

I had forgotten all about the kittens we bought in Paris. I am glad they won first prize.

I suppose you would rather come home on the train December 18th, if not I will be glad to drive down and get you.

Never mind about getting A's on your report, what I want are B's. Don't attempt too much and try to "get" what you do take.

Did you get Christmas check from the bank? I have started one for you at The First National for next year.

Lots of love to you my Darling.

Father.

To: Miss Dorothy Danner
Gulf Park College
Gulfport, Miss.

GULF PARK COLLEGE

Mr. Father Darling Danner
1954 Government Street
Mobile, Alabama

Dear Mr. Father:

Miss Boots accepts with pleasure your kind invitation and all the marvelous things that go with it, especially the "spoiling." It is not certain but most probable that her roommate will accompany her for a few days but not the entire time. She will bring her riding habit in case Mr. Darling would like some rides with her at the "Bit and Spur" and she is dying of excitement to get there and loves you more than anyone in the world,

Boots.

P.S. Arrive on Bus.

Paul Danner
Merchants National Bank Bldg.
Mobile, Alabama

Friday, Jan 9, 1931

Dear Darling:

Don't bother to write often, once a week will do. Just *think* of me often.

I had a delightful trip to Gulf Park with you, and as the weather was so nice, I wasn't one bit tired on my return. Reached Mobile just at one o'clock in time for lunch.

I have told the girl at Reynalds to be on the look out for some new records for you.

Love,
Father.

To: Miss Dorothy Danner
Gulf Park College
Gulfport, Miss.

Paul Danner
Merchants National Bank Bldg.
Mobile, Alabama
Tuesday, Jan. 13, 1931

Dear Darling:

You are awfully good to write me so frequently, and I appreciate it and enjoy your letters.

Yesterday I motored to Stockton over an abominable road. Came back covered with yellow mud but hungry and happy. Was in bed, after a nice hot bath, at 9 o'-clock and never waked until 7:30 this morning. I read your letter just before going to bed.

Your writing about Tut reminds me that last Sunday, "The Bit and Spur" Club rode from the stables at Springhill to "The Cabin" at Dog River. There we all had breakfast. It was lots of fun.

I hope they don't send home the girls who were smoking. It would be hard on their parents to have just paid about $400.00 and then have their daughters returned, as I don't suppose the school money would be returned with them. I have just stopped smoking, which I try to do every so often. I get to the point where I am nervous and can't sleep then I have to stop

Continued

and it is quite a struggle to stop, as it is to give up any habit.

I shall drive down to see you next Monday. Write me and tell me just what time I should arrive. If you want to ask any of the girls to dinner at the hotel do so.

I can't close this letter without saying how much I enjoyed your visit home Christmas, and you would be surprised if I were to tell you how many people have said nice things about you.

Lots of love, and write me as to when you would rather I reach the college on Monday.

Love,

Father

To: Miss Dorothy Danner
Gulf Park College
Gulfport, Miss.

Paul Danner
Merchants National Bank Bldg.
Mobile, Alabama

Friday, Jan 17, 1931

Dear Darling:

I expect to see you Monday so will only write a short note.

The college has sent out a circular letter to all parents, saying that the semester after Christmas is always hardest as everyone has been having fun at home. The circular suggests that parents write to daughters encouraging them to work during this period especially. So I have written. A few "B's" will be Okay.

Lots of love to you my dear.

Father.

To: Miss Dorothy Danner
Gulf Park College
Gulfport, Mississippi

Athelstan Club
Mobile, Ala.
Tuesday night, Jan 27, 1931

Dear Darling:

Although I wrote you this morning I must write again tonight, because I have just opened your last letter, the one telling about the sorority party, and you are so sweet about writing.

Your letters are always a great pleasure to me, and if they are short it makes no difference I just like to hear from you.

Robt. thought you all looked fine at Edgewater. There was nothing to be embarrassed about.

I don't know just when I'll get down again as I must leave soon for a trip north, however I will not be gone long. And may get to see you before I go, even if only for a brief visit. I may drive down Friday evening. If I were to do this what time would be best, 3 or 4?

My yachting trip upset me terribly—nothing at all to drink, but too much rich concentrated food, after two days I am feeling much better. I am thinking of sailing all the way to Havana next March on the same yacht. We would first go to St. Petersburg, Fla. and then enter a race from there to Havana. If I decide to

Continued

go I will keep you posted, but it is a long time off.

Did you notice any increase in your school bank account? It ought to be fat, as your Christmas savings card money was left there.

Today I rode "Darling," not many people riding now, but I enjoyed being out. Hope you are having lots of good rides.

A heap of love to you my Darling, and good night.

Father.

To: Miss Dorothy Danner
Gulf Park College
Gulfport, Mississippi

DELTA LOGGING COMPANY
Chickasaw, Ala.

Tuesday, May 12, 1931

Boots Dear:Miss Ramsey, from the College, telephoned me yesterday just to say that you were looking fine. She was in Mobile to see about new students for Gulf Park, especially from "Wrights."

Today I mailed a check to New York paying for your trip. I have reread the itinerary, and I know that you are going to enjoy the whole trip. Try to get all you can out of it.

It seems silly, but I can hardly keep from crying when I even think of you being over there alone, but of course you won't be alone, and besides you are nearly grown. I am just a silly old Father who only has one child. You are all I have Darling, and I love you so much. Do take care of yourself for my sake, as I am trying to take care of myself for your sake. Tomorrow I leave for Louisville to be gone until next Monday or Tuesday, as soon as I return I will drive down to see you, and I expect to telephone you tonight.

Lots of love.

From,

Father

To: Miss Dorothy Danner
Gulf Park College
Gulfport, Miss.

June 19, 1931

Dear Darling:

I was so sad to miss you last night and I cried after I got on the train. We've had a marvelous time and Miss Adams is awfully sweet. We're just on the other side of Gainsville now, still on the train, of course, which is a little excuse for this writing. I'm having a marvelous time and can't wait to get on the ship.

Tell everybody hello. There're lots of things I want to tell you darling but really it's too hard to write so I'll wait till New York.

Love,

Boots.

To: Mr. Paul Danner
1954 Government Street
Mobile, Alabama

[NOTE: This was written on the way to a conducted tour of Europe. Mary Bacon and Nini Bacon Gaillard were also in the group. They sailed on the SS *Berengaria*.]

HOTEL YORK,
Berners Street
London, W.1.

July 1st, 1931

Dear Mr. Danner:

London has been a lovely experience. We've had fair weather and happy days here. I'm afraid I shall be completely spoiled after this trip and shall never want to see Europe again except with a group of girls. They have been so enthusiastic and so appreciative.

We're leaving for Holland. I shall try and write you from time to time and shall certainly let you know if the slightest thing goes wrong. Dorothy is a very adorable person and I can easily see how anxious you feel. You would think that your three girls had known the others always, so completely are they a part of the group.

With best wishes,

Sincerely,
Irma Baumgartner.

To: Mr. Paul Danner,
Merchants National Bank Bldg.
Mobile, Alabama.

Friday, July 31, 1931

Dear Darling:

Everyday I wonder just what you are doing at that time in Paris. I know you have done a lot of window shopping. You must have many funny experiences with the language in the restaurants. If you feel as silly as I do when I hear a foreign language, you will cone home determined to study French and learn it. I think you should. Have you been for a boat ride on the Seine? I always wanted to but never did.

Will $75.00 be enough for the dress? If not tell madame I will stand for $100.00.

I wonder if you have seen the McClures' (R.L.S. McClure) whom we crossed with on the "Paris," and with whom we dined one day.

Colleen Ireland is in Paris also. You might possibly see her. Mrs. Perdue has sailed for the same city. Try to remember a lot of things to tell me when you get hone.

Love,
Father

P.S. *Lots of Love.*

Paul Danner
Merchants National Bank Bldg.
Mobile, Alabama

Saturday, August 1st, 1931

Dear Boots:

This is August and you will be leaving France in about 20 days, which means that I cannot write you later than the Eighth with any assurance that you will receive my letter, as it is a 10 to 12 day period between writing and receipt in Paris.

Yesterday I received your letter from Florence, Italy. I am always awfully glad to hear from you.

Did you find your lipstick? And what is more important did you ever find your watch? Have you had any goodies from Rumplemeyers?

Don't forget to write a short letter to Mildred McIntosh. She has improved very much though still somewhat whiney. Little Sara is rotten spoiled, and losing much of her charm on account of it.

Love from,
Father.

To: Miss Dorothy Danner
Students Travel Club
19 Avenue de L'Opera
Paris, France.

Mobile, Alabama
January 8, 1932

Dear Boots:

Your vacation at home was a great pleasure to me, and you are a precious girl. I only hope I can be of some help towards your getting a great deal more pleasure, enjoyment and benefit, for a long time. Send me the key to front door, and write me about anything you want, or anything that may trouble you at any time.

Don't ever let anything destroy our delightful spirit of frankness and comrade-ship. This is a silly and "Dumb" letter, but you will just have to remember it is from a Father who doesn't want to spoil his little girl, but who would certainly like to.

Love,

Father

To: Miss Dorothy Danner
Gulf Park College
Gulfport, Mississippi

Paul Danner
Merchants National Bank Bldg.
Mobile, Alabama

March 16, 1932

Dear Love:

You are awfully good about letter writing. I don't want to appear sentimental by repeating that your letters are a source of great comfort to me, but they are.

I am sorry about the girls being shipped, be careful. It is difficult to get into many schools after being shipped from one.

About Latin, C+ is OK. Keep fighting it the balance of this year and maybe we can switch to modern language next year, however French will be difficult without some knowledge of Latin. Don't neglect it this year.

Darling, about the Horse show, none of the directors, as far as I can find out wanted it to be held, and it will be, I am sure, only a 2nd rate exhibit, although probably a good deal of fun. Elizabeth and her mother are bossing the whole thing, trying of course to make some money out of it, for which they can't be blamed.

I, for many reasons cannot afford to have you ride this year on Tut. It is not altogether the cost but, borrowing large amounts of money as I necessarily must do in my business, and being unable to pay back at this time, it is or would be very bad taste and also bad policy, from a business view point, for you to be "written up" in the paper as riding your own horse in a horse show. People put wrong impressions on so many things, and exaggerate grossly. Tell Elizabeth I can't

Continued

afford it this year, or tell her anything else you want to. The best thing to tell her would be no!

My plans are to be in N.O. [New Orleans] Saturday, drive to the Edgewater or Buena Vista Saturday night and come for you about 11 am. or 12 a.m. Sunday. We can have dinner together and spend the evening (afternoon) at Elizabeth's horse show. You can dress either in riding clothes or otherwise if you are not riding, probably "otherwise" would be best.

Love to you my angel.

Father

To: Miss Dorothy Danner
Gulf Park College
Gulfport Miss.

Saturday, Jan. 13, 1935

Dear Precious:

It was fine to get your interesting and cheerful letter, and I am glad that things seem easier at school. I knew that the little hard shelf in the drawing room was going to be a pain to somebody. It really was never meant to sleep on, just to rest on, during the day.

I don't know about Bermuda. Business is pretty rotten. If I can spare the jack will be glad to go, but don't count on it.

Bake has probably told you that Aunt V & C are planning to board with Manger. Poor sweet Manger seems to be in a tight place for money.

I am having Neenie, Laura Jackson and a few of their friends in for cocktails Sunday morning, as a sort of going-away party for Neenie.

I hear that Bailey is going to fix up Dandelion and try to conduct a first class Tavern, as he calls it. He will lose all the money he puts into it, as the location is poor for that, but he can afford it.

Love to you from your Devoted old

Father.

To: Miss Dorothy Danner
The Holton Arms School
2125 S. Street
Washington, D.C.

ATHELSTAN CLUB
Mobile, Ala.

Feb. 14, 1935

Dear Darling:

What do you want for a birthday present? No diamond rings this year, but just as much love.

I want you to go to West Point if your roommate is going. I think it would be an opportunity that you will probably never get again. It should cost about the same as your trip to Vassar as it is very near Vassar.

I think being nineteen is wonderful, but looking back from my fifty three years I know it is still awfully young. The next few years will offer many opportunities to make mistakes. Try not to make any more than you can help. You will find it easier if you don't drink anything.

I want you to have all the fun you can but make the fun last over a long period of years. Don't crowd it.

When you get all the plans for the West Point trip, write me and tell me how much you need, and I will be

Continued

glad to send it, and of course you will need a new frock & etc. which will be OK too.

Everybody here is well, except Danner, who has a cold.

I think of you always Darling, and love you more than I could ever tell you, or ever write you.

Devotedly,

Father.

To: Miss Dorothy Danner
The Holton Arms School
2125 S. Street
Washington, D.C.

Mobile, Alabama
March 8, 1935

Boots Darling:

Just a line to say how much I enjoyed talking to you over the phone.

Of course you get depressed occasionally—everyone does. We have to fight it and stay cheerful. It's pretty hard to stay depressed when we are feeling well physically (at least I find it so.)

Business is such that I have some doubts as to whether it would pay me to call on customers near Washington at this particular time, and it might be better for you to come down for Easter, see your friends, and let me drive up about April or May. That way you could see me twice. Think about it.

I plan to drive to Bhmg. [Birmingham] tomorrow for a weekend on Temple's farm. Am taking my riding clothes.

Am looking forward to the picture of my sweetheart, and am very interested to hear about the W. P. [West Point] Trip. I am sure that you will always remember it, with a lot of pleasure.

You are a sweet happy girl, and a great comfort to

Continued

me, and don't ever hesitate to write me when you feel blue. I can always help, and I always will.

Love,

Father

To: Miss Dorothy Danner
The Holton Arms School
2125 S. Street
Washington, D. C.

Mobile, Alabama
April 22, 1935

Dear Boots Darling:

The more I think of The Frontier Nursing Service the more I think it would be all right. The Executive Committee seems to have some prominent people on it. The main thing would be your environment, that is the girls with whom you would be associated in the work. I presume they would be congenial but unless you know some of them it might pay to make some inquiries. In selecting the terms (periods) on application, make a selection that would not conflict with college. Very likely some of the applicants will cancel as is usually the case.

I ought to hear from Louisville in a few days, and will write you. Six weeks in the mountains ought to be very beneficial, and I could spare you. Some weeks ago there was an article in "Time" about Abyssinia. They are a bunch of Negroes, whose king claims to be descended from Moses, I think.

I will be glad to get the box you are sending. I am sure it will be large enough. What I am trying to get is

Continued

something small, so as to occupy less room in my bag.

Everybody is well. Manger was so glad to have you that she positively refused to accept any payment for your last stay. I let Danner and his friends use the Cabin last week end.

Love,

Father

To: Miss Dorothy Danner
The Holton Arms School
2125 S. Street
Washington, D. C.

Tuesday, May 7th, 1935

Dear Boots:

I will mail checks to Dr. Morrison, Dr. Little, and to the Breece Riding Club.

Application blank F.N.S. [Frontier Nursing Service] is enclosed, never have heard from Louisville, but feel sure it is OK, am only apprehensive about the hard work, and exposure to weather such as is sometimes encountered in the mountains.

Robert has started a dime chain letter and expects to get rich.

Business in our line remains almost nil, but a man in business must necessarily be an optimist.

I don't know what to do about moving to The Cabin. At present the apartment is very comfortable, so I don't think I shall move until I return from Washington, that is one reason why I want to know just when I should be there (Washington). Ethel has some relatives she wants to cut on the job and I am not going to hire and feed them while I am away, and have them do nothing.

The public schools here must be nearing a close as I see all sorts of Field days, and other evidences of Commencement.

I am greatly interested in what you write about

Continued

having had tea with Eleanor [Mrs. Franklin Delano Roosevelt]. It is a privilege, and an opportunity to know the real person instead of the picture lady.

Aunt Mildred has malaria, a troublesome and slow illness though not considered anything to be alarmed about. She contracted it, I am sure, at The Camp last summer in the swamps.

A great many people ask me about you, and I think about you very very often, frequently wonder what you are doing "Right now."

With all my love,

Father

To: Miss Dorothy Danner
The Holton Arms School
2125 S. Street
Washington, D. C.

Paul Danner
Merchants National Bank Bldg.
Mobile, Alabama

Tuesday, June 11, 1935

Dear Darling:

I have been head over heels in work since my return, and have shamefully neglected writing you.

My trip was a pleasant one, all air-conditioned cars, try to get one when you start home, though I fear you cannot, as the L. & N. have only a few. Danner and Fred met me, as arranged, in Atlanta. They exhausted their gas and had to stop just two blocks from the depot at Atlanta; were also busted, had six cents between them, we reached Mobile Sunday night at 8 pm. over good roads, and through cool weather. No tire trouble, or any other kind.

Am now at The Cabin, my cook "Ella" is OK, but so far I am not favorably impressed with the husband's industry, but he may prove to be all right.

Have had no company yet but expect the old Bridge gang down tonight.

Have ordered the telephone installed, and also an electric range. Cook is scared to death of the gasoline stove, and it is pretty much of a pain in the neck, with its smells and dirt.

I feel sure that you will pass the college exams, but if you fail, I promise you that, I won't worry, and I don't

Continued

want you to worry. There are many other more important things than college exams.

If you don't make them we won't pretend that we don't care, but will simply say, and know, that it was due to lack of proper preparation in the poor schools here and at Gulf Port, where one doesn't have the proper opportunities, the proper training, or the proper environment.

I love you always.

Father.

To: Miss Dorothy Danner
The Holton Arms School
2125 S. Street
Washington, D. C.

Dec. 13, 1935

Dear Darling:

I know you enjoyed seeing Mary Boland in Jubilee. I read that it is the best of the musical things being done this season.

I would like to see Jumbo, and when I make my trip to New York in March, we will have to see some of the shows together.

Hope you didn't catch cold sleeping on the floor.

I doubt there would be much saving in carrying a balance at the Vassar Bank. To be certain of maintaining a balance of $100.00 we would have to keep nearer $150.00 and the loss of interest on $150.00 @ 6% would be $9.00. You probably will not pay that much in charges. We will talk about it when you are home.

I think tutoring is a good investment in almost any subject as it is individual instruction. Go to it.

I am sure Alabama is a grand place to have been, but it is only one kind of fun—a repetition day after day of the same parties—no shows—no big stores to shop in. I believe you are having more fun than you realize, especially as you get some of the light social life at home, to balance things.

It seems that I was not so right about you enjoying your visit to Helen's.

The girls in The North seem to have a different life. Not many parties until they make their debut. Perhaps your visit will give you a lot of pleasure by offering a

Continued

contrast to the life at home in the summer, and during holidays, as we live it.

If business continues to improve I shall never have to be away from you as long again. I mean that next year I hope to visit New York say in October, and again in March. This, with Christmas together, will break the year into about three month periods.

I am sending your regular allowance Ck. $12.00 and "extra" for Pullman and incidental traveling expenses $25.00.

If you think it safer you can keep these checks until you reach Mobile and then cash them, spending part of your Christmas saving $100.00 for fare home, and replacing with funds after you cash the checks at home.

You would really be astonished to know how many people say to me "I never would have thought of Dorothy going to Vassar" and similar expressions.

I am awful proud of you.

Love to you my darling—

From,

Father.

To: Miss Dorothy Danner
603 Jewett Hall
Vassar College
Poughkeepsie, New York

Dec. 16, 1935

Dear Boots Darling:

I will tell Ethel that you enjoyed the pecans. They are cheaper this year than ever before so will send you some more after Christmas.

Use your return R.R. ticket. It was on a "school rate" and nothing would be gained by keeping it. We can get the same rate for a round trip school ticket from Mobile, when you return to school.

I have not been active in school work a sufficient length of time to speak with any knowledge on subject of Federal Control of Education.

Years ago there was much discussion on "States Rights." A Civil War was fought, over the states right to secede, and the decision was in the negative. Alexander Hamilton once said that the "Best Government was that which governed least," and the Democratic Party has always claimed that there would, under their administration, be less interference by the Federal Government with affairs that could be better managed by the states themselves, but under our present Democratic Administration the emergency has been so great that there has been more Federal Control than ever heretofore.

As the country becomes one of lesser distances (figuratively speaking) on account of more rapid transportation and communication, there will be a growing demand for a more and more centralized form of government, or in other words Govt. Control in everything.

Glad you are getting some tutoring. I believe in it. I have signed the accident and health insurance application and forwarded to comptroller.

Continued

Your Christmas ck. was mailed, I think last Thursday. Hope and suppose it reached you about Christmas; remember that people, except very young children, appreciate the *thoughtfulness* shown by the sender of a present, far more than the *intrinsic value*. Send many, but inexpensive presents.

We will give Bake an afternoon party in the apt., and talk about a Cabin dance after you get home.

So glad you can make the 2:30 Friday afternoon. That will put you home about 5:30 Saturday, and will be the train Jane Darrah and others will be on. I suppose you have to transfer from The Grand Central Station to The Penn. Station, but you know about this, and will allow yourself time I am sure.

A lot of girls have asked me as to how long you would stay home before returning to school, and I have to tell them that I don't know, but I hope you will have a long stay.

Went hunting Saturday but didn't kill anything worth speaking of. The woods were beautiful, and I enjoyed being out.

You won't have many more days after you receive this letter, and I probably won't write you again, but shall expect to see you on Saturday evening. I can hardly wait.

Love always,
Father.

To: Miss Dorothy Danner
Vassar College
603 Jewett Hall
Poughkeepsie, New York

7 Caroline Rich
(neé Carrie Mae McCants)

In June 1974, EBONY *published an article entitled, "The Adoption Controversy: Blacks Who Grew Up in White Homes." Caroline was featured. She had just resigned her position with the federal government to go into business for herself. Later, "A Black Cinderella Grows Up in a White World," was published by* SEPIA, *in January 1977. The article was occasioned by the opening of Caroline's new business, "Ego Tours by Caroline," in Philadelphia. The following account is reconstructed partly from those articles and partly from insights gained in my own interviews with Caroline.*

I was adopted by Dorothy Trabits, whose husband had died and left her the family fortune, which had been made in the lumber business. They had no children of their own, and they always liked me, so when I was five years old, they told my mother they wanted to adopt me legally. They explained to my mother that they could give me everything any child in the world could possibly have, so she allowed them to adopt me.

I lived the life of a rich kid. Christmas was especially great. I'd write a letter to Santa Claus about the things I wanted, and I'd always get those things and lots more. As a teenager I got many expensive presents such as tape recorders and expensive clothing.

I attended the finest schools in France, Italy, and Switzerland. In Europe we always stayed at the finest hotels and ate at the fanciest restaurants. I picked up the native languages without too much trouble, and I was the object of great attention from the Europeans since many of them had never seen a black child before. It was quite ironic because in the South I was just another black child, and Boots was thought to be exceptional, but in Europe I was considered exceptional and Boots ordinary.

When I returned from Europe, I had a good vocabulary, spoke five languages, and had better manners than Amy Vanderbilt. But many [black] kids said I was trying too hard to "talk proper," so I would lock myself up in my room and practice incorrect English so I'd sound like everybody else. In trying to be like everybody else, I used a lot of profanity too. But stringing together $5 adjectives with "motherfucker" finally lost its image, so I let it go. It took me a long time to learn who I really am.

Boots herself was an only child from a very rich family, and she had little regard for society's prohibitions. She was always an independent freethinker who was gutsy as hell, and I hope I will always be like her. She did what she believed in, which is the way everybody should be.

I was married twice and divorced twice before I was old enough to vote. No reasonable person would hold against me the mistakes of my youth. My first marriage was very stormy. But at sixteen, how cool can you be? I'm calling having married my last husband a mistake. He's a great person, a good man. It's just that different blacks reach different levels of awareness at different times. That was one of the levels when I was married to him.

When I was twelve, the Klan burned a cross on my guardian's lawn. A car load of blacks from the North armed themselves and drove down to Mobile, ready to die for me. That was in the back of my mind when I was going through all of those changes, trying to find myself and married to a white man.

I probably went through an anti-black period, too—I was being put down so much by black people.

I have been exposed to the best of everything, so I am not concerned anymore about places and things, but about people. I think I am a better mother for having had such advantages. My son is attending a private school in the North and spends part of his vacation with my guardian in the South. He is eleven and identity is not his problem because he comes out into a different world.

I've gotten over the resentment I once had for my guardian. And I now realize that when my mother had me, she was a child herself and did what anyone would do to get their own life. I have located her and recently visited her. Gradually, we are getting close. It's really kind of hard. Please soften this: I'm not knocking my mother, but I know that had I stayed with her, I'd probably be a welfare mother now.

It took me a long time to know who I was. In the old days, in the white world, if you had written a vicious story about me, after I'd read it and cried, I would send you a thank-you card because that is good manners, and, as a little girl, good manners were instilled in me by my white guardian. Now, if you had done a horror story on me, I would let you know, whether by phone, wire, or letter what an obnoxious bitch I thought you were. Colored? I've gone beyond that. I've gotten black!

Caroline Rich

In the 1977 SEPIA *article, Dr. Napolean Vaughn, a black psychologist, spoke about trans-racial adoptions. The National Association of Black Social Workers strongly opposes the adoption of black children by whites under any circumstances.*

I don't doubt that Ms. Rich was treated very well by her mother, but there has to be a feeling of isolation later on. In a way these people are neither white nor black as adults. They're not completely accepted by either blacks or whites, and they're in an emotional no-man's land.

[Trans-racial adoptions] can be a positive experience, but it can also be very negative. Much depends on the motives of the adopting parents. Nowadays, for example, many white parents are adopting black kids because no healthy white ones are available. As a result, they raise the child as if he were white—with white mores and folkways—and then that child has a very difficult time coping with his or her blackness as an adult.

I've known many, many blacks who were adopted by white parents, and many have rebelled against both systems since they were rejected by both. Many wind up punishing their parents or themselves by boozing it up or not being gainfully employed. You'd expect them to be successful because of all their advantages, but the opposite is often the case.

Last year I gave a talk to a large group of white parents who had adopted black children, and it was obvious from their words and actions that they doted on the children to an excessive degree. They were extremely overprotective, not letting the kids stand on their own two feet and making them very dependent. They're well-meaning people, but this approach can do serious harm later since a black adult needs to be tough in order to cope with a racist society.

I spoke with Caroline in a Mobile nursing home on June 28, 1988. She had a room to herself, and it was clear that she needed a lot of help getting about. I explained what I was doing and got the consent form signed—Dorothy had prepared her—and she seemed glad to talk, but she couldn't or wouldn't give a lot of detail. I felt very sad when I left her.

I was born on July 4, 1944, and my mother's name was Hazel Thomas. Hazel Lee Thomas. I mean Hazel Lee Everett. She married Thomas later. That was after I was born.

Boots—Dorothy—got me when I was five. I felt very confused because I really didn't know what was going on, and I thought she was the evil white lady that made my mother "sho' do scream" [laughs].

My mother was working for Boots when she took me over. My mother was gone pretty soon after that. She moved into town with my grandmother.

I'm writing a book about it, and you'll find out a lot from my book as soon as I get it out. I was going to show you the letter because, when I started writing, a lot of ideas, things started flowing, and I've told my pen pal I must be working too hard because I jammed my typewriter. My deacon put the typewriter in the shop, the office machine repair shop, but having it repaired costs more than the typewriter's worth.

Well, I'll be telling you in my book exactly how I felt, and I suppose I'm lucky because I remember everything. I even remember when I was in the cradle and shocked my mother when I asked who the young male was that used to throw me up in the air and catch me. So, I can tell you how I felt when I first lived with Boots—it was fun! She used to sing my song that I wrote real well. But, it bothered me that my mother disappeared. And nobody told me.

I saw my mother once, when I kept insisting, and Boots broke down and let me go see her. Boots looked very heartbroken when I went to see her. Now, my mother, as I realized as an adult, was pregnant—my mother was always pregnant—with my third sister, and I think she was going through some conflict with my stepfather, so my mother wasn't that friendly to me when I came to see her. I never asked Boots if I could see my mother again.

Why did Boots take me to Europe? Well, Boots liked to go out to dinner at these first-class restaurants in Mobile—and I know the restaurants by the quality of the kitchen—and at that time in life, I liked Boots and wanted to be with her and didn't like having to eat in the kitchen while she and Mildred ate in the restaurant. They were going through that segregation insanity, and she took me to Europe because it wouldn't be like that over there.

Boots had said at one time that if she could put me in a maid's uniform, then I wouldn't have to be separated from her so much when we ate at restaurants. [Fine restaurants let maids eat in the dining room with their ladies.] But, I was five or six, and even a small maid's uniform wouldn't fit. So we went to Europe to get away from this Southern insanity about segregation that was so depressing to me.

I think Boots got involved in race relations when we came back from Europe, and she entered me into this white school. It was frightening. Well, for one thing, when we came back from Europe, I was very out of touch. I remember my girlfriends were talking about this big-deal white singer—and I must be the only person in the world who said, "Elvis who?" It was frightening.

It was frightening, too, because Boots was a mean person. And, as soon as I got it together and could speak one language, then the next day it was a whole different thing, and I really felt a kind of a relief when I heard some people, some black workmen cursing each other out, and it was in English when we came back from Europe.

Boots was mean. Boots expected things of me that I couldn't really deliver. It's true I spoke languages well, and without an accent, but that's because I learned them, for instance, French, I learned my French from French kids. Because I was speaking different languages well, without a foreign-like accent, she thought I could speak the language, whereas, I learned really just conversational things.

I just got into wherever we were and what was going on around me, and it was fun because in the States Boots was looked upon as a saint, because she took me in. If they could have built a statue, it would have been to St. Dorothy. But in Europe, I was the big thing, and she was like a nurse or something.

In Mobile everybody thought she was a saint for taking me into her house. She was greatly admired by black people. I didn't feel like an experiment then, but I did later after she took in Phil, the little white boy.

She didn't explain this place (nursing home) to me, naw, she just does stuff to me. She doesn't explain anything. She didn't explain why my mother disappeared.

I heard about when the Klan burned the cross. I didn't really know what was going on.

After that I went to school in Maine, yeah. I was about thirteen. And, then I came back. I went to school in New Orleans for a year, in ninth grade, and then I came back and I went to school in Mobile, in tenth grade. I felt like, if I could have lived a normal life, by the time my son was born, I probably would have been first year in college. But Boots kept putting me back—like in eighth grade in Mobile. Boots took me up North, and I was in the eighth grade, and then when I went to St. Mary's Academy in New Orleans and was in the ninth grade—I was making like straight A's—and I think the next year I was in the ninth grade again, and I just couldn't live. I just was confused because I was going to school and doing school things and making good grades, and I was still repeating.

Even after the *Brown* decision, I went to black schools in Mobile. It didn't make any difference; it was all the physical things going on in me. I really would have liked to understand.

It was around puberty, then, and I didn't. . . . I remember when I was twelve and a half, I had my first period, and she never said anything. I didn't expect nothing, and when I saw this blood, I immediately put a bandage on it [laughs]. Then, Boots gave me all of this information that's in a Tampax box and said "Read it." I didn't know what the words meant. She was no help.

Later on, when I was sixteen, I got pregnant and married a disk-jockey. Boots had me marry him. I wasn't really that particular. I didn't really get to know him. I wasn't in love with him. My grandmother—my mother's mother, Carrie Everett—took me into her home, and my child was born in Chicago. I lived with other sisters of mine (I think I had four sisters) when I was with my grandmother. My mother was down South.

I just wanted to find out what was what, and begin living a normal life, because I felt like I never got that with Boots. I think she just wasn't any help. And after Alpha-Omega—Boots called him Alfred—was born I went back to Mobile, and then, I think, I began college. Because it was easy to do. All you had to do was take a test, and if you passed it, then you got in college. I had been taking tests lots [laughs], in all different schools, so that was no big thing.

This was Daniel Payne College in Birmingham, and after I finished there I . . . oh I went to Tuskegee, Alabama. When I finished there I went to Howard University.

Ralph Rich comes into the picture when I left Daniel Payne: I married him. That was probably '63.

I met him in Mexico. When I was going to Daniel Payne. Boots was in her magnanimous mood. She was always doing things to blow my mind, so she had me go to school in Mexico to improve my Spanish. So, Ralph was the bus driver from Wisconsin. These kids paid to go to study in Mexico, and I met Ralph there.

I married him in Kankakee, at my grandmother's place in Kankakee, Illinois, where she was staying. It's like girls have babies and leave them with my grandmother. She takes care of them. Several of my first cousins' children were staying with my grandmother.

So it looks on the front end like, here's a rich white woman who's trying to really educate a black child, a poor black child. Trying to give her every advantage. But that doesn't work very well because I have

Caroline on the
front lawn of the cabin
at Dog River, 1958

a good mind, and the more important things you need to learn were interpersonal relations, and I never learned even how to consider other people's feelings until recently.

I was very selfish. I mean Boots, whatever she did she got away with because she was Danner's daughter, and richer than everybody I know. So, she was a very haughty person.

I was that way too, because that's what was around me, and I was not exposed to love, no compassion or affection and why. . . . When she first took me—sure it was fun, but it wasn't real. For instance, my mother, when I was still staying with her at the servants' house at Dog River, used to do things like go to work everyday. Boots never cared. She didn't have to. Why should she? So, I grew up to be trifling like that. I made a very bad employee. And I'm just now getting over her at my age. I'm saying she was a very superior-acting person, and I was too. Until I learned better.

Yeah. I only found out recently. Boots thought religion was foolish. When I first came here, she is very good with threatening people and lording it over people, and the Doctor here that I had, I used to call him Dr. Echo, because whatever she said, he did. I think that gradually, and it's kind of tragic this late in life, I'm getting to be my own person. I have something, it's a signed and sealed document, that says that Boots is not my sponsor, so I'm my own sponsor. At first, I couldn't go out anywhere, and then I got to the point where I was going to leave regardless and go to church. And then my deacon got the pastor to come here, and I told the pastor that Boots might sue you if you take me out of here, and my pastor said something like, "Come on," and I said, "No. Even God couldn't stand up to Boots" [laughs].

You see, my mother had a big lap; she was a big woman and she was very affectionate and leaving her to go with tight-lipped, unaffectionate Boots was really hard.

Boots married Larry Patrick, and I think he was a young drug addict. That was when I needed her, but she never has been worth a damn. That was when I was young, before I got pregnant, when I really needed somebody, an adult to talk to me.

She married him because I think that they had the hots for each other, and Boots liked young, rough, men: and that was Larry Patrick.

I think when Boots first took me—she must have found out back then that she was barren—and she married Larry to check on it, to see if she could get pregnant, and when she couldn't, I don't think she had much more affection for him. Boots "whored" my mother to me, because my mother was always pregnant. Well, how else is she going to get nine children, unless your mother's always pregnant? She never pointed out things, like all my siblings have the same sire, my mother was legally married and all, while she whored my mother to me. She probably whored me to my son. I think she told him that Larry Patrick was his father.

She was an evil person, and I think, can't prove, but I think she was more involved than she says when her first husband croaked. Now Nicki, what's his name, DaPonte, died before Boots took me in, and her story was that he was cleaning his gun and shot himself. I think Boots wanted him dead because he beat her up, and her daddy covered for her. It's something I surmise. Also, it was something told to me by my family: that her father had a name for her. She was very spoiled. It fits that he would have covered for her. And I think that's one of the reasons I got so much hell when I was with Boots, because she had that guilty knowledge. Now, I'm sure this is just an accusation, that I have no facts, but seeing the way she is and the way she was with me, I think so.

Because Boots can impress people with her bounty, she probably had my mother convinced that she could give me everything, and my mother went for it, and it's true she could, but she wouldn't, because she's not worth a damn! [Laughs.] That was fun saying that and don't you dare put that in your book.

I finally finished at Tuskegee. But when I went to Howard University, I found out I hadn't. So what Howard did was take some courses that I took at Tuskegee and applied them to Howard. I stayed at Howard until I finished law school, but I didn't pass the bar. I never practiced. I went through law school because I was mad with Boots. She had said that black people weren't that bright in an interview she gave with *Ebony*, that I liked Ray Charles when I was a teenager, and she said I liked the savage beat of the tom-tom. So, I felt a compulsion to keep going to school, to get all the degrees, and they came pretty easily because I'd gone to school lots [laughs].

Then, I started working for the Federal Government in Washington, D.C., at the Federal Trade Commission a year or so, and then I went to Philadelphia and started trying to run my own business. That was a failure, so I went to Phoenixville, and came back to Mobile from there.

I started writing my book after Boots tricked me into this place. I was staying at the Mobilian Motel, and we left one day, and I found we were going for a ride in Boots' car. Boots left me here. But I have managed to take this time to regroup, and I've started the book, and it was good even though my typewriter got jammed, because of working too hard on it. It was a great relief to start getting this out.

Boots was into experimentation. I was into life. She was taking care of a white boy, and he had the same time I did. The white boy has been dead since the late 50's. You could probably find out the date. She was just a person without feeling and without compassion that perhaps was conducting this experiment, but her experiment got in the way of life. Yes, she cares far more about animals than she does about people. I think, I guess . . . if you knew she had eight houses in Mobile and I'm in here. . . . That might tell people something about the depth of her feeling and compassion.

You might say I let Dorothy Danner down, but I would say, remember in the Bible where it says, train a child in the way they should go. Boots never did anything that a parent would do for a child, and she doesn't do anything, and she had an obligation. It's not all my fault. Some of it's her fault, and it's not over, that is the most encouraging thing I can say.

There's a fellow in my church I have a crush on, but if everything works out, we'll get together, and he has his own house, and she won't be needed. She was needed in the past, and it was a disappointment, and when my book is out, it will be laid out for everybody, and I feel good about it because other people can judge, and like when I was five, I'm going to be the teacher again.

You ask about my son Alfred. No, I didn't have him with me, not for any length of time. I was trying to get it together, and I've only gotten it together around now. I just forgave my mother, which is something I thought I'd never do in life, for leaving me with this evil serpent, and I think Alfred will forgive me.

I had been an alcohol and drug abuser before, because I used to hear Boots' voice in my head when I was younger. I know that Boots was reading this book called *Brave New World* and about how I used to be a very heavy sleeper. I think I woke up one morning and heard that part of the book saying "SOMA," and now I know that I was a junkie for years. I think I had a lot of promise I didn't realize because I became a junkie.

The problem we had, it's a human problem. And you can give my story a happy ending because of my mother and her interest. My real mother. I got into the religion she belongs to. I got baptized in it, and subsequently I laid my burden down, and I feel so much better.

8 Ralph Rich

I had a hard time finding Ralph Rich, Caroline's husband. Neither she nor Dorothy had heard from him in years. Dorothy thought he was a veterinarian somewhere. I called places without much luck. People in his hometown confused him with his father, who had died. Finally, by chance, I was given a city and a firm. When I called there, I was transferred to another city and questioned pointedly about my interest in him. Finally, I was given a phone number. When I called and spoke to him, he was incredulous. He kept asking how I had found him. I interviewed Ralph Rich on March 5, 1991. He was very security conscious. He set up an appointment for the lobby of a carefully selected hotel. He brought his seventeen-year-old son. Both of them wore guns on their belts. But Ralph did have a lot to say when we got to a room.

Yep, I tell you what—I'm a rambler. I started at the University of Wisconsin in 1958, and in the year '61-62 I was taking Spanish, and they wanted two drivers to drive buses from Eau Claire, Wisconsin, to Mexico for Wisconsin's Language Centers Abroad, and our payment was room and board and six weeks' tuition at the University of Jalapa. We brought about fifty students down there. That's where I met Caroline. She was an independent student—she was not with our group. Dorothy had sent her down there.

I was raised in Sheboygan, Wisconsin, which was a totally white town. In fact, we had an ordinance up there that if you did not have a relative in town, you could not stay overnight. When black people got a train or a bus to come into Sheboygan, there was a phone call made, and a committee met them and informed them of this ordinance, and, of course, they didn't have any relatives, so they were put back on the train. Our town was 100 percent white. The first black person I'd ever seen was at the University of Wisconsin. I started asking this fellow about black people, and he kept looking at me and saying to himself, "What in the world is wrong with this fellow?" He was from Nigeria. So, when I got down to Mexico, I had no idea what was going on, and over the six weeks, Caroline and I got to know each other. Another fellow and his girlfriend and Caroline and myself went to the Gulf, then we climbed up on a mountain, and—I'm just trying to think what other things that went on down there—the memory of the romance part of it—a lot of fun things. I was only twenty-two years old, so there were a lot of fun things.

When we came back, we had two black students on our bus, and I remember as we crossed into Texas, all of a sudden they had to sit at the back of the bus, and when we went into the restaurants, they could not come in. We had to buy food and take it out to them, and for a Wisconsin boy, that had quite an impact. I stayed in touch with Caroline. She was going to some university in Birmingham.

Oh, Caroline was very flamboyant—very attractive. She'd already had Alpha. She was married to Lester Foster, and Lester Foster was a disc jockey. She was in the process of getting a divorce. She told me that she had hired two lawyers, because the first one was dragging his feet, so she hired a second one. When the second entered into the case, the first one would not drop it until he had been paid. So I paid for both lawyers. I never saw any receipts or anything, but I believed her, and I paid for them. Then, she told me she was pregnant by Lester, and she had to get an abortion down there in Alabama. And again, I don't know shit from nothing about what's really going on. This was after we had returned.

I went back to the University of Wisconsin. My father died in '62, so my education came to a screeching halt. I was on my way to veterinary school, and I didn't have any money to go after my father passed away, so I went back to the University of Wisconsin, and I switched my major over to dairy science and got my degree there.

Caroline had come back from Vera Cruz to Birmingham. She was going to school there. We wrote each other through the year, and also she came up there for Christmas, and I can't remember what else. She came up for a couple of days and spent some time with me. I was living in a little itty-bitty, one-dollar-a-day room right off the campus while I was going to school. I was driving school buses after my father died, and it took me six years—a total of six years— from '58 to '64—to get my B.S. degree.

She was quite a fascinating young lady, O.K.? Very flamboyant. Very talkative, and she was quite fluent in different languages. I saw all the pictures where she was educated in Europe—in, I believe, Italy, France, and England. This is why I am so *stunned* to hear where she is, you know?

I have a lot more memories of Wisconsin than I do of Jalapa, Vera Cruz.

I sent for Caroline, and we rented an apartment at the University of Wisconsin. She got into political science, and I completed my degree. It was '63. In '64 I graduated from the University of Wisconsin, and I went to work for Clinical Oncology doing experimental surgery.

We wound up in the hospital, beaten up, and all sorts of good crap up in Wisconsin. Oh, several times. First of all, this gal—why in the hell I didn't get killed with her, I don't know.

Well, I'm a very introverted fellow, and I'll ask my son to say—I don't go out very much, do I? I don't party. I like to fish, and I like to hunt, but I don't party. With Caroline I partied my heart out. And, like, a group would come in—some of these singers would come—we'd go down to the theater—she'd work her way into the backstage. Next thing we knew, we were at their party, and I had to keep my eye on her, because they'd be heading for the bedroom. I had to step in and say, "This is my wife"—even though we weren't married at that time. They'd apologize, and she'd say, "I was so drunk I didn't even know where I was." O.K.? She'd get into a discussion with somebody—these are separate instances—she threw beer in this guy's

Ralph Rich,
1963

face. He turns off and smacks somebody, and there's a fight all over the place. At another party she took a cigarette and went right into this guy's bare chest, and he turned around and hauled off and put her head right through the banister, and off we go to the hospital and get some more stitches. Then she gets a job as a go-go girl at a bar near the Air Force base. And I'm settin' back and I'd hear some white boy saying to another guy: "Why don't you ask her?" He said, "All niggers fuck," and I turned around, and I don't remember what the hell I said to him—I said "That's my wife." She changed her clothes and went out to the car, and they waited for us and beat the living shit out of us again. She knew how to egg people on, and then she would step out. We would be walking down the street—we both carried switch-blade knives, for instance, and she taught me that when somebody came for us, you never stood together. You separated and you opened up your knives together. This is Madison, Wisconsin. And when the guy realized that if he attacked one, he was going to get a knife in his back from the other. Then they would back off and leave. I mean, this is the kind of shit we were into. And like I say, I'm doing clinical oncology research, experimental surgery, and I'm going to work, you know, and trying to prop my eyes open—trying to figure what the hell to do next. If I don't go with her, she goes by herself. If I go with her, I can't get up in the morning, you know, and I'm trying to take a course in histology and stuff like that. I'm trying to take some real stuff.

When we got married . . . I remember one little girl there had been caught up in a fire, and she was totally burned, and they were going to have to have her sterilized, because the doctor said that if she ever got pregnant, she would die from splitting open . . . and I remember going down there, and it was in a slum area, and Caroline had made all these arrangements to get married in the Methodist Church in Kankakee, Illinois, and I have no idea where she spent that night, but we got together the next morning. We went down to this church, and the minister had a hissy fit when he saw the two of us. I'll never forget being in his office with a big desk with a big picture of Jesus Christ carrying a cross, telling us that his parishioners wouldn't understand. Then, we had to go get a Justice of the Peace, or something. I've got the documents, but they're in storage. I don't know, maybe nature has a way of blotting out a lot of this stuff—and anyway we got married, and we got some gifts, and she comes out of the bedroom, and a hundred dollars has been stolen. Well, we rented a car, and we went back to Madison, Wisconsin, and she pulls the hundred dollars out of her girdle. Because after she claimed it was stolen, they took up a collection and got another hundred dollars. That was on her wedding day, O.K.? I can't remember the date I got married or divorced, but that's the part that stuck in my mind, that she actually accused somebody of stealing the money, got a collection up, and got two hundred dollars instead of one hundred.

At this time I'm still not tumbling to all the different crap that she's pulling. I'm still under the impression of this lady that I'd met in Mexico, who I thought was so educated and had the standards I have. Now, I'm up a creek. My father has just died in California—my mother has bought a house up in Madison—she sees the pictures of Caroline, and she has a hissy, and she throws me out. The more my parents and grandparents got on my case, the more I defended Caroline and me. If they had shut their damned mouths, I would have quickly found out what Caroline was all about and kicked her ass out and gone on about my life. But it became a—what's the word—"cause célèbre"—I can't say it. I was not gonna have anybody tell me that I couldn't have this lady.

I'm about as bad as Caroline. All I've got are fragments for you, you know. I've just got lots of fragments.

We met Robby and his girlfriend—she was white. Hewett Robinson, Sgt. Hewett Robinson: he was an Air Force man. He was fresh over from Spain. Anyway, the two of them and Caroline and myself—somehow or another we got invited to the party with the Harlem Globetrotters. On the way, he said he had to make a stop. And we went up to a place, and they were gambling with loaded dice, and Robby slipped new dice on the table and grabbed the old dice and put them in my pocket—and in a voice that everybody could hear, I said, "What's this?" And Robby kicked me in the shin, and when we got outside, he said, "You have no idea how close you got to having us all killed." I have no street sense. I had no idea what I was into. Robby knew about what was going on—I didn't—if he had just told me, but I felt these dice go in my pocket, and I reached in to see what they were, and he says, "Later!"

And then there was this club not far from the University of Wisconsin, near where Abe Lincoln's statue looks down the mall through State Street right up to the capitol. I don't know if those clubs are still there, but we would go there at night, and they would close the bars around one o'clock in the morning, and there were these four black musicians, and from there we went to a white professor's house, and they would switch over from bar music to just pure jazz. We would sit there 'til the sun rose. I didn't do any drugs, but I often wonder—I know there was marijuana—and back in those days marijuana was something else, boy.

I'll never forget it was the first time I ever heard a black person call another black person "nigger." One of the guys had borrowed money, and this woman was downstairs, and she wanted her money, and he told her he didn't have it, and she grabbed a wooden coat hanger off of one of those racks and, I mean, put holes in the wall, calling him a nigger as he went up, back into the bar and back outside again. I'm standing there—I didn't know that black people called other black people "nigger." I take it you can understand that my son—his mother is black. I don't know if you noticed that or not. So, anyways, I learned an awful lot.

Robby invites us to go out to California. We go out to Sacramento. (To son: You remember Robby, right—he owns the radio station.) Caroline wants to stay in California. This is the summer of '65. And, Robby told me that she tried her damnedest to get him to go to bed with her, because of Hilda. Hilda was the girlfriend. Hilda hated Caroline's guts, so Caroline was going to take Robby to bed to get back at her. We rented an apartment from them for just one month, and I mean I busted my tail off trying to get a job. I couldn't find a job.

We write back to Don Shaw at the University of Wisconsin to ask if he knows anybody out there in California. By then, he's moved to Tuskegee Institute down in Alabama. The letter is forwarded down there, and is given to Dr. Blackledge. Dr. Blackledge gives it to Wayne Durdle who says, "Go get this guy for a master's candidate." Now, way back, when I was trying to become a vet, I had written to all seventeen veterinary schools, and I got a letter back from Tuskegee. It said, "Traditionally we do not accept students of your color." I'm saying, "Where the hell is Tuskegee?" I have no idea. Anyway, they wanted me now for a master's degree program, so I left Caroline in Sacramento, and I took the car and I drove. I think I did it in about two days, without any sleep. Got on over to Tuskegee in order to get registered. Then, I sent for Caroline. It turned out that Wayne Durdle, Don Shaw, Cayce, and I can't remember who else, were the only five whites down there.

On the way down to Tuskegee, I had a couple of "hard hats" in the back of my car. I had Illinois plates on the car, and they were asking me where I was going, and I told them, and they said, "Well, just remember, the only good nigger is a dead nigger." "If you shoot 'em and they live," he says, "they'll take you before a Federal court and sue you for civil rights violation. If you kill 'em, you get tried by your friends and neighbors in a state court, and you go free." So this is the kind of shit I heard.

When I got there, I was driving around looking for the place, and I said, "Well, hell, I'm in the white neighborhood." I was so prejudiced, because I thought that black people lived in shacks, and when I saw all these brick homes with little Ford cars instead of shacks and Cadillacs, I thought I was in the wrong place. All right? Tuskegee has its own credit union, has its own VA Hospital, and the whole thing. George Wallace split Tuskegee into Tuskegee town and Tuskegee Institute, and put two post offices down there in order to segregate whites from blacks, because Macon County is 80 percent black. I didn't know diddly-squat about where I'd gone. However, I also found out that I could not get a job anywhere else because I had a C average and a B.S. degree in dairy science. Graduate education at Tuskegee looked pretty good to me. I was there from '65 to '69.

Now, Don Shaw and Wayne Durdle are my professors, and Caroline now goes to work for Don Shaw. She gets into school, and I can't remember what else. But down there our life got to be pretty hectic.

At Tuskegee, while I was in graduate school, I was pulling a 4 point until the shit with Caroline went down, and then I dropped to a 3.75 grade-point-average. What I was doing—I was going to school at six o'clock in the morning and wouldn't come home till one or two o'clock at night. So the reason we got divorced was because she got frustrated and started looking for outside comfort. I discovered her one night in the apartment of a professor, and that's when I divorced her.

Before Tuskegee, Caroline had me convinced that all of this stuff that had happened in Wisconsin and California was because she was black. All right? When I get down there, I find out that's a bunch of bullshit. Black people are just like white people. There is a variety: there are educated and uneducated, there are wild, and there are black people who love Beethoven, Mozart, and every other kind of classical music, who enjoy opera and fine paintings and all the rest. But until then I didn't know. And here I go up against Dorothy Danner DaPonte, and it took me that experience to figure it out.

Before I went to Tuskegee I had heard about Boots, that's what Caroline called Dorothy, but I'd never met her. And this is when I found out that a white liberal is just as dangerous as a Ku Klux Klanner, a bigot. They are mere sides of the same coin, and I discovered *I* was one: a white liberal, O.K.? And they are just as despicable as a bigot, because they both regard black people as inferior.

Now, up until this trial happened, we went down to Mobile maybe two or three times. And then after the trial, we made five more trips down there. The relationship with her fairly well deteriorated rather quickly.

I can't give you the address where she lived, but I do know that the street that she lived on was one-way southbound, and it was also on a fairly main east-west street. And this white boy, with his girlfriend—I'd say he's about seventeen, eighteen years old—somehow or another he was on his way to church or some damn thing, and he turns down this one-way street the wrong way. If he'd been going the correct way, there was a stop sign right there. And, this old black man, who'd been let out of the hospital to go home for Christmas—who'd had some kind of surgery—was driving a car with a door that did not shut. The handle was all rusted out. When they collided, nose to nose, Caroline and I were sitting on the front porch, and I turned around, and I saw it. I saw all the skid marks and everything. In the collision that old man's door opened up, he apparently fell out, and when the cars came back together, it crushed him. He was in the street, right? He clipped a fire hydrant, and I don't know where the hell they all went. It's all in the trial transcripts. But I came out of the house, and I held him while we got ambulances there.

They brought criminal charges against this white boy, and I was supposed to testify against him in the trial. The defense attorney was trying to make out that I was having sexual intercourse with Caroline on the front couch when the accident was occurring, that I had to rise up off of her body to look out the window—on Christmas morning.

Well, I was telling my son Howard here that during the trial there was this young black kid in there who was a high school student who was speaking in clearly enunciated English with all the proper usage—I mean nouns, pronouns, verbs, and everything—the right way. Whenever the defense attorney would use the word "nigger," in the transcripts it came out "Negro." This kid—every sentence of his was turned into "Massa talk" in the transcript. They brought this piece of white trash up there—this woman—I don't know how they got her—either they paid her or whatever—to testify that the black man was ricocheting down the highway at reckless speeds one block before the accident. Her language was converted into proper English by the person who does the transcript. I got the transcript—they didn't want me to have the transcript, but I got the transcript.

You gotta remember, too, that when I went into the trial, first of all, I checked my gun with the police department, and then I went into the courtroom, and there it was—all the blacks on one side and all the whites on the other, and here I am with my black wife, not knowing which side to sit on. So we both sat on the black side, and you should have seen—even the black people were upset with me sitting there. It was racist beyond words, and what they did was, they kept postponing. They said they'd have the trial, and then they postponed it, and they postponed it until finally I was the only witness who showed, and then they dropped it for lack of evidence.

When we went down there on the Greyhound bus, and we got to Evergreen, Alabama, we hit typical discrimination. There's a bus depot there, and we were not permitted to go in the front door. We had to go around to the back. And, as I was telling my son Howard, the room for blacks was about the size of this room. It was cement, cement block, and there was a hole. If you wanted food, you had to pay for it *before* they started cooking it. The white people got their bill at the end of their meal, but we had just this wet floor. That's where the black people went to in Evergreen, Alabama.

Wayne Durdle took me to a cattle auction once, and I walked up and got a drink out of the colored fountain, and he grabbed me—this is a white man—and, he says, "You don't drink out of that fountain." He said, "What do you want to do—get us both hung?" I was telling my son about Sammie Young. Sammie Young went down to the Amoco station in downtown Tuskegee. That's when they had three bathrooms: Men, Women, and Colored. He would not go in the Colored side. He went into the Men's side. The owner of the station shot him in the back of the head, and through a trial, right there in Macon County, he was exonerated. The guy went free, and that's when Tuskegee rioted. They painted a big yellow stripe down the Confederate soldier's back—you know, the one that's down at the courthouse.

Someone smashed in the windows of our house because we were working with Sheriff Hamerson, trying to get him elected. He was the first black sheriff since Reconstruction times. He issued me a pistol permit—I mean I carried a .38 and I carried a .25. When the trial started approaching, we would hear rustling in the bushes outside the house. I kept a loaded shotgun at the head of the bed just in case. Finally, we found out there were police coming out around our house at night—to protect us.

The white boy on trial in Mobile was a part of the Ku Klux Klan. I didn't know that I had stepped in where I wasn't supposed to, just by witnessing the accident and volunteering to testify. I did tell you, didn't I, that the first ambulance that pulled up was a white ambulance, and it would not pick the man up. We stood there, and we waited for a good fifteen to twenty minutes 'til a black ambulance came, and I looked down and I saw the man urinate, and I knew he'd died. 'Cause that's the first sign of death—is urination. So, if they had gotten him in the ambulance, or if they had done *something*—but they *stood* there—I mean, it was just race, race, race. . . .

See what I mean: Leroy Bouldin and Hector Anderson and I damned near got hung in Goodwater, Alabama. I'm fresh out of Wisconsin, one guy's from Jamaica, one's from Trinidad. We took a trip up to Gadsden, Alabama, for the Institute. We got Army surplus—our refrigerator, and a freezer, and a stove and four wooden boxes that we'd filled up with electronic equipment—and on the way back that night we stopped to get hamburgers in Goodwater. We went into a white restaurant, and all the local patrons got up and left. And Andy looks back, and he sees this pretty little fry cook, and she puts her thumb and her second finger and makes a little circle and goes back and forth with her hand like this to Andy, and he says, "Hey, maybe we ought to spend the night here." And pretty soon I saw this old black man walk in front of the place, and he went like this to us with his eyes. [Gestures] And I'm sittin' there with a big old cowboy hat and a great big old beard and an earring hanging out of my ear, and cowboy boots. Then, here comes this cop and he's got this thing in his hand, and pretty soon we started noticing all these cars are pulling up. And their headlights go out, but nobody comes in. So we walked outside, and the cop comes right behind us. He says, "Where you boys gonna set up?" And we say, "What do you mean—we ain't settin' up." He slapped that big billy thing on his hand, and he says,

"Don't lie to me." He says, "You with the NAACP, SNCC, or CORE?" We said, "We're from Tuskegee." He said, "I ain't never heard of that one." "Now don't lie to me," he said, "Where you gonna set up?" And we said, "We aren't settin' up anything—we're going home." And he says, "Don't lie to me." He says, "I see your refrigerator and your stove and all your clothes." And that's when I took the bill of lading and opened up the trunks and explained to him that we were in school one hundred miles away—can you imagine he had never heard of Tuskegee—that we were students, and all we did was stop to eat. He made a wave with his baton, and all the cars started up. He said, "Good niggers don't eat here—the last one who tried, we found hanging in the woods." We got back in that truck. Leroy was supposed to have driven—but he said, "No, you drive." So I got in there—this is the Talledega Forest—and got about two miles outside town, and then it hit me. You know, my body loaded with adrenaline, and I could not keep my foot on the accelerator, it was bouncing so bad. And we pull off to the side of the road, and all three of us—we just cried. We had come that close to getting hung.

And, then, there were five more trips down to Mobile for the trial, until all the witnesses disappeared, and the trial was declared a mistrial. I can't give you the legal terms. They just terminated the trial for lack of evidence. It was interesting.

Dorothy was sort of a blondish-haired woman. She was not overweight, but she sure as hell wasn't underweight. I remember her kind of being fairly full-bosomed, wearing these, what I considered, old-women's clothing. Now in 1965-66, I was born in '40, so I was twenty-five, and here we are in this house sorta built up on stilts—blocks—an old house—the outside looks like hell and it's in a black, I mean all-black, part of town. And she's got this fine Thunderbird sittin' out there. Old furniture, old bathroom utensils—you know, everything is just yecch—O.K.? I mean, I can't say it was dirty, but it was soiled. It just didn't have that comfortable feeling.

Dorothy informs me that the reason she is there is to give these black people an example of how to live right. They can see her, the way she lives, and they too will have hope and inspiration. She was telling me her views: like Caroline would have washed out her nylons or something and hung 'em up, and Dorothy said, "That's the mark of a prostitute." Well, I'm saying, "What the hell are you talking about," you know, "Where you coming from?" I mean, always putting her down, every chance she got, she was just putting her down.

Boots was into animal rights, and she got on my case because, hell, I was raising kittens, and I was killing 'em at the seventh week—you know, sanguinating them through their hearts, taking all their tissues out. I was doing Vitamin A analysis, and you can't do that unless you take the livers out. The conversations with Dorothy were just like, "Oh, please, not again." I mean, you know, I wasn't there to be lectured to. I went down there for Caroline, not to see Dorothy.

The only other big event, of course, came when we went to this civil rights thing. It was Prattville. We pull into the parking lot, and we get out, and as we start towards the door—it's Johnson's Barbecue or some damn thing like that, and he slams that door shut, and he locks it. Slams the door, and locks it, and gets out a bucket and a mop and says, "You can't come in." Now, there are customers all over in there, but all of a sudden he says that we can't come in.

Boots summons a cop and puts a citizen's arrest on him. And, Jesus, now I'm gettin' scared. Down we go to the police department, and I don't know what all else she does, but she goes through a bunch of stuff. (It was just after Viola Liuzzo had been killed. You remember her? The Klan pull up alongside, and they put a shotgun through there and killed her as they were going along the highway.) So here I'm going to Birmingham, watching every car that passes me, trying to steer and see if there's a shotgun coming out the window, because we're in this Thunderbird, which I'm driving. Damn, I *swear* I have no memory of what we did in Birmingham—or coming back.

Then, later, came the trial in the Federal Courthouse in Montgomery. We went before Federal Judge Frank Johnson. He was the big liberator of Negro people on the courts down there. He was talked about for the U.S. Supreme Court, later. Dorothy brought the restaurant owner up on a violation of our civil rights, and I mean we had it going our way. The other side brings these field hands in who testified that they ate there all the time. And he said, "Where did you eat?" And they said, "Well, at that window out back." That's where he was serving them. As far as he was concerned, he was serving all the black people. But it was only the takeout window out back.

Dorothy got up there on the stand. Attorney Fred Gray just dropped his head, because everything that had been rehearsed she threw off to one side. Again, I cannot quote anything. If you can dig up the transcripts, you'll find it there, but she went into integrating schools, and it went into this political thing—the *Pittsburgh Courier* and animal rights—and she just became a crazy person. And, I mean, Attorney Gray, Caroline, myself, even the jurors started talking amongst themselves. The Prattville guy was acquitted. It was over with, because she had this speech and she gave it on the stand.

We figured out she was looking for a podium, and the trial gave it to her. I think she genuinely believed in what she was doing, and I think that she was a white liberal, and I think that she firmly believed that black people were niggers—from the flip side of the bigots' point of view—that these people were genetically inferior to white people. She wanted to do everything she could, and . . . I often wonder if she didn't do all this to prove that these people were inferior. These are some of the weird thoughts that go through my mind—O.K.?—when I look at her.

I feel that way because I was with other people. I've been around so many white people who are not bigots, and they're not white liberals. I haven't got any word for what's down the middle of the road. And I'm not religious, so I don't know if the word is "humanism"—I don't know what it is. It's just that because my background is in genetics and biology I recognize that we are a species—a singular species—and, by definition, a species can have offspring by any other member within the species. The way you know that you've crossed species lines is when you put a donkey and a horse together and you get a sterile offspring. At the University of California, where I worked for Environmental Toxicology, we would artificially inseminate partridges and chickens. The chicks all died exactly on the nineteenth day. I mean, hatching after hatching after hatching. With almost all other cross-fertilizations, there's no result—because of the chromosomes. I come from the point of view that the only difference between races is the different concentration of melanin in the skin. Beyond that, we are a species, and I look upon environment and culture as what really splits us apart. But, because I've been in the academic end of this thing, my encounters with black people have been among educated black people. You know, like the state of Virginia, I mean, the head of the department of Accounts was a black man, and one of the things I've been telling my son, for instance, is when you see Bryant Gumbel and Connie Chung, it's their speech that makes them. But if all of a sudden we hear what we, what black people call "Massa talk," an immediate discrimination comes out in whites. Including me.

I think that Dorothy's point of view was that black people were inferior, absolutely inferior. But now don't forget, my contact with her was extremely short and extremely hostile. Very hostile. Because Caroline said that I could not argue with her, and I just found her to be totally repugnant. Then, I started looking in the mirror, and I started seeing myself. And if it hadn't been for Dorothy, I think I would have made some awful mistakes.

See, my thing was whenever black people did something that was wrong, I forgave them, including Caroline. So when Caroline would misbehave, sleep with somebody else, I'd forgive her because she was black. "Blacks should be forgiven." That's the flip side of a bigot. But, they're both racists. Both the Klan and the liberals, yeah, because they do not give the black person the dignity of being a human being.

"Eccentric" was Caroline's word for Dorothy. I don't think I ever saw them embrace—excepting maybe when we first came in, to maybe lean over and they might buss each other on the cheeks. But I never saw any real hugging. I didn't see any real discussion about "How are you doing in school?" or "How's your career coming?" or "Do you need anything to further your career?" I never heard any of that kind of crap. But we did hear a lot of stuff about animal rights.

Oh, yeah, I remember going to a ball—in Mobile, Alabama, there must be a convention center or some damn thing. Anyway, I remember going downtown to see something like that. Dorothy was involved in debutante-type stuff. The community-type stuff. I don't know if she was trying to integrate that too, or not. You know, that's a white-only, social-type thing.

Integrating schools. Deliberately finding an all-white school, I mean, all-white, period. That says it all. And then enrolling Caroline there. I was to presume that the reason was for integration. But that was one conversation. Then would come the other conversation about why she was living in this all-black neighborhood: because these people couldn't live right. You had to take care of them like children. Even as adults they were children.

Caroline viewed this as a gravy train. I don't think I sensed any bitterness in her. Yeah, Dorothy was "a source." And, as I look back over my time with Caroline, I see now she used everybody she ever touched. Thank God I went to Tuskegee. If I had not gone to Tuskegee, I probably would not have divorced her for years, because I would have continued to believe the bullshit she was feeding me: That black people have to do this—it's in their genes: "We gotta go party," We gotta drink," "We gotta screw," and every other damn thing. "Because it's in our genes."

Now, you're giving me some insight. I wonder if this wasn't from Dorothy. I wonder if this isn't where Caroline got her stuff from, or did Caroline view me as another white person—an ignorant white person. Some of her thing was, "You're white and twenty-five and male—why aren't you making lots of money?" That was what some of our arguments came to, O.K. So, racism comes on every side of the coin you can think of.

Alfred—his name was Alpha Omega really—he came up to Wisconsin one time. We sent for him, and he came there, and he was only there for a couple of weeks, and it just didn't work out, so he went back. But where he was, I don't know. I honestly don't know. Because, when we lived in Tuskegee, I never saw Alpha. The only time I saw Alpha was in Wisconsin, and then he was gone.

My philosophy of civil rights when I was with Caroline was to lead an exemplary life on the correct side of the law. So, we never joined any protest marches in our entire marriage, nor did we go to any rallies. All our people were university people, those whom we associated with I mean. It was always integrated. We got into some real deep religious discussions in some of these parties we went to. Half of them were very intellectual parties, and half of them just turned absolutely wild. Those were debaucheries—I mean, getting stoned-ass drunk, fights, and blood all over hell, knives and guns.

I got lots of reports when we lived down in Tuskegee about what Caroline was doing. There was several motels on the outside of town, and I would be told that Caroline's car would be seen here and be seen there. One night I came home and her car was gone, and I went driving around looking for it, and I went down to this apartment complex, and I saw her car. I lifted up the hood, and I pulled the distributor wire from it and shut the car down. And then, I waited. I was told where she was, and I walked up to the door and knocked on the door, and a professor came to the door. He was a white man. He said no, she wasn't there. I said, "Well, if you see her, let her know that I'm looking for her." I went out behind the bushes, and I waited until she came out the back door. And I remember tearing off her dress, tearing the front part of her dress off, cocking back, and I was going to hit her, and then I said, "No, I'm just gonna divorce you." And proceeded with the divorce. That was the last straw, because by that time, I now knew that black people were just like everybody else, and that the other shit was just a goddamned excuse to get over on me.

I'm trying to remember how it was, because we met again in Montgomery, and Dorothy took us to a Holiday Inn, and I remember she let me order filet mignon, and they had lobster or something. This was after we were separated. And I remember going back up to the hotel room, and somehow or another Caroline and I wound up hugging and kissing, and all of a sudden she pushed me away, and she said, "I had to do this to know that it was over because," she said, "I have the same feeling I had with Lester, and I now know it's over with." God! I can remember that. I can remember that! But I can't remember the date. I do know it was after we were separated. I know it was in Montgomery. I know it was a Holiday Inn, and she was all dressed up. She and Dorothy were very dressed up. And how I got to Montgomery and how I got back to Tuskegee, I don't remember that. So there are all sorts of these little clips coming in now.

After I set the divorce in motion, Linda Montgomery was working at the cattery, also. This cattery was a building built by Booker T. Washington, hand built out of bricks and was once the cannery for the Institute. We gutted it out and built animal rooms and a research laboratory in there. And I was going with this girl, and Mallory, Linda's daughter, was in there, and Caroline came in there and got on my case for something. And if you work at Vanderbilt, I know damn well you've been in some of these research labs. They have lamps that have clamps on them. She grabbed one of those things and busted it and came across my face and sliced me up, and I whupped her one—got her on the floor—I was kneeling—and I had my fist cocked back, and I was going to kill her. Linda stepped in and very quietly said, "Ralph, Ralph, think of spending the rest of your life in an Alabama jail." And, I let her up. I think that was the last time I saw Caroline.

When Caroline got ready to leave town, I found out about it, and I checked with the person, Mr. Foster, who she bought a car from. And I said, "Do you know that she's leaving town with your car?" And he said, "No," and he went and got his tow truck and towed it away from her. And, I checked with the bank, and, my God, I don't know how much money she borrowed off the bank. She split town and went off to some place near Washington, D.C., by herself, on a

Greyhound bus.

After we got our divorce, Attorney Gray had me give him a part of my stipend monthly, and I was only making $2,400 a year. I had to move out of my apartment. I went into my office, I locked the door, and I put a bed in there.

I went on with my life. Years later she tried to contact me and said, "Do you remember that hundred dollars from our wedding?" I said, "Yeah," and she said, "Well, I want it back." I said, "What the hell are you talking about?" I said, "You're wealthy now. You're a damned lawyer, and you've got this travel agency, and you've got this employment agency, and you're making big bucks," and I said, "For one thing, that money was ours and," I said, "it was spent." This happened about 1970, '71, '72—somewheres in there. I was on my way to Minneapolis.

I wouldn't let her know where I was, and the only reason she called my mother was to try to get some money out of me. I was just flabbergasted, because, I mean, hell, everything I had heard from her was she was going great guns in Philadelphia. She sent me some articles that she cut out from *Sepia* and another one from *Ebony*. This was the early '70s when she was still appearing in these articles.

I now view these magazines as being extremely racist, you know, because my kid is by definition in America, he's black. (Son: I'd prefer "Mulatto.") Well, Americans don't give that option, unless you want to check "other." But we've had a lot of talks on this: like we look upon Black Education Week and stuff like that as "Hey, let's have White Education Week, too." Granted, why can't we have our education in such a way that says "American" and put a picture of the person—O.K., fine, he's black—O.K., fine, he's white. But hey, we are Americans. I got that from Dr. Ron Chung, because I asked him, I said, "Are you from China?" He says, "I am a Jamaican." He says, "In Jamaica we do not distinguish." He said, "We are Jamaicans first." He said, "Here in America you are Afro-American; you're Euro-American," he said, "You put American second." He said, "As far as we're concerned, we're Jamaicans." And he hit me real hard, you know, in my brain. So, I'm looking at a whole lot of things. I'm hoping Howard here has picked up on a whole lot of this—because we are Americans and not black and white and everything else. Our brains are what really count.

What would my father have said? My father—my father—my memories of my father. First of all, he was an athlete, which obviously I'm not. He was a track star. He was the recreation director for the City of Sheeboyagan. He was coach and all kinds of things. My father was a sprinter. He had a wall full of medals from the University of Wisconsin, but the only thing he ever was proud of was that his face was in the same picture as Jesse Owens crossing the finish line, and nobody got that close to Jesse Owens to get their picture in the same frame. He almost could have gone to the Olympics.

He had an Asiatic Indian exchange student stay at our house in Sheeboyagan, Wisconsin. Now, he's an Indian, but he's as black as your briefcase over there. My father came home furious, got on the phone and called a bunch of barbers, because our family barber would not cut this "nigger's" hair. Then, another time, Reverend T. Perry Jones brought up a quartet of black gospel singers, took 'em to the hotel, and they would not register them, so my dad and Reverend T. Perry went all around town until they made certain everybody had a place to sleep that night, so they could sing in our church the next morning. Also, I met Mary Crabb, from East St. Louis, and my dad took pictures of her and me together. She's a girl I studied with for a couple of nights. And my mother had a hissy. Mary Crabb. And then Johanna, my girl, saw those pictures, and we broke up. [Laughs] Mary Crabb and I were standing together at the University of Wisconsin—just standing together—that's all the pictures were. So, I grew up with a lot of racism, but my father—his hero was Truman, because with the stroke of a pen, he integrated the United States Navy, without any publicity. It was done silently. And I guess, that's pretty well the key to where I'm coming from—quietness, just easing, breezing along. But you don't force, you don't jam it down someone's throat, and then, it just happens.

I don't think interracial marriage is for everybody. I don't think that's right. I just think that the workplace and where you live and where you get your education from and the benefits that society has to offer should be out there for everybody. I know a lot of Jewish people who will not marry outside their faith. I know there's a lot of first, second, and third generation Japanese and Chinese and a lot of the other oriental people who will not cross-marry. But that doesn't mean that they're not integrated into our society for jobs and education and purchasing and health insurance and medications and all that kind of good stuff. You don't physically have to have children amongst all the different races. Eventually, it's just like Governor Wilder of Virginia said, "We will be truly civilized when the color of a man's skin has the same significance as the color of his eyes." It's the brain that makes us human beings.

I guess I'm a little sorry that I can't give you more of a handle on Caroline. I think Caroline was always searching for that magical discovery. If you look at Dorothy DaPonte's father, he probably made a lot of money through manipulation of a lot of contracts and purchases and land and everything else. But Caroline probably has no concept of the amount of work that went into making a veneer mill and all the chances that that man took, all the ups and downs financially and all the nights he laid awake making certain he had loans. I think that was what made her "Ego Trips" so appropriate. I mean the very word that she used was *ego trips* for her travel agency. And I mean, when I saw that, I said that fit right into her personality. What she wanted was to find something that you could put down a dime and make a million, and put in an hour-and-a-half and then lay back on the Riviera while your business was making dollars, and while somebody else was doing all the work. I mean, when we lived together in Madison, when we had a nice apartment for $45 a month, and I came home one day, and there was this stranger standing up there ironing shirts. And I said, "Who the hell is this?" And she said, "Well, I'm not gonna do this," she said, "I hired her to do the housework." In Madison. Oh, yeah, she was *not* going to do any of this stuff. Unh unh, she was not going to cook, clean, wash, do dishes—nothing. I can't remember what happened, but I put a stop to it.

You're just bringing back things that have been forgotten many, many, many years ago, and you're just bringing out. I don't know how you're triggering 'em, but they're coming out. But, yeah, that's part of her personality. So strange.

So I was involved in four events down there, all because I was just in the wrong damned place at the right time, you know? We were at Dorothy DaPonte's on Christmas morning when the accident occurred out front. Another time, I was selected for Grand Jury duty, and then when I went down to register to vote, and they wouldn't register for me to vote, and then my professor, Don Shaw, got into it, and he raised all sorts of hell and pulled a knife—and so we wind up in the court trial in Macon County. Then we're just with Dorothy DaPonte on our way to Birmingham, and all we're going to do is get a bite to eat—that's all we were gonna do—so that's the way I just kept falling into the shit. And like I said, I was never in a civil rights march—I never went to any rally—never got involved in any of that stuff. And yet, I wind up in *Jet* magazine, and then I see my name shows up in *Sepia*. What can I say? And then when *you* called! [Laughs] You don't know the buzz that went on at our house when you called. . . . (Son: He looked like Bart Simpson with his eyes all bugged out.)

No, don't get me wrong. I'm not wanted for murder or for tax evasion or anything like that, but Big Brother's out lookin' for me, and I thought I had left a complete void. I'm living on cash—I have no cards—nothing. And then, Wham! So what we've concluded is that if Big Brother really was out lookin' for me, they would have gotten me by now. I had no idea it was that easy to find somebody.

9 Mary Bacon Barney

(sometimes called Bake or Mary Bake)

When I approached Mary Bacon, Mrs. Howard Barney, she did not want to talk about Dorothy at all. She said she did not want to remember painful things. Still, in time, she relented. I interviewed her on July 17, 1991, in the living room of her home looking out on Dog River, south of Mobile. Her husband Howard protectively sat at her side and jumped into the conversation whenever he could not contain himself.

I remember that Dorothy was always difficult. She was always somebody you had to sort of go over, or get past, and her mother was always worried about what Dorothy was going to do, what she was going to say. You were always making allowances trying to get along with Dorothy: that's what I'm trying to say.

I can remember one time we were all playing at Dorothy's house, a lot of us, four or five, and I don't know whether we put her in a closet or what, but I do remember the maid coming out and saying, "No, you mustn't do this, you mustn't treat little Dorothy this way, she has to be treated differently." I don't know, I guess the point was that they felt that she was too scared or too high-strung or something. That is the memory I have from the time we were probably six or seven. Little children.

She threw temper tantrums, and she'd be mean, and she was just difficult, that's all. We had to placate her.

My mother was proud of her as time went on, because my mother was sort of a crusader herself, for the blacks, from the time when blacks first used rest rooms downtown and things like that. So she sympathized and empathized with Dorothy in a lot of that stuff, but I don't know how she really felt about Dorothy. She also used to say to me, "I have to keep remembering that she's my mother's granddaughter" [laughs]. You know, she would say that lots of times. But, all of us were sort of wishing Dorothy were different, always.

Her mother's last words, when she was dying, and I've told this to her too, was, "Pray for little Dorothy." That's sad, isn't it?

I don't know if Dorothy would have been any different if her mother had lived. She's bound to have been different in some ways, but she was already different, and not like everybody else. I don't know how she would have turned out, she might have turned out worse, who can tell? [Laughs.]

I don't think her father was ever able to love anybody but Dorothy. He loved her, and of course he probably loved his wife, and he was crushed when she died. He was a little cold, but her mother was more affectionate, more empathetic towards Dorothy, and that's why I think she attributed so much of her loss to her mother's death early on.

We had a doctor in our family, Emmet Frazer, and he was young, just back from Mayo, and he said that he could tell that Aunt Antonia was dying for five days; her charts were showing it, and her doctor wasn't aware of it. She shouldn't have been cut, because she was so young, thirty-five or six, I think.

When we were at camp, I could do everything well. And I say that in all humility. I was so full of enjoying life that I didn't pay too much attention to Dorothy. I can remember that she didn't bother me there, she was no problem to me at all.

Well, we all just loved that camp. It was just wonderful. Those were some of the happiest days of my life. My husband Howard talks about college, but *we* had a wonderful time at *camp*. Dorothy loved it just as much, too.

When Dorothy's mother died, she got sent off to Gulf Park College. I'll tell you about that. Dorothy had an aunt that lived with her

Dorothy's cousin, Mary Bacon,
with her sister, brother, and parents,
ca. 1927

family, her mother's sister, Aunt De De. De De had always been babied because she had TB when she was young. She didn't ever have to do any work. She didn't want to lift her finger. She was waited on. Antonia and the whole staff waited on her, and when Antonia died, Uncle Paul couldn't wait to get rid of De De because he had had to support her and take care of her all her life. He just told De De that she would have to go get a job someplace, so she went to New Orleans without any skills at all, and became a librarian. That was why Uncle Paul had to do something with Dorothy, and he sent her to Gulf Park College.

Dorothy was kind of excited about going, though. She got beautiful clothes. We were all envious of all the pretty clothes she got. There was a nice woman down in one of the clothing stores, Edwina Marks, who helped her. Dorothy really had a beautiful wardrobe, and I think that she was thrilled about going down there because she was kind of the center of attraction, everybody was going on about her, and would drive down on weekends to see her at Gulf Park, and all that fuss. It should have been a good time for her.

I loved Holton Arms. I had a grand time there. It was the kind of school that took care of individual needs, and if I wasn't smart in something, they would fix it so I could be; it was that sort of thing. It was a good school.

By the time Dorothy came to Holton, I had been there a year, and I was president of the student government, and I was having a grand time, and again Dorothy did not feature much in my life. I would see her, and we would be pleasant, but she was not in any way in my life. I remember when we graduated together, somebody said, "It's the first time that I've ever thought that you looked alike—I could see your family resemblance," but I have no recollection of going places with her or doing things with her then.

Mrs. Jessie Holton, the director of the school, said a little something personal about everybody at the end of the year. She said about me that I had a talent for friendship, and about Dorothy she said that she had never known someone so young who had such a social consciousness. Those are the only two things I remember.

In our teenage years, when we all went around together, Dorothy probably didn't have as many dates, but she was always included, but it might be with just some lone boy, you know. Everybody had a boyfriend, and Dorothy never did really; she was just sort of on the fringe.

I don't know, maybe she wasn't attractive. She should have been attractive. I don't know what it could have been. . . . Maybe they were afraid of her [laughs]. I don't know, that was just a remark. Dorothy had a mean streak. I cannot tell you why she wasn't popular, unless that she was just strange. The boys didn't feel at ease with her.

(Husband: Maybe she didn't have the sex appeal that you all did, who knows, I mean. . . .)

Yes, I would probably say that. Yeah. I'll tell you, she says that she thought she might have been a lesbian. I don't know, I just don't know. I really can't say that.

There was Payton Bush. He was my brother's friend, nine years older than Dorothy, I would say. I thought that was a very strange relationship. By the time I knew him, he was drunk all the time. At the time, I remember, everybody thought, well, isn't this grand, Dorothy and Payton are together, they are probably a good team.

Didn't she go to a psychiatrist at that period when she was in New York? Un huh, I remember her talking about that: all he wanted to do was make her fall in love with him, and she couldn't or something like that, she told me once. The psychiatrist felt that he couldn't help her unless she could fall in love with him and really identify with him. She told me that. And, she could not do that, she said.

I want to say something about New York. Lots of people went to New York. Everybody went to New York; that was not unusual at all. I mean I went to New York and spent two months before I got married. For people of our social class, that was not in any way unusual.

Sarah Harris was Dorothy's friend who went to New York with her, and Dorothy's closest friends were always easy-going, nice, happy people. A lot of people couldn't put up with Dorothy because she was too hard to get along with, but somebody like Sarah, who is really easy-going, could.

Well, there was another one, too, from right here in Mobile. Lib Radcliffe. It was the same kind of thing, and they were always good to Dorothy, and you know, they didn't mind her, shall we say, idiosyncrasies. They could put up with her.

Is someone an old maid at twenty-five? I think so. If you haven't gotten out of school and gotten married, you were pretty much worried about yourself. In my day, you would marry almost anybody rather than be an old maid. [Laughs: Why? I don't know why you asked me that question.] I don't know why she didn't marry.

She could have done it, but she just didn't want to. But, she did get to lead the Strikers Ball, which was a big social event. If you did that, you were supposed to be pretty fine, so that was good [laughs]. But, you know, she did things that seemed to put men off. I remember one man came to call on her—she had a date with him—and he had on a brand new suit, and he was a very poor boy, and he walked out to where she lived at Dog River, and she pushed him overboard into the river. She ruined his brand new suit. She would do things like that. This was when she was seventeen or eighteen years old.

I mean that's what is so funny about it all, she has all this advantage, yet she would do cruel things like that, to men anyway. Maybe it was just sort of an impulsive, funny thing, but it wasn't funny to this little boy. He still talks about it to this day, but I'm not going to tell you his name.

(Husband: Ask her next time you meet her about her aggressiveness with the opposite sex. Not sexually but physically. She hit one man with a broom.)

Oh yes, but you can read about that in the paper. Well, I don't know any more than the paper, because I wasn't in on any of that. I read the same thing you did and heard about it.

She took earnest money. . . . . She gave this man a little note on this paper bag or something agreeing to sell some of the Dog River property, and she dishonored it. He was going to hold her to it. See, anybody else who had known Dorothy and Uncle Paul would have let her get out of it, and she expected to be let out of it, and when she couldn't she was furious.

(Husband: She hit him with a broom, and I think broke his glasses. Ask Dorothy.)

Then, there was a lieutenant in the Navy, I don't remember his name. She struck him once, but he hit her back. It happened across the river in the middle to late thirties. I don't know how much she was drinking, but it was mostly a beer parlor anyway. He was a flyer from Pensacola, and it wasn't an argument or anything else, but she just off and impulsively hit him in the face with her fist, and he didn't take it. He just knocked her down. She went around with a swollen jaw for a while. When he came back to Mobile six months later, he said he was ashamed of himself for striking a woman, but everybody congratulated him. That's why I don't want to get too involved in talking about Dorothy.

I would say she has an inability to form close relationships. Definitely. With men and women I would say.

(Husband: Yeah, and I think she is now just reaching out.)

I really wanted to be close to her for a long time, and I tried to be. And, then, she would turn on me and say mean things. I can't remember: see I've tried to forget all that. I really have put it behind me.

(Husband: What was the instance when she came out of the bushes here? What had she done?)

Oh, that was so horrible, but I can't remember that either, except she just came screaming through the bushes. Dorothy lived just up the road. I was here with a friend, and we were getting ready to go to an art show, and Dorothy said, "Bake, Bake," and she was screaming and furious, and she said something about how she was locked out, and I have forgotten what all it was, but I said, "I have to go or we're going to be late, but I will take you to get someone," and she got perfectly furious because I wouldn't do whatever she wanted me to do. I have forgotten now, but she talked horrible to me, and . . . I can't remember all the horrible things she said, talking about her father's will and all sorts of horrible stuff. Just wild talking.

When her father died, like a fool . . . they said who will tell Dorothy, and I didn't do right. I should have gone to her house, but I telephoned to tell her, and she lambasted me over the phone, saying why are you telling me this way. So that's the kind of thing that she was saying when she got so angry at me for not helping her right then. After awhile you just want to spare yourself that kind of treatment. I think she acted that way another time when she was buying a refrigerator; she just went all to pieces over something like that. She had that erratic behavior. She did have it, but probably doesn't have it anymore. I hope not.

I don't remember much about Dorothy during the war years. I remember when she was married to Nicki, she was so happy, seemingly, and she was so pretty then. She seemed very happy for a long time. Of course, she wanted to have a baby very much, and I remember one time Nicki said in his European way, "Well, the keel has been laid," and everybody was so thrilled, but of course, it turned out not to be true. Dorothy wasn't pregnant. Then, of course, it went from bad to worse. One time she said, "You don't know what it is like being married to a European man. He expects me to drop everything the minute he comes home." And, he would say, "I come home and Dorothy is lying in bed reading." I guess he wanted her to be up fixing his dinner. Well, I don't know what happened after that.

When he killed himself, we always heard that she went down there and, uh, picked up the gun, so she destroyed the finger prints. Wasn't that it? I think it is. She picked up the gun. There was a doctor there, too, I think. He must have been there at the same time. And, Nicki's head was in a basket, and nobody can understand that unless he—how could he put his head in a basket? Maybe he planned it that way. Would he plan that? In a wicker basket? Anyway, that's what we've always been told.

That's the story, but I don't know. We were not there, we didn't see it. And I tried. The doctor that was there is dead now, but I know he saw the note that Nicki had written. His name was S. S. Murphy,

Dr. Murphy, but he is now dead, so you can't ask him.

(Husband: I think he was the one that told us he had fallen in this wicker basket.)

Yeah.

That was so sad and horrible. But Nicki called up several people and said that he was going to kill himself . . . my Aunt Mainger for one, he called her. She was begging him to come up to her house and spend the night with her. He was despondent. He said he would lose his job and lose everything if Dorothy left him, and that she couldn't leave him, and Dorothy was saying that she was going to leave him. But anyway, Dorothy got very thin after all that, and Uncle Paul was so upset. I remember how we were all very upset about it all, naturally, and sorry about it, but that was that. Poor man.

Everything Dorothy did was distressing to her father. And when she took over the little black girl, Carrie Mae, he nearly died, he was so distressed over it. It was pitiful, he was so upset.

Mother was more aware of it all than I was, but Mother was always trying to desegregate the churches, too. I wouldn't have been aware of what Dorothy was doing because I was too busy in my own life in those days. Raising children and having fun.

What do you suppose went wrong with Dorothy and those children that she brought up? Why didn't they change? I haven't any idea.

I have three girls and one boy. I certainly know something about raising children, and mine didn't turn out like Carrie Mae and Alfred, thank God! I don't know, I guess it wasn't a normal environment. One thing: maybe Dorothy didn't know how to treat people . . . children.

Dorothy said to me once that she hoped that Carrie Mae, whom she raised, would make a contribution to her race, but that she didn't have it in her—Carrie Mae didn't have what it took. But that was Dorothy's ideal. I think that was her real plan; that was what she hoped to do. It is sad that it didn't work out for her.

If you had seen Dorothy coming into concerts and things with Alfred, dressed up like a little baboon. He was so tacky looking, you couldn't believe it. He wasn't dressed like a nice little boy. He would have on a funny little hat with a feather, and he just looked awful. Dorothy would walk down the aisle, sit on the front row practically, so everybody would see her come in with this little black boy.

(Husband: Somebody said, "I am glad she is exposing him to culture, but can't she make him take off his hat? There he sits on the front row with his hat on.")

It was pitiful really. It was sad.

I think a lot of Dorothy liked to shock people, don't you?

When we saw her written up in the *Press Register,* when the Klan burned a cross in her yard, we were terribly embarrassed, wishing it weren't so. I remember that, and I remember being over at my sister's house, it was right next door, and I think the phone was ringing all the time. I can remember that there was a lot of confusion, and we were very embarrassed.

People teased me about Dorothy always. I can remember when I would go to a party, people would ask me, "What's Dorothy doing now?" that kind of thing. You see, we were all a very close group and everybody, even though they loved Uncle Paul in a way, and they loved all of us, were sorry about Dorothy's misadventures. But it was done in a kind way. People really were good to Dorothy, even though she did these things. They took it. They didn't ostracize.

I loved what she was doing about the dog pound, but I hated to see her dragged along with her legs sticking out all over . . . pictures in the newspaper. Horrible! [Laughs.] It was very undignified! Oh, I felt terrible. I thought, Dorothy, why did you do that? I mean I just hated her doing that, I despised it. It was just undignified, and there was no reason to do that. She could have just walked out in a nice way, she didn't have to be dragged off by the police, do you think?

She doesn't seem to have the same kind of pity for human beings. I mean, I told her one time about a cousin we had that was very poor, after Dorothy had told me she was a millionaire many times over, and I made a little hint . . . and I suggested that she might could help this cousin, and she was not in the least bit interested in it.

That's another funny thing about her. She is weird about money and always has been. I can't imagine why. Uncle Paul was always very generous with her. This is something else I was thinking about, how she never could make up her mind shopping. To go shopping with Dorothy would just drive you crazy because she couldn't make up her mind what she wanted to buy, and she also lost a lot of things, growing up. I remember we went to Europe together, and she would lose her evening bag one time and lose something, a watch, the next. She was always losing something. That's strange, too. I wonder if she still does. But she was always very tight about money, very tight.

She was really mean to her father. She was always putting the knife to him and turning it in him, over everything. And, he was long-suffering—it is the only way to put it. He told me that when Dorothy was sitting there, and Alfred came in from school and kissed her on the back of the neck, that he could hardly stand it. Both Carrie Mae and Alfred were so unattractive. If they had been better-looking blacks, it might have been easier to take.

But going back to Dorothy, I can remember as a child, that she couldn't bear to see anyone take a hook out of a fish's mouth. So even then, she couldn't stand it. So she has always felt that way about animals.

She is a mixed-up person, isn't she? It is interesting but sad.

Uncle Paul didn't know what to do with her. I don't know that he knew what to do with anybody. Uncle Paul was a strange man. He was just a cold, mean sort of man. He was always mean to my mother. He was unloving—let's don't say he was mean; let's just say he was unloving, and he was kind of obtuse in lots of ways. I just think that he was not kind.

He had an affair with somebody. I know who this was. They were in New Orleans together, and she said they spent the night together, and the next morning he got up and left a twenty-dollar bill [laughs]. What kind of man would do something like that. Imagine being that dumb and unfeeling. I don't think he meant it to be cruel; he just didn't know, and probably thought that would be a nice little way to express himself instead of going and buying her a present or something. But imagine such behavior. Doesn't that tell you a lot about him?

Now Uncle Paul had lots of friends, and lots of people loved him. He was a courtly, gentlemanly man. Lots of people thought he was a wonderful, old Southern gentleman. But, he also had a lot of people that thought he was kind of hard to get along with. Women more than the men, maybe, wouldn't you say that? [Husband nods.] But he was not a very kind brother to my mother, not a kind brother at all. He was just aloof and cold and not loving.

Didn't Dorothy tell you that she never felt too close to her father? Is that what she said or not?

Dorothy's mother was a charming, lovely, pretty person, but she was also very high-strung. I can remember her having nightmares and crying out in the night. I remember her having sort of a temper fit one time when we were off in North Carolina together. So, I would say she was not your everyday normal sort of person either. I wouldn't say normal, that's not the word I mean. But she was excitable, that's the word I'm looking for. And when Dorothy was little, she would say her prayers, and say her prayers so long that her mother would beg her to get up off her knees. Dorothy was always doing things like that. And then she would turn around and say, "Don't stick a pin in me," and nobody was thinking of sticking a pin in her. She would say her prayers for hours. [Laughs and mimics] "Don't stick a pin in me!"

Un huh, and then she would take forever to eat her lunch. Her mother would say, "Hurry, darling." I would finish mine long before, and Dorothy would still be eating one green pea at a time. She did all sorts of things to annoy people, always [laughs]. You are making me remember things I've been longing to forget.

She took lipstick and painted some little boy's penis like a barber pole. When they were little teeny children, they were like three and four. That was the story we always told. I wonder why we knew that story, but we did. It was better than playing "Doctor" I guess. Playing "Barber."

Dorothy feels like she was well provided for in some ways, but she did not get control of her father's estate. I know about that because you see, he had already given her a certain amount of money; she had some money of her own. When he died, the estate was left in trust, because he knew she would squander it—he thought she would anyway—and he said he had worked hard for his money, and he didn't want it left that way.

(Husband: He was afraid that she would give it to some of these causes, I think.)

I don't mean squander it, that was the wrong word. But, she was supposed to have had a good income all these years, and she told me that Arthur Trabits made wonderful investments for her, and that is why she got interested in him [laughs].

But Uncle Paul's will was very sad. There were five nieces and nephews, and . . . I shouldn't tell that. . . . . Well, anyway it is nothing except that my sister and brother and I were left a quarter of the money, divided by three of course, and then the others, Anne and Danner Frazer, were left with 75 percent of the money, which was so mean because we were really closer to Uncle Paul than the other two. But he had thought that we didn't need it, so he left it very unfairly. Now, they turned out to have more money than we do. If I outlive Dorothy, I will maybe get $80,000 from Uncle Paul's estate. She will hate that. I hope I will outlive her just long enough to spite her.

I'll hate it when you publish this book. I don't suppose I'll hate it, but I won't want to read it, I'll say that. That's not true, I will read it. But as long as there isn't anything too horrible about her, I won't mind. And there won't be anything too horrible because I haven't told you anything too terrible. No, there are a lot of little stories that are bizarre, but not worth talking about. I've told you all I can.

She used to be lots of fun. I used to love to be with her. She could be so companionable and fun, and you just loved this woman, and then the next time you would see her she would slap you down for no reason that you could think of. You never had any security in your relationship with her.

Three

THE RESPONSE

10 Confession

Have Caroline and I been a great experiment in integration? No, not particularly. As an individual case, we know each other very well, and Caroline says that I'm still prejudiced. I guess I am.

Is she? I never ask her anything like that. I just don't think I can talk about it. I have a lot of political actions I can point to without getting into all this analysis. [Becomes angry.]

Listen, I don't care what people want to know about! Tell them you couldn't find out! I don't owe it to anybody! I don't have to give people what they want! I don't have to answer questions! I don't have to defend my stand! I just did it, and they can make what they want to out of it!

I don't feel that they're a bill collector, and I owe a debt, and have to give it to them. I did what I did, and I don't owe them any explanation.

So what if my life is misconstrued in some way? It will be! But not everybody gives all this total, transparent, perfect communication. We all keep hidden a lot of things all the time. You can't just get truth by asking for it.

This is for publication—this communication. I'm not going to put it on "off the record" either. But I'm certainly not going to say everything I think for public consumption. The place I say everything I think is after Mildred and I get alone in a room—we can say all sorts of negative things then, because that's what we want to say, and we can relieve ourselves of them.

I really would hate to have the book be too white supremacist, but I certainly think that . . . If I'm going to say anything . . . I just don't think I can say. . . .

Here's what I can say: The black people are aware of their power, politically. I helped them get the vote. I helped them get the schools integrated, which has certainly lowered the public school system's accomplishments—their scholastic averages. Blacks have great consumer power, and they've learned to use it politically. They've got representation, like Jesse Jackson, and they've got their issues. They're one faction politically, and we're another. I don't think there's a strong push, particularly, for complete integration.

I'm talking about blocks—political blocks. Of course, if white people wanted integration, we'd have it! Instantly! Of course it's the white people that don't want it. Oh, I wish you wouldn't make me get into all this. I can't say anything about what black people want! Talk to Jesse Jackson and ask him.

I enjoyed many of my contacts with the black race. I never really became totally a pacifist, and I'm not as far out in the animal rights movement as some can be, because I can't sacrifice that much. Almost everything we do exploits an animal. I got a big thrill out of both of those causes. And I got a lot of thrills in my black relationships, too. So did other people that I've run across.

I don't think there's competition between the races. If it were naturally competitive, the black people wouldn't have to have affirmative action or be able to get anywhere. We would have all the good jobs—we can beat them every time—except basketball and football and dancing.

I'm not going to get into all this! I'm just not going to do it. [Pause] I don't like affirmative action. . . . I am *not* going to do it! I am not going to say all the things I think about black people! They are too negative, and I am not going to put them in my book. If you don't stop trying to dig them out of me and make me say them—I'm simply not going to say them. I hate your questions. You're always making me say . . . making me think about things that I didn't want to think about.

I'm bored with my life. [Resigns] Let's quit. You've got enough, haven't you?

I want to talk about what I want to talk about instead of being taken down other tracks by your mind. I'll talk about plenty.

I enjoyed my lawsuits, but it was a vice to enjoy them so much. I wouldn't call them self-indulgent or self-promoting. No, I don't think it's either one of those. I think it's—a natural vice. In our nature we're corrupt and carnal, and politics is very close to armed combat. These lawsuits of mine are very close to a substitute for bloody battle. That blood lust is a very primitive animal instinct. It's natural to kill and to eat meat and to drink and to do all the other things that are not elevating spiritually—that don't take us to the better part of our mind—parts that are reptilian instead of cool, logical, and compassionate. Our natural vices are exciting, stimulating.

Oh, it's human. I didn't say *not human*; I said it was not elevating. And I'm just not going to answer any more questions. Just let me talk without asking questions.

I see the comfortable lives people around me live. I think it would be very foolish for me to think that my sort of uncomfortable life is morally superior to theirs. But that's the kind of statement it makes.

I have likened my protests and my lawsuits to combat, I know, but I wasn't thinking of Valkyries and Amazons. More like Joan of Arc.

I was influenced by a picture of Joan of Arc, which is in Paris. I've got it in my scrapbook. She's looking up sort of, and it's like a light from heaven coming down to it—a voice or something. I had that conceited, morally superior feeling, and I'm not so sure that these feelings are valid guideposts to action. I'm not so sure that it isn't neurotic compulsiveness that keeps me from relaxing and enjoying cooking and sewing and reading and bridge, that those things aren't just as deserving of our time and attention as these more dramatic things I've done. I'm not sure I can get away from—can control—these urgencies, but I don't think they're divine. I don't believe in divinity.

I went to a Quaker meeting once, a Quaker wedding—I've forgotten when—and one of the old Quakers broke the silence with a remark and later on, at the refreshments, I said, "I liked what you said." He said, "That wasn't I speaking—that was God." I thought that was very foolish, to really persuade yourself that, even though it's your deepest concern, that it's some morally superior assertion, something that has a certain authority.

I'm just trying to take myself off of the pedestal and to look on these things I've done as probably substitutes for marriage and children and good housekeeping and wonderful parties and social life.

I'm really not very brave. I pass up many opportunities to speak. I'm silent when words need to be spoken. I've got a very cute new T-shirt—it's anti-fur. I wore it in church last Tuesday, and one of the women who wears a fur stole, Martha Callahan, whom I've given an animal rights leaflet to before, was interested in the shirt and felt it, and said it was pretty. Well, it's dripping blood. It's got fake fur on it. I'm not sure that she even got the message that that was against her stole. And I didn't make her get it. Then, another time, two of the women were talking about how the crabs ran away on their counter, and they'd have to catch them, to boil them alive and all that. I was silent as a tomb. Those are life forms that have me for their defender.

I think we all struggle—I know I do—against total animal protection at all times, and I know I don't speak up as well in face-to-face confrontation as Mildred does.

I don't feel that I'm putting out a message. I feel that I'm just dressing myself up in an image to display myself. Yeah, that's it, probably.

The causes I've supported will outlast this book. The book is me: a person's life. My life is like a book. I can get interested in it—then, you can feel like you've read it enough, and then you go on to another one. I've kind of had enough of my life, almost.

Have I done any good? Of course, absolutely. I look at myself as part of a group. All these pressures have resulted in a great difference

(photograph by Victor Calhoun, courtesy of the Mobile *Press Register*)

Caroline and Dorothy,
1989

in the racial system—integration of public facilities and schools. And voter registration. And because the black people have the vote, they've gotten a lot of these programs passed which have resulted in their walking around in nice clothes. They're living in apartments that have the general amenities of refrigeration, heating and cooling. And, they are greatly overweight; it's turning into their largest single health problem, especially for women, because of food stamps and welfare.

Pacifism—well, the Fellowship of Reconciliation was the parent group of CORE, the Congress of Racial Equality, and Amnesty International came out of it. I saw CORE's work in all these civil rights things—bus rides to Montgomery and so on. And, then, the Vietnam War protesters went far beyond the Fellowship of Reconciliation, but certainly it was connected with the idea of pacifism. And the animal rights movement is just beginning to get its full force.

Yes: I have a sense of satisfaction.

But, Caroline and I go to different churches now. If I had stayed true to my initial actions with Caroline, I would have gotten her into my church. The preacher asked her to join. The congregation wouldn't have liked it, but I guess they would have accepted the situation. There're a couple of black men there now, but they're not regular members of the church. They're in a retarded group that gets brought in by bus: two black men, there might be three sometimes.

11 Atonement

In July, 1991, I went to see Dorothy for what I imagined might be the last time as her biographer. It had been two years since I had last visited with her.

Let me tell you about Alfred. He was convicted of possession of stolen property and burglary. I think he was sentenced to ten years. He served only a portion of that, which is very alarming for us outside the prison system to realize. The judge doesn't have any control over that. Other people do. Prisoners don't serve but a tiny bit of their sentences.

One year ago Alfred got out on probation. He was here on my birthday just by accident. That was February 24, 1990. Well, they just put him out with nothing at all: no place to stay, no family, no job or anything. He came over here. I gave him a little of whatever we were eating, and he walked off again. He stayed at some horrible place over on Davis Avenue.

I hated it over there whenever I had to pick him up or drop him off. Apparently he took up with some girl that offered him a place to stay, and it wasn't hers to give, and when the owner came back, she accused him of I don't know what all, but he was just out of jail, so they put him right back in again. Actually, I believe he was innocent of burglary at that time. And he could have defended it in court and won, probably. But, he chose to plead guilty, which was very foolish. He was pleading innocent when he was guilty and now guilty when he was innocent. He thought the sentences would run concurrently. He just thought he would outsmart them, that pleading guilty wouldn't mean anything anyway. But he's been in jail ever since. That was a year ago in February. It's going to be August soon—a year and six months in jail.

See, I wasn't in touch with him for years, and then he called on me . . . and started phoning me and writing me. Telling me all these prison plans: the ways you can get out. There are many different types of plans apparently. I responded to his wanting to take up that relationship again. He wanted me to visit him up at Atmore.

He's been all over the state of Alabama; I can't name all the different prisons he's been to. He's close to Atmore on work release now. He's been home on furlough, a seventy-two hour furlough, over at that house I'm giving him, and I can go up to see him any Sunday, or I can take him out for eight hours, I think, on Saturdays.

I've been to see him two or three times, I've forgotten which, and I've taken him out twice. One time was last Saturday. Anyway, he'll be at home soon. Maybe in two weeks. As soon as the parole board decides on his case. This time it's so much more sensible: he has to have a job plan, which he's got. He's working in Flowerwood Nursery. Greg Smith owns it, and he is married to my cousin's widow, and some of them are going to get a large part of my estate, so I think that influenced him to hire Alfred. I hope. I mean it's only logical to think it would have some influence.

And, then, Alfred has to have a place to live and a telephone, and I've talked to the parole officer, the man that will be in charge of him, but he can't do what Alfred may need. The parole officer told me what his job was like at the prison where they kept Alfred. He said he was a baby-sitter for all these convicts. That he had to tell them when to get up, when to take a bath, when to eat, when to go to bed, what television programs to watch, and he couldn't do that for Alfred in Mobile. He has too big a caseload. We can only come twice a month or something—very long intervals anyway—to check in with him. Somebody else has got to get Alfred waked up for work.

When he came home on the furlough, we had some bad moments. I lost my temper with him and told him that it was absolutely hopeless to try to relate to him because he'd just shut the door on every single thing I would suggest. It's hard to be around somebody and not suggest little things: would you like to do this or see that person? No, no, no, he'd say. It's real hard to say I won't suggest anything to do, and so I really was very angry. I've never been that openly angry with Alfred before, and it may have done us some good, brought us closer together. He wrote me a nice letter, I can show it to you, and he apologized in a way.

Anyway, I have been working on this house. I've had it since about 1960. And Alfred, when he was just a toddler, was sitting on those steps and he said, "Don't give me this one." I reminded him of that the other day, and he said he's changed his mind now.

If he has a car pool, that may help get him up for work. I don't know what he'll do for transportation otherwise. If I help him get a car, he might try to drive to work himself, and it will all fall to pieces.

No, I don't think Alfred is going to be straight this time, or that it's all going to work out fine. I don't feel that he's proved himself.

Oh, it's sad. And Caroline's story is sad, too. There's nothing new that's sad, I mean it's just turned out so bad. . . . I saw her this morning. I just washed some shoes for her. She's still in the nursing home. That's where she will live for the rest of her life.

She makes up all sorts of things. She phones real estate agents, and they've taken her out to see places. She thinks she can make a down payment on a house with the SSI and keep house, when she can't even get up out of bed very well. She's using a wheel chair now. She will always. She'll get worse.

Yeah, we get along. I think we get along well, but she says bad things about me all of the time.

What do I think? Well, she's a person that has a great deal of self-confidence in a way. She's very much at home with white people. She speaks English well. That's all I can say. I think her sisters have done better than she has, most of them. The ones I didn't bring up. One of them is earning $35,000 a year, and another has a master's degree from LSU, has been teaching, and had a stable marriage and legitimate children.

My father would have been harder on a male child than he was on me. He would have taken a male child into the business and trusted him with family money and business decisions. Yeah. If I were male, it would all be mine. I would be running it all. But his way with me was typical of his generation of men in Mobile. Actually, I don't think men have changed that much. Women are not at all able or interested in running big businesses.

Yes, I do live frugally. Does that bother you? It bothers some people. But you don't need to ask why. You know my ideals and ideas. I don't live frugally compared to the Quakers and the Fellowship people. I just don't want to be a big consumer. Consumerism just isn't my bag.

No, I don't believe that talking about my life with you over the years has made any difference in the way I see it. I just wish I had lived differently. But the moving finger writes, and you can't change a bit of it. I'd say I had so many opportunities to form a stronger community network for Caroline and Alfred. And, I think *that* is one of the main things that is wrong with this situation: our being in a racially divided country. And, especially, in this state and town. There is no place where we three really fit in together.

I had various opportunities, and I didn't take advantage of them. I was almost a Quaker, and we could have made it, and then I could have become a Catholic. I was going to church with Mildred and Frances all the time, and they would have accepted us more or less. Little Mildred, Frances' youngest child, was Alfred's age, so they could have played and grown up together. She was the most outstanding student at McGill's. She's a lawyer in New York now, and Alfred's in jail. I really think I brought him up to feel he wished he were a white person.

I know I didn't have Alfred all the time. He suffered a great deal, those years I sent him back to Mother Dear, and I don't know why I did it. I wasn't exhausted. I didn't have any health problems. I mean everybody gets tired of little children, but that doesn't mean you have to give them away. Caroline . . . she really didn't want him, she wanted to give him to Mother Dear. It was my choice, though. I had the authority.

My life doesn't have a theme. Not a very clear cut one. I've had several causes—race relations, animals, and pacifism, and trying to be a mother, wanting to be one. I haven't been totally *committed* enough to any of them.

I did feel a sort of a calling or something. I have been moved to strong spiritual feelings sometimes, and I have been thrilled, too. It's a feeling of leadership! of movement! of influence!! Dedication or something. And I certainly felt this in one of the cathedrals in Guatemala or Mexico with Francis. We saw a crucifix . . . you know they are very realistic over there. And that crucifix when I looked at it made me burst into tears. That was a real religious experience.

I wish that my heart were pure enough to feel that response again. To be worthy of it. I mean, I know that was *goodness*, what I felt. I felt love or something. An appreciation of sacrifice.

I believe in spiritual experiences. I believe in the churches, too, but I don't think there is any Creator . . . no afterlife. Probably, I shouldn't be in the church.

I didn't bring Caroline and Alfred up right. I wish I had brought them up in the church. There is just nothing else that makes you concentrate on your ethics once a week in an organized fashion, and celebrates the important occasions in your life and the special occasions of the year. I think it is very important, even though I shouldn't be saying the Creed and all of those other things. I know I don't believe them. I told Alfred that, and that is no way to bring him to religion: Saying I am a Christian atheist.

Well, when I look back on my life, I think it's been a big mess. All of my decisions have been wrong. That I should have become one thing or another instead of remaining with one foot as a Southern belle and another in all these different things. With each of these different causes I can see the outstanding people leading very satisfactory lives, but I haven't really committed myself totally to something.

I think it's not the way to live. It's the broad path that leads to destruction, instead of the straight and narrow.

That's my life then. Now, I've got to get ready for Alfred.

Conclusion

INTERPRETING A LIFE

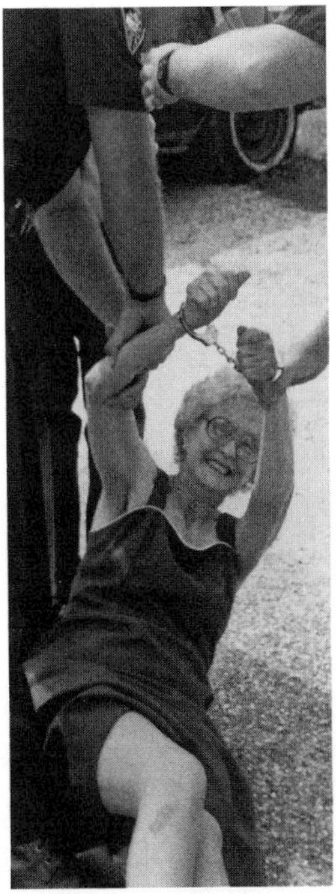

12 The Crisis of Biography

Dorothy and I don't see much of each other any more. Our work together is done.

I have visited her from time to time, though, just to catch up. Dorothy stays busy. She successfully protested a bear wrestling contest put on by a Mobile nightclub. She received the M. O. Bealle Scroll of Merit for contributing $38,000 for the more humane euthanasia of animals at the Mobile animal shelter.[1] She lovingly assembled and privately published *Songs of an Untrained Voice*, a chapbook of sad, lyrical poems by her namesake, Dorothea McIntosh, dear Aunt De De. Dorothy has a larger project, too. She plans to dispose of her estate in a meaningful way and struggles fiercely to find the right monument for her life among the causes she has favored. She has negotiated and rejected agreements to endow professorships at Vassar and the University of Alabama at Birmingham and has sought consultants to help her set up an animal rights museum and education center in Mobile, but nothing is settled. Most mornings she teaches reading, as a volunteer, at a local public school.

I have visited Caroline, too. Mostly, she looks forward to her physical therapy at the pool and to her meals, although she has trouble feeding herself now. Church remains central to her life. Dorothy continues to visit her often and tries in little ways to make Caroline's life more interesting and joyful than it would otherwise be. Each year

1. *Mobile Register*, Mar. 28, 1994.

Dorothy teaches
reading, 1994

Dorothy puts together a little birthday party for Caroline and once got Alfred to come.

Dorothy was right about Alfred. After his release, he soon became a fugitive from the law again. I tried through relatives to find him in Mobile, but he never made contact with me. In 1994 he was arrested on federal charges involving the sale of drugs. In 1995 he pled guilty and was sentenced to ten years in federal prison. As he awaited trial, he called Dorothy often and asked for small favors.

Final Questions

Over the years, and particularly during the many long drives up I-65 toward Nashville, I thought about Dorothy's story and what it all meant. I wondered, too, about why I was so fascinated: What did that say about me? I cannot answer these questions, even now, but I have had a few ideas.

Dorothy had strong moral convictions, and she made public commitments out of these principles that served to cut her off from those around her. For my part, during the 1970s and 1980s, when busing for desegregation and hence support for public education itself were such deep issues in Nashville, my wife Dana and I had put our children on the front lines of the cultural struggle. When friends, neighbors, and associates played it safe and placed their children in private schools or moved to the suburbs to escape the fear, we remained committed public spokesmen in the pro-schools movement, and our children were bused for racial balance. Did we use Ethan, Sarah, and Katherine just as Dorothy used Carrie Mae as means to a greater good? Could that be the "hook" that brought Dorothy and me together? Or, maybe, it was something more personal and elusive: righteous public anger masking complex private doubts? Or perhaps our relationship was based on more prosaic stuff: I am a scholar who writes because it is my job: Dorothy was willing to bare herself to me; and I took the opportunity to make a book, to put another line on a résumé.

From the first, I shared Dorothy's story with others, and I was constantly challenged by those who had their own particular feelings about her as a person and who advanced interpretations of her life that were sharply different from my own. I came more and more to see that making meaning from a life is not an easy task, nor necessarily a benign one, especially in our time.

Several aspects of the story stimulated ambivalence among those who heard her tale, and these feelings often implied three questions not always put directly to me, but which nevertheless caused me to look deeper and think harder about the complex task of telling a life story.

Why is Dorothy important enough to have a book written about her? Some among those who heard the story were vaguely embarrassed and disappointed at having seen Dorothy this closely. They were initially intrigued by her principles and her political stands, but in the end they were not sure they liked or respected her, especially after they heard the harsh words of Caroline, Ralph, and Mary Bacon. More important, Dorothy has not accomplished very much of lasting value. She is a mixed role model at best.

A second reason for unease is deeper still. *What is the truth of her life?* There are too many unanswered questions in her "confession." Is she sexually confused? Clearly, she has had unsuccessful relationships with men. Why is that? Did she have a more direct role in the death of her first husband, as some of her relatives have wondered? That's a serious charge, but there is no evidence offered. Where does the truth lie, and does it matter? Which is more important to the unfolding of a life: what *really* happened or what one thinks happened?

Why was Dorothy's story set out in terms of a confession and not a traditional biographical narrative? At root, most readers want to be reassured that there is a pattern to things, one that can be reconciled with the values of his or her own life. The confessional approach leaves many people wanting a more coherent story of Dorothy's life, one that ties down loose ends and arbitrates among different themes. Traditional biography does this through both tight narrative structure and thematic clarity and consistency.

Dorothy's worthiness as a biographical subject and the truth and form of her story are clearly matters for extended discussion. These very questions imply that some lives are more valuable to us than others, and some stories more truthful and satisfying.

There is a crisis in biography today whether seen from a humanistic or social scientific perspective. Over the past century biography has changed its boundaries, focus, and purpose. Everything is contested. Lives are contingent.

A History of Modern Biography

In *The Troubled Face of Biography*, Eric Homberger and John Charmley invite contemporary biographers to comment on the current discontent.[2] Underlying their concern is a paradox embedded in twentieth century intellectual life: as biographers have moved increasingly into the most private aspects of a person's life in a search for truth, the notion of truth itself has become problematic.

The biographical impulse is ancient, and one of our oldest written records makes clear that a "great man" notion of historical development gave it impetus. *Sirach [Eccleseasticus]* 44:1-2: "Let us now praise famous men, and our fathers in their generations, / The Lord apportioned to them great glory, his majesty from the beginning." Great works were made by great men, and lesser men could be comforted by signs of their ancestors' legitimate authority. Now we, their cultural descendants, recognize and learn from the stories; we are encouraged to support their values. Individual lives may have had their own problems, purposes, and meanings, but most biography that has come down to us from biblical times through Victorian England has had twin purposes: to ground hierarchy in divine or natural order, and to provide role models for the young to learn to accept that private virtue leads to public achievement.

Like the ancient Hebrews, the Victorian English valued public achievement, and they assumed that great men had good and strong characters. Biographers supported that view. While they insisted on

2. Eric Homberger and John Charmley, *The Troubled Face of Biography* (New York, 1988).

writing biographies from diaries, letters, and personal papers, they routinely covered up unpleasant facts about the protagonist's private life. "Lives were cleaned up not just because readers 'shrank from indecency' (though this was certainly important) but because they were expected to exemplify virtues, private and public. It is often forgotten that public lives were whitewashed just as much as private ones: public men always acted from the highest motives."[3] In this phase, the real struggles of lived lives were suppressed; lives were socially constructed to support the cultural assertion of the ascendancy of virtue.

Some Victorian men and women undoubtedly believed that private virtue as well as public character were inevitably manifested in an individual's life works. Good men had good characters and good works. Others, who knew better, wanted not to call into question the fruits of the social order.

Lytton Strachey was an intellectual radical, and he turned biography upside down in 1918 with the publication of *Eminent Victorians*, the first "modern" biography.[4] Strachey's project was "truth-telling." "Truth-telling for the modern biographer was not simply fidelity to the facts or scrupulous reliance on 'original sources': it was to do with correct moral evaluation."[5] He sought to expose eminent characters as humbugs and prisoners of false values when judged from a position of moral elegance.

The Victorians were concerned with character; the modern biographer is focused on motive. Unmasking private motive became a preeminently modern trait with the ascendancy of Sigmund Freud. Post-Freudian biography still centered on lives of significant public achievement, but it asserted that the will to achieve was an expression of sublimated or frustrated sexual energy, diverted from immediate gratification into socially approved tasks. Psychological

3. Robert Skidelsky, "Only Connect: Biography and Truth," in Eric Homberger and John Charmley, *The Troubled Face of Biography*, 5. I use and extend Skidelsky's three "stages" in this chapter.

4. Lytton Strachey, *Eminent Victorians* (New York, 1918).

5. Skidelsky, 6.

reductionism became the hallmark of this second stage of modern biography. "Every achievement is actually 'something else' displaced, and it is this something else which ought to be the focus of biography."[6]

As an explanation for political behavior, psychoanalytic psychology was given impetus by the publication of Harold Lasswell's *Psychopathology and Politics* in 1930. Lasswell issued, "The most general formula which expresses the developmental facts about a fully developed political man: p}d}r= P." Private motives (p) are displaced onto a public object (d) and rationalized in terms of the public interest (r).[7] This meant that all political actors, whatever their office or station, unconsciously worked out their private, personal issues in public space but unknowingly masked them under actions they justified as a public good.[8] This formulation dominated political biography for decades.[9]

In the third stage of modern biography, the criterion of biographical worth itself shifted. "We write biographies of people not because they achieved great or unusual things, but because they led interesting or unusual lives."[10] The rise of popular culture after World War II replaced the aristocratic notion of "achievement" with the democratic notion of "fulfillment" as the measure of biographical worth. And, a fourth stage ushers in a postmodern era, one where life is seen as the ultimate failure of both achievement and fulfillment. At the end of the twentieth century we celebrate victims of social and political

6. Skidelsky, 12.

7. Harold D. Lasswell, *Psychopathology and Politics* (Chicago, 1930). Reprinted in *The Political Writings of Harold D. Lasswell* (Glencoe, 1951), 75.

8. The self-defeating behavior of President Woodrow Wilson became widely discussed in these terms. See Sigmund Freud and William C. Bullit, *Thomas Woodrow Wilson, Twenty-Eighth President of the United States* (Boston,1967); and, Alexander and Julliette George, *Woodrow Wilson and Colonel House: A Personality Study* (New York, 1957). For criticism see: Bernard Brodie, 1957, "A Psychoanalytic Interpretation of Woodrow Wilson." *World Politics* 9:413-22.

9. Fred I. Greenstein, *Personality and Politics: Problems of Evidence, Inference, and Conceptualization* (Chicago, 1969).

10. Skidelsky, 13.

oppression in order to mobilize moral judgment; the biographical project that uses sympathy not only for symbolic reassurance but also to even political scores is not uncommon. Just take a look at recent titles: Rose Mary Denman's *Let My People In: A Lesbian Minister Tells Of Her Struggles To Live Openly and Maintain Her Ministry*; Chris Glaser's *Uncommon Calling: A Gay Man's Struggle To Serve The Church*; Joseph Steffan's *Honor Bound: A Gay American Fights For The Right To Serve His Country*; and editor Louise R. Noun's *More Strong-minded Women: Iowa Feminists Tell Their Stories*.

During the twentieth century, the very grounds of biography shifted: biography democratized. Biography's central justification had been rooted in the "great man" view of history—that knowledge of the life illuminated great achievement—but in our time the "great man" idea was rejected in favor of the notion that circumstances, not individual attributes, produce the great individual.[11] This change was not happenstance. If authors write mainly about the dominant group, as the Victorians did, then one might conclude that great ambition set this elite apart from others in society. The fallacy of this logic became apparent when studies of women and other marginal people showed that they too had ambition.[12] It became clear that intense ambition was not a sufficient cause of personal or gender power. Hagiography, the idealization of the subject, which subsumed most Victorian and pre-Victorian biography, gave way to a "debunking" and "demystifying" biography in the middle of the century only because the intellectual privilege and power of the new authors lay unexamined, as was the case with Freudian interpreters of life. With the coming of postmodern critiques, however, justification for the biographical enterprise itself could no longer rest on either the high social position of the object of biography or on the expertise of the author of the study.

Over the past century, populations became more aroused and more insistent on voicing their own views in societies' transforma-

11. Skidelsky, 3.

12. Estelle C. Jelinek, *The Tradition of Women's Autobiography: From Antiquity To The Present* (Boston, 1986).

tions. Increased literacy and new media of mass and interpersonal communication enlarged the attentive audience; rapid mobilization led to social, economic, and cultural dislocation. Meaning-making and meaning-sustaining acts became more important to individual and collective survival, which made them all the more problematic. All manner of biographical objects and subjects became possible as expectations rose. A century that began with biographies celebrating great accomplishment ends with biographies touting interesting stories. As one respected biographer declared, "A good biographical subject, it seems to me, is simply one that stirs much feeling and provokes much thought. . . ."[13]

A new ethos has emerged. Societies change, and we ourselves change them by the stories we tell about our encounters with each other, with nature, and with God. What passes for good biography at one time will be rejected at another time. The stories will be thought to be wrong; the moral lessons judged to be inappropriate.

A Postmodern Critique

During the last decades of this century the intellectual edifice of humanistic and social science studies has been torn from top to bottom by a postmodern critique.[14] The postmodern critique has diverse sources and many components, but two general themes stand out: everything in culture is "text," and all texts are inherently political.[15]

The postmodern critique rests on the mutability of language. Traditionally, it was argued that language conveyed interpretations and meanings directly and consistently. Derrida, among others, challenged this view.[16] He said language is problematic. A word is itself contingent on other words for its meaning, words that are themselves

13. Michael Holroyd, "How I Fell Into Biography," in Homberger and Charmley, *The Troubled Face...*, 97.

14. For useful summaries see: Norman K. Denzin, *Interpretive Biography* (Newbury Park, 1989), and Robert Hollinger, *Postmodernism and the Social Sciences* (Thousand Oaks, Calif., 1994).

15. Larry Reynolds, *Interactionism: Exposition and Critique* (Dix Hills, NY, 1993), 232; Reynolds' summary and critique are succinct.

16. Jacques Derrida, *Positions* (Chicago, 1972/81), 26, as discussed in Denzin, *Interpretive Biography*, 45, and in Hollinger, *Postmodernism and the Social Sciences*, 96ff.

equally contingent. Therefore, words have no stable meanings but only traces and mutations of prior meaning at each iteration of use. Words make sentences, and from them we *adapt* meanings rather than receive them. If words as signs have no stable meanings, then texts have no center, no essential structure. But writers and readers nevertheless proceed to "read into" texts a structure anyway. They construct "real" authors, intentions, and meanings. Derrida argued that Western literature and science were based on this fallacy of misplaced *presence*. Authors and readers came to believe that real subjects could be found in the real world and then be relocated in texts. Postmodernism says they cannot be so relocated because they cannot in fact be found.[17]

The logocentric bias of Western culture has other implications for a biographical project. First, "Every representation is always a representation from some point of view, within some frame of vision."[18] Hierarchies and oppositions are embedded in texts by authors, knowingly or not, and these take the form of self versus other, deviant versus conformist, reason versus emotion, and so on. These concepts give order to what would otherwise be disordered experience, but they are also highly ideological. Some ways of looking at the world are set above others; some categories of people are dismissed. *Deconstruction* is the process, invented by philosophers and literary critics, by which one makes clear whose point of view is privileged, and whose made marginal, by the frames of reference adopted in texts. "Texts," including biographies, shape the values we seek to live by, and making texts is a deeply rooted political power.

Humans in society generate and receive unequal material resources and social respect. Politics is about getting and keeping physical goods and social deference in the struggle over our collective destiny. Political power has three general manifestations within

17. Denzin, *Interpretive Biography*, 45.

18. Richard H. Brown, "Rhetoric, Textuality, and the Postmodern Turn in Sociological Theory," *Sociological Theory* 8:188-197 as discussed in Larry Reynolds, *Interactionism: Exposition and Critique*, 232ff.

the patterns of conflict.[19] First, power is exercised directly when officials use or threaten to use the ultimate power of government to get someone to do what he or she would not otherwise do. When we pay taxes or obey trespass laws, we are responding to the coercive power of the state. Money and votes are typical measures of this form of power. Second, political power is exercised when officials and others, particularly in the communications media, do not permit issues to be placed on the public agenda: they ignore some complaints and rule others out of bounds, and thus they make marginal those persons whose interests are deflected. When officials state without serious discussion that child care is a private matter, not a responsibility of the community but clearly the responsibility of the parent alone, that is an exercise of power. There is yet another face of political power that is more pervasive still: political power is exercised when Party A can get Party B to do something not in B's own interest by shaping B's values and the way he views the world. John Gaventa tells the story of Appalachian coal miners who continued to live out the stories of competitive individualism in the mining camps when those values served only to keep them in bondage to mine operators. The miners' distress was not coerced by the power of the state or the boss; on the contrary, the boss's political and economic power had been internalized by the miners.[20]

Those who tell the stories or write the curriculum, literally the "texts" of our culture, have great power because they create the images and markers by which we define and direct our lives.

The postmodernist argues that no way of knowing, no epistemology, can escape the fact that it is created by a human being through a linguistic convention that has been shaped socially, culturally, historically, and politically just as has its author. All accounts of reality are not just social constructions but political constructions.[21]

19. John Gaventa, *Power and Powerlessness: Quiescence and Rebellion in an Appalachian Valley* (Urbana, 1980), 5-20.

20. Gaventa, *Power...*

21. Reynolds, *Interactionism*, 235.

Currently, debates over multiculturalism, political correctness, and other manifestations of culture wars signal contests for control over fundamental "texts" in schools and universities.

Language is not a benign vehicle for transmission of intention and meaning; language itself constitutes particular ways of looking at the world. According to this argument, truth and knowledge are ideological constructions; they are constructed by those with power in the world to serve a system that benefits some more than others.

Through deconstruction, all texts are relativized; their connections to culture, class, gender, race, ethnicity, ideology, sexual orientation, religion, history, linguistic conventions, author, and reader are exposed so that readers and critics alike knowingly participate in the problematics of representation even as they come to be armed against the subtle uses of real power.

The Need for Story

Humans need stories. We strive always to find meaning in life; indeed, meaninglessness is practically intolerable. Stories supply meaning to life for those who hear them, and they establish meaning for those who have the energy, courage, and talent to create them. Our need to understand our own location in time and space compels us to interpret lives, both our own and others, and to participate in the generation of a common understanding of the pattern of all our lives. We make stories—we do not discover them in nature—and with them the meanings we have established are passed from one to another. Our stories shape our community and our culture.

Biography is story. *Generic biography* comes in three forms depending on who "authors" the text in some formal sense. *Autobiography* is a narrative account of a person's life written or otherwise recorded by oneself. *Biography* is a narrative account of a life written by a second person and reconstructed mainly from documents. *Life history* is an account of an individual's life as told interactively to another person. Generic biography is a stylized rendering of a life, and whether it takes the form of traditional biography, autobiography, or life history, there is a creative interaction between the protagonist, the writer, and the reader. Inevitably, the three separately and together participate in the meaning-making enterprise. The real life is always remote from each of the three. Not even the autobiographer can capture life as it was actually lived or intended: the acting self, the reflecting self, and the writing self are separate and necessarily distant.[22]

There is a disciplinary predisposition among the three forms of biography. Life history has been used by social sciences; biography by the humanities; autobiography by both.

Whatever its form, all biography is an imaginative creation; it is therefore a fiction that hopes to create an "essential" life for a person through narrative. The "truth" of a life is not found in fidelity to facts, since these are almost always unrecoverable, but is the ordering of both known events and those subjective realities hinted at by choices made in the present or by recollections offered later.[23]

> Perhaps our fascination with these subjects of biography is that we can contemplate in their lives an apparent being-as-a-whole, whether real or illusory. This possibility for being-as-a-whole inspires us with the sense that our own lives might be focused, too, in this manner. Perhaps the recurring themes in Western culture of chance, luck, destiny, and fate have a hidden meaning, then: a desire for our lives to reveal a design that might release us from ambiguity and the painful wrestling with conventional values as we struggle to become whoever we may be. People in all cultures seem to desire, even need in order to survive, patterns that give meaning to their lives.[24]

22. L. Langness and Gelya Frank, *Lives: An Anthropological Approach to Biography* (Navato, Calif., 1981), 105.

23. Victoria Glendinning, "Lies and Silences," in Eric Homberger and John Charmley, *The Troubled Face of Biography* (New York, 1988), 49-54.

24. Langness and Frank, *Lives...*, 116.

Biography, as a cultural artifact, supports us by making clear that life is not random, that there are connections over time between what we feel and think and do, on the one hand, and what actually happens to us, on the other. Dorothy is not very good at making meaning. She has invited us to participate with her in the process.

If we were to make a traditional biography out of the elements of Dorothy's life, we would need to be self-conscious about the enterprise. Biography interprets a life and makes meaningful otherwise inchoate experiences, but the pattern and range of possible stories is culturally constrained. Some stories—some biographies—are acceptable because they reinforce important cultural values; others are entertaining largely because they depict outrageous, that is culturally aberrant, behavior. In either case, there must be an interpretive theme and a recognizable structure if readers are to engage the life.

> The facts do not speak for themselves. A biographer who tries to avoid interpreting them is abdicating his central task. It may be difficult to make an interpretation. It may be the case that two (or even more) interpretations are possible. What is sure to kill a biography is to make no interpretation at all.[25]

Interpreting Dorothy's Life: Four Themes

Four interpretive themes offer themselves immediately from Dorothy's account; each is by now a cultural paradigm:

(1) *Arrested development*: Dorothy was a wounded child and was dealt a traumatic blow when she was thirteen. Her mother unexpectedly died; her dear Aunt De De was removed; Dorothy herself was sent away to school. Her losses were not grieved; the wounds never healed. She spent her life seeking worldly excitement because she could not face the pain within. Dorothy felt like such a victim of fate that she over-identified with those who were themselves victims of

25. Robert Blake, "The Art of Biography," in Homberger and Charmley, *The Troubled Face...*, 77.

war, racial injustice, and exploitation. She was not able to grow up into wholesome maturity. She remained an immature and spoiled child, protected by her wealth from the consequences of her actions.

(2) *Rebellion against patriarchy*: Although largely unmentored, Dorothy intuitively tried to throw off the repressive Southern patriarchy of her time and place and to become her own person. Unlike other young women of her class and culture, Dorothy wanted more than was traditional: she accepted the challenge of the Frontier Nursing Service; she pursued intellectual and social freedom at Vassar; she sought out adventure and personal liberty in Greenwich Village; she publicly and persistently opposed military service, racial supremacy, and hunting and fishing—all defining issues of white Southern manhood. Throughout, she embraced ideas, values, and people who were clearly disapproved by her own community. Dorothy was keenly aware that at crucial points in her life, her father undercut her principled stands, and this angered her greatly. Her quest for husband and children was an illusion sought only as a misguided attempt to relieve the loneliness of her personal rebellion.[26] Nevertheless, at the end she is nearly defeated and vanquished:

> Well, when I look back on my life, I think it's been a big mess. All of my decisions have been wrong. That I should have become one thing or another instead of remaining with one foot as a Southern belle and another in all these different things. With each of these different causes I can see the outstanding people leading very satisfactory lives, but I haven't really committed myself totally to something.
>
> I think it's not the way to live. It's the broad path that leads to destruction, instead of the straight and narrow. (Pp. 223–224)

(3) *A personal myth*: Dorothy was early and powerfully moved by the story and image of Joan of Arc. Joan was a simple soul who was

26. Carol Gilligan, *In a Different Voice* (Cambridge, Mass., 1982).

moved by God to rouse and lead her people against a strong enemy, only to be betrayed and martyred for her unwavering commitment to her convictions. It is a story of spiritual inspiration, martial courage, and utter sacrifice. Dorothy was struck by paintings and statues of St. Joan when she visited Paris as a child and ended the story of her own life with a reference to Joan. This may signal the power of personal myth to give shape and meaning to her life. Interpreters of the human mind reinforce this notion.[27]

> So each of us has his or her myth around which we pattern our lives. This myth holds us together and gives us our capacity to live in the past and future without neglecting each instant of the present. The myth bridges the gap between conscious and unconscious: we then can speak out of some unity of the tremendous variety in each of our selves.[28]

(4) *Sin and redemption*: At some level Dorothy cannot shake her Christian upbringing, despite her principled rejection of its creed. At the end of her account of her life, she said:

> We saw a crucifix . . . you know they are very realistic over there. And that crucifix, when I looked at it, made me burst into tears. That was a real religious experience.
>
> I wish that my heart were pure enough to feel that response again. To be worthy of it. I mean, I know that was *goodness*, what I felt. I felt love or something. An appreciation of sacrifice.
>
> I believe in spiritual experiences. I believe in the churches, too, but I don't think there is any Creator . . . no afterlife. Probably, I shouldn't be in the church. (P. 223)

27. Joseph Campbell, *Archetypes of the Collective Unconscious* (Princeton, 1959); and in psychology, Eric Berne, *What Do You Say After You Say Hello: The Psychology of Human Destiny* (New York, 1972); and more recently, Rollo May, *The Cry for Myth* (New York, 1991).

28. May, *The Cry for Myth*, 33.

In this view, Dorothy's life is structured around sin, and guilt, and confession, and atonement. She rebelled against God and taunts Him still. Dorothy sought her own glorification, not loving kindness; she used Caroline as an object in a social experiment. Dorothy used others, too. She sought thrills, and now she feels bad. Penance is required. She atones for her guilt by continual service to Caroline despite the resentment and accusations she makes against her and by reaching out to Alfred despite her disappointment in his failure to respond.

Those who have read Dorothy's story are often troubled by what they have been told and by the manner of its telling. Their ambivalence has a common root: this "confession" does not seem familiar. The story of Dorothy's life, or of any other person's, helps us to understand what has happened only if it makes use of one of the structures and themes embedded in our own cultural heritage; otherwise, the narrative itself is entirely problematic and the "text" will probably remain unpublished and unread.[29] Dorothy's story badly needs an interpretive theme and a recognizable structure.

A traditional biography could adopt any of the foregoing themes—trauma, rebellion, myth, or guilt—or still others, but in any case an interpretive theme must be chosen. The theme gives order, and therefore comfort. Nevertheless, it must be clear to all that the price of reassurance is often deception by authors and willful ignorance on the part of readers to the thematic possibilities not explored, to the contrary information not given, and to the biases left unacknowledged.

> I believe we know, as any historian does, that history can deliver no final truth about motives or anything else. Some readers may seek for a final truth, and even find one—but that is their private adventure.[30]

29. Patricia Ticineto Clough, *The End(s) of Ethnography* (Thousand Oaks, 1992).
30. Glendinning, "Lies...", 49.

There are other issues, too. Dorothy is made an example through biography, and the theme chosen to illuminate her life will necessarily strengthen some subcultural perspectives and undermine others. It matters to a great many people whether Dorothy is seen as a crippled neurotic, an exhausted rebel, an inspired hero, or a repentant sinner. And it matters to the interpreter, too. He is revealing something of himself in the process.

> As he pursues his research and finds out more and more about his subject, the biographer makes discoveries about himself. Features below the conscious level of his personality emerge, and what they are will depend upon the forces released by the meeting of two lives.[31]

The Biographical Project in the Social Sciences

In the social sciences, life history and autobiography, more than traditional biography, are the forms by which lives are apprehended and interpreted. In classical social science, the story of a person's life is turned into data so that by aggregation across many cases researchers can discover regularities, using valid and reliable measures of key concepts, to make law-like generalizations that are integrated into general theories.[32]

If a political scientist or sociologist were to ask why Dorothy became a political protester, he or she would seek explanation within a literature almost barren of intelligence or meaning. The dominant paradigms in mass political behavior stress social class explanations. Dorothy ranks in the top two or three percent of all Americans in her political activity: she has worked in campaigns, made financial contributions, attended meetings, written letters, and so on. Sample sur-

31. Michael Holroyd, "How I Fell Into Biography," in Homberger and Charmley, *The Troubled Face...*, 97.

32. Denzin, in his *Interpretive Biography*, summarizes this argument very well.

veys tell us that high-level participants tend to be better educated and feel more personally efficacious than most other citizens, but little else.[33] According to political science, Dorothy's life of protest is largely a product of her income and education. What kind of explanation is that? It clearly does not get at the central dynamic of her personal or political life. Dorothy herself is aware of this notion and discounts it: she tells us that some people think everything she has done is because she went to Vassar, but she notes that Vassar has turned out many conventional people too.

Somehow, mainline social science, with its emphasis on quantification, large samples, and hypothesis testing, has missed the essential point: humans are moved by complex forces that lie deeper and farther from our intelligence than social class explanations. Certainly this is true of Dorothy. Comparing her answers on a questionnaire to those of 100 others would be misguided because the core of each of the 101 would be reduced to static, non-essential characteristics.

There are also social scientists who use autobiography and life history to get at underlying dynamics. These less quantitative social scientists nevertheless seek to *explain* human behavior by objective approaches.[34]

The classical natural history approach given shape in sociology by Thomas and Znaniecki in 1918[35] and the most recent attempts to use life histories by the German sociologists who practice "objective

33. Margaret Conway, *Political Participation in the United States* (2nd edition) (Washington, DC, 1991).

34. See Denzin, *Interpretive Biography*, 49-58; Michael Mumford, Garnet S. Stokes, and William A. Owens, *Patterns of Life History: The Ecology of Human Individuality* (Hillsdale, NJ, 1990) 1190; Michail V. Angrosino, *Documents of Life: Biography, Autobiography, and Life History in Social Science Perspective* (Gainsville, 1989); Ken Plummer, *Documents of Life: An Introduction to the Problems and Literature of a Humanistic Method* (London, 1983); and Daniel Bertaux, *Biography and Society: The Life History Approach in the Social Sciences* (Beverly Hills, 1981).

35. W. I. Thomas and Florian Znaniecki. *The Polish Peasant in Europe and America*. Volumes I and II. (Chicago, 1919-20), Volumes III-V. (Boston, 1919-20).

hermeneutics"[36] both compare individual lives to analytical ideal-types, and therefore both approaches shape the life story to the interests of the researcher. Both diminish the subjective meanings of that life and privilege their own viewpoints, even though in some very important respects the classical and the hermeneutical positions are different.

Diversity within social science means that its own "truth" is also relative; social science itself is one form of intellectual game that has implications for society because it shapes our viewpoints and values about individuals and their interactions.[37]

What Do I Make of Dorothy's Life?

Aspects of the postmodern critique have made the biographical enterprise entirely problematic, whether seen from a humanistic or from a scientific perspective. Both truth and meaning have been undercut. Choosing one interpretive theme over another and adducing evidence to support that interpretation inevitably represents the life in power-filled ways.

Where does that leave us? In brief, humans need meaning and purpose in life. Stories are the repository of meaning. Language does not permit our understandings to be sealed in time; texts are not truth-filled by authors. Instead, each individual creates meaning for himself or herself from an admixture of culturally received "texts" and personal experiences. Meaning-making is political in the sense that it is based on our own interests. There is no solely objective interpretation of life. We are each configured by our station and its interests. At the end of the postmodern critique there is no community interest, only the aggregation and separation of self-interests. Communication, meaning, and community are not likely; they are only longed for.

36. Ingeborg K. Helling, "The Life History Method: A Survey and Discussion With Norman K. Denzin," *Studies in Symbolic Interactionism* (1988) 9:211-243.

37. Clough, *The End(s) of Ethnography*, 1-3; Denzin, *Interpretive Biography*, 58.

The postmodern conundrum is this: We need meaning, but we cannot have it. This position is humanly untenable and culturally nihilistic, but where is the way out for those who are responsible for asking questions and giving answers? Is there a naturally privileged position? The answer is a qualified "yes."

Empathy

In the current debate, language and interpretation are not trusted. Words are thought inevitably to shift meaning with time and distance and use. There is no standard of meaning through words as there is a standard of weight and measure in physics. The National Institute of Standards and Technology in Washington, D.C., retains the actual physical standards of weights and measures for all time in a secure vault, but there is no secure standard of language. Our dictionaries reflect the changes in meaning instead of countering them. Interpretation is merely aggrandizement.

There is, however, a standard of human communication which is pre-verbal, or at least extra-verbal, and reliable: that is *shared* emotion. Empathy does not depend on language, but on the capacity to share epiphanies.

Epiphanies are interactional moments and experiences which leave marks on people's lives. In them character is manifested. They are often moments of crisis. They alter the fundamental meaning structures in a person's life.[38]

There are different kinds of epiphanies: they range from those that touch on the center of a person's life to those that are minor or peripheral issues, and from those that culminate long-festering conflicts to those that are immediately traumatic.[39]

Epiphanies are moments when a person's ground of meaning shifts. We can find evidence of them in artifacts, but if we encounter the person at these times and share the emotional content of the ex-

38. Denzin, *Interpretive Biography*, 70.

39. Denzin, *Interpretive Biography*, 71.

perience, then we have given and received deeply human messages that are not dependent on words for their content or effect. Empathy—our capacity to feel what others feel yet not to lose our selves in the process—privileges us. Those who empathize share meaning before language gives name to the body's movement.

Lives can be interpreted from a variety of positions. Meaning can be imposed on lives by those who write or tell the stories, but these stories should not be given special privilege unless they are assayed for the immediacy and authenticity of their emotional content.

Dorothy has told her story, and any one of four paradigmatic themes seems well-suited to frame an interpretation of her life. The consequence of any choice is to advance some worldviews and some values over others in the contest for the social and economic rewards that come from interactions with each other. In that way, willfully or naively, biographical interpretation is a political act. So let me ask: When we write Dorothy's life, shall we advance therapists, feminists, mythologists, or Christians? And can we do otherwise?

Empathy is pre-political because it is unselfconscious. The life history is created through interaction, and on those occasions when distance between the subject and interviewer is lost, political agendas are shed in favor of shared humanity. Pain is pain, and loss is loss.

During the years that Dorothy and I talked with each other, there were moments of epiphany. Perhaps the most important was in her "confession" to me that she had used Caroline (née Carrie Mae) to test her sociological notions and that she was, at the end, a closet racist. Dorothy was pushed to face herself, and she did: her feelings of anger, fear, acceptance, and loss came in their turn. She *felt* what she had otherwise only intellectually entertained. The text does not bear out this interpretation quite as fully as our feelings did. I provoked the anger, but I shared the agony and the release. I empathized. I felt, if only for a while, the pain of that awful but liberating recognition.

Dorothy was different with me after that confrontation. She no longer exaggerated her public face to draw attention from her private wounds; she did not stridently defy and then retreat from her interlocutor, a Southern male after all, and one who could betray her trust, but became more and more unwilling to reenact old gender games; and she gave up St. Joan. From time to time she sought to recover the high ground of moral superiority in the telling of her story, but that did not last. What did last was the change in her relations with Caroline and Alfred. The experiment was over. She no longer sought to control them. She accorded them real dignity and equality as fellow human beings. More and more, she shared her true feelings: she was not the teacher/mother/experimenter/redeemer any more; instead she was herself, and dealt with them as autonomous adults whose behavior she might dislike but whose fundamental right to direct their own lives she accepted. They were separated from her, yet reconnected in some new way. In freeing herself from the burden of hypocrisy about race, she could accept the natural obligations of real relationships. In her own life Dorothy had made decisions that affected deeply the lives of others, and now she could choose to live out with care the implications of those decisions.

That is the meaning I make from Dorothy's confession to us. It is not a story about the truth of a past life so much as it is an inspiration for a new one. A life is continually being re-written; there is always more to say.

Epilogue

A Biographical Voice

After I met Dorothy that first summer, I did write part of her story in the traditional biographical mode, and in my own academic voice, for my book about Mobile's racial politics. What I said there was grounded in public documents and that first, traditional interview. What follows is that preliminary biographical sketch. Only the last paragraph is a recent addition. Some will say this biographical sketch is not enough; some will say that it is too much.

Mobile's First Attempt at School Desegregation

The letter, dated September 3, 1956, was addressed to Kenneth W. Reed, President of the Mobile Board of School Commissioners. "Dear Mr. Reed," it began, "I am asking you as president of our school board for individual placement of my foster-daughter, a little Negro girl. This child is named Carrie Mae McCants. She is twelve years old and has been educated in various schools in Europe for the past two years."[1] This simple request broke a cultural taboo. It was a first attempt to desegregate the Mobile public schools, and it was made by an upper-class white woman. The writer, Mrs. Dorothy Danner DaPonte, then forty, was the only child of a wealthy Mobile businessman, and with this petition she stepped firmly outside the magic circle of Southern society.

The United States Supreme Court had rendered unconstitutional "separate-but-equal" schools in 1954, but it had not fixed a specific

1. Copy in Pride files.

date for this to happen. Instead, the court ordered segregated school systems to desegregate "with all deliberate speed." In Alabama, as all across the deep South, public officials adopted a policy of massive resistance to court-ordered desegregation. Newly enacted state laws and local policies would serve as renewable barricades behind which the norms of the old South could be protected. Lengthy litigation over the constitutionality of these laws meant change would come only much later, if ever.[2]

Alabama enacted its Pupil Placement Law in August, 1955. It placed final authority for student assignment with local school boards who were to study the issue and make policies affecting pupil placement that took into account available space, the effect of new pupils on the established or proposed academic program, the scholastic preparation and ability of the student, the effect of admission upon the prevailing academic standards, the home environment of the student, and the possibility of friction or disorder among students or others, among many other considerations.[3] Although racially neutral on its face, there could be no doubt what was intended by the law. In August 1956, Alabama voters amended the state constitution to empower the legislature to abolish public schools if necessary to prevent integration. The amendment also authorized state aid for private schools, the sale or gift of public facilities to private owners who could operate them as segregated academies, and freedom of choice for parents to send their children to schools attended only by members of their own race.

That DaPonte Woman.

Who was Dorothy DaPonte and why did she challenge the established patterns of Southern life? Mrs. DaPonte was born Dorothy Danner in February, 1916, into a conventional and well-to-do Mobile

2. Harrell R. Rogers, Jr. and Charles S. Bullock III, *Law and Social Change: Civil Rights Laws and Their Consequences* (Boston, 1972) 72; Charles S. Bullock III and Charles M. Lamb, *Implementation of Civil Rights Policy* (Belmont, Calif., 1984) 56.

3. Alabama Code 58 Title 52 Section 61 (1) et seq.

family. Dorothy's mother died when she was thirteen, and Paul Danner, her reserved and sometimes bewildered father, did the best he could to raise his intelligent and strong-willed daughter in the manner of Southern women of their station. He sent her to a private boarding school in Mississippi for a few years, but she was not happy there. Ultimately she was permitted to return and graduate from Murphy High School, the jewel of the white Mobile public schools. She went to Holton Arms in Washington, D.C., for a finishing year. She participated in the social seasons of Mobile, and her relatives were queens, maids, and knights at Mardi Gras—honors seldom given to those who did not have the traditions of Mobile and the South near their hearts.[4] But unlike her nominal sisters, who would marry and settle down, or sometimes go to Agnes Scott or to Sweet Briar for further education, Dorothy Danner chose to attend Vassar College in Poughkeepsie, New York, where she was graduated in 1939.

What was a well-educated, free-thinking, and unmarried young woman to do with herself in Mobile, Alabama? After a summer marked by indecision, her father encouraged her to take a job with the WPA in Jasper, Alabama, where she interviewed country folks who needed government assistance. There Dorothy became isolated and bored, and after many months she quit. In the company of a friend, Sarah Harris from Tuscaloosa, she took off for Greenwich Village. In 1941 she celebrated her twenty-fifth birthday amid the adventures of New York City.

With the outbreak of World War II she returned to Mobile, but she was never again to fit comfortably into the culture of her birth. She remained unmarried until 1944 when, after a very brief courtship, she married a Dutchman, M. Nicolo DaPonte, who worked for the Royal Netherlands Steamship Company in Mobile. DaPonte proved to be a heavy drinker and killed himself just six months later with a gun given to him for Christmas by Dorothy's father.

4. *Alabama Journal*, Sept. 15, 1956.

EPILOGUE

Motherless, childless, and now widowed, Dorothy retired to the family cabin on Dog River, just south of Mobile. She became a pacifist and in the late 1940s refused to pay her income taxes in protest of war, until the government compelled her to do so. She became antivivisectionist and still later an animal rights advocate. Perhaps because she felt like a victim of cruel fate herself, she began to support others diminished in life, including blacks. When Marie Gayle was beaten and kicked by a bus driver and other white men for refusing to move to the back of the bus, Dorothy Daponte paid $1200 to a Birmingham attorney to prosecute the bus company; the verdict was that no more force had been used than necessary. This incident fueled her outrage, and she began to fight for the rights of other black people armed with her own money and the law. She found her only comfort within The Fellowship of Reconciliation, an inter-racial pacifist support group.

In 1949 she began her relationship with Carrie Mae McCants, the five-year-old daughter of her servant. The need to love and be loved gave impetus to the relationship, and in time she took Carrie Mae into her home and like a distaff Henry Higgins began the slow process of creating Caroline out of the rough stuff of Carrie Mae. She wanted to show, her friends later said, that culture and graciousness could be brought into being by environment as well as by heredity.[5]

The journey embarked upon was both literal and figurative. Carrie Mae lived with Dorothy DaPonte but went to "colored" schools in Mobile during the early grades, where she excelled. Mrs. DaPonte then took her ward to Europe, and the schools Carrie Mae attended show the pair's itinerary and Carrie Mae's progress. In sixth grade: Ecole de Fils, Versailles; American Community School, Paris; Miss Barry's American School, Florence. For summer school: La Chatelainie, Neuchatel. For the seventh grade: French Lycée de Londres, London; American Dependent School, Heidelberg; and Ackworth Friends Schools, Yorkshire. For the eighth grade, the peripatetic pair were back in Mobile. Carrie Mae was ready.

5. *Ibid.*

Dorothy DaPonte knew what she was doing when she wrote her letter to the school board. She knew the Southern way of life and she knew the law. She wrote, "I have brought up Carrie Mae myself since she was six-and-a-half years old. Her background academically, morally and socially is adequate for her entrance into an integrated school." She continued:

> The "psychological effect" on her would be good as she has attended schools with white pupils for two years now. She would understand the significance of her position and is prepared by personal character, intelligence, and training to conduct herself in such manner as to minimize the possibility of friction and disorder.
>
> Such acceptance of her would give the Negro race an opportunity to show what their development can be under favorable circumstances. It would give Alabama a chance to show good faith in a case where there is no danger of large numbers or lowering of standards.

Mr. Reed, president, replied for the board. He said that acts of the state legislature and recent revision of the state constitution had yet to be fully studied. In the meantime, planning for the current year had been done "on the basis of a continuation of the segregation status that was maintained during the last term. It is physically and financially impossible to make any change during the current term. There is a pupil-load in this county in excess of 52,000, and a material shortage in physical housing." Reed concluded his letter by saying that "it is not possible . . . to make exceptions of this type."

A policy adopted by the board in 1955, following the Supreme Court's decision in Brown II and close upon the passage of Alabama's Pupil Law, more than the letter, showed the board's thinking. The policy statement included this rationale:

> It must be recognized that integration is not acceptable to the major portion of our people. This is a factor that can-

> not be ignored, as was recognized by the Supreme Court in its decree implementing its decisions. The accomplishment of a full and complete result; which the bulk of our people feel was imposed on them by a superior power that, as they see it, was without adequate appreciation of the sociological, factual and psychological conditions of our people; may not be had with one blow. The traditions of two centuries can be altered by degrees only.[6]

Denial of Carrie Mae's assignment to a white school was not a matter of inadequate space; it was a matter of cultural norms. That a well-prepared black child sponsored by a privileged white lady could not be reassigned was a sign of how slowly the board was prepared to turn away from segregation.

Others in the community made it known that even to have asked was too much. On September 12, 1956, a small story was printed in the local newspaper summarizing DaPonte's petition.[7] On the night of September 12, eighteen cars with about a hundred white-robed men drove into Mrs. DaPonte's driveway with horns blaring. They erected and ignited a ten-foot cross.[8] After milling about and shouting, the caravan left. "That DaPonte woman" and Carrie Mae were not at home. Days later another cross was burned at the home of a friend with whom she was staying. Reflecting in 1956 on her experience, she said, "The main reason my friends and relatives are afraid to mix with me is because they are afraid to be burned out."[9]

The burning of crosses was not all that happened. "Obscene calls and letters flooded my home and the homes of my friends and family," she recalled. Her father, one of her sharpest critics, fled to Mississippi to get away from it all. "Of course I know the rumors that are being circulated by low-lifes and trash," she said. "My friends and some of my family are beginning to believe some of these awful accusations that I'm Carrie Mae's mother." Salacious gossip argued that

6. Copy in Pride files.
7. *Mobile Press Register*, Sept. 12, 1956.
8. *Mobile Press Register*, Sept. 18, 1956.
9. *New York Post*, Nov. 11, 1956.

her husband had committed suicide when he found out the "true circumstances" surrounding Dorothy and Carrie Mae. "I can prove any time that I am not the child's mother. But I won't give anyone that satisfaction until I'm forced to," she said.[10] She vowed to press for Carrie Mae's reassignment in court. In the meantime, Carrie Mae would once again attend black schools in Mobile. Over the years, Dorothy and Carrie Mae faded from public life in Mobile and became increasingly estranged from their roots and from each other.

The marauding Klan harassed Mrs. Daponte, and it signaled to others that the color line was not to be broken with impunity. They burned other crosses in the city; at night they paraded in full regalia down the main street of the city; they ran ads in the local newspaper; and they bombed several black homes. A newly organized Mobile Council on Human Relations, an affiliate of the Alabama Council on Human Relations and the Southern Regional Council, petitioned the city commission to pass ordinances curbing violence and intimidation by the Klan. This led to more disturbances and greater efforts to cow white liberals sympathetic to school desegregation. City fathers vowed to keep order but otherwise did not address publicly the underlying issues of race and class.[11]

School desegregation in Mobile subsided as a focus of concern. Between 1956 and 1963, under the state's Pupil Placement Law, not a single black child was admitted to a white public school.[12]

The experiment in living that was begun so impulsively and hopefully in 1950 ended regretfully and unceremoniously in 1990 with Dorothy's "confession." But the complex relationship of these proud women, Dorothy and Caroline, forged by the stress of intense social and personal conflict, continued to unfold as each came to fashion and to refashion her life in the telling and retelling of her story.

10. *Ibid.*

11. Albert S. Foley, S.J., "The Dynamics of School Desegregation in Mobile, Alabama," National Insitute of Education Project, Harvard Graduate School of Education (Boston, 1978), 6.

12. Foley, 8.

BIBLIOGRAPHY

INDEX

Bibliography

Aaron, Daniel. *Studies in Biography*. Harvard English Studies, no. 8. Cambridge: Harvard University Press, 1978.

Abbott, Shirley. *Womenfolks: Growing Up Down South*. New York: Ticknor and Fields, 1983.

Alexander, Maxine, ed. *Speaking for Ourselves*. New York: Pantheon, 1983, 1984.

Angrosino, Michael V. *Documents of Interaction: Biography, Autobiography, and Life History in Social Science Perspective*. Gainsville: University of Florida Press, 1989.

Ashley, Kathleen, Leigh Gilmore, and Gerald Peters. *Autobiography and Postmodernism*. Amherst: University of Massachusetts Press, 1994.

Barnard, Hollinger F., ed. *Outside the Magic Circle: The Autobiography of Virginia Foster Durr*. University: University of Alabama Press, 1985.

Baron, Samuel H., and Carl Pletsch, eds. *Introspection in Biography: The Biographer's Quest for Self-Awareness*. Hillsdale, N.J.: Analytic Press, 1985.

Berne, Eric. *What Do You Say After You Say Hello: The Psychology of Human Destiny*. New York: Grove Press, 1972.

Bernhard, Virginia, and Betty Brandon, Elizabeth Fox-Genovese, and Theda Perdue, eds. *Southern Women: Histories and Identities*. Columbia: University of Missouri Press, 1992.

Bertaux, Daniel, ed. *Biography and Society: The Life History Approach in the Social Sciences*. Beverly Hills, Calif.: Sage, 1981.

Bleser, Carol, ed. *In Joy and in Sorrow: Women, Family, and Marriage in the Victorian South, 1830–1900*. New York: Oxford University Press, 1991.

Brantley, Will. *Feminine Sense in Southern Memoir*. Jackson: University of Mississippi Press, 1993.

Brown, Dorothy M. *Setting a Course: American Women in the 1920s*. Boston: Twayne Publishers, 1987.

Campbell, Joseph. *Archetypes of the Collective Unconscious*. Princeton: Bollinger Press, 1959.

Chernin, Kim. *Crossing the Border: An Erotic Journey*. New York: Fawcett

Columbine, 1994.

Clough, Patricia Ticineto. *The End(s) of Ethnography: From Realism to Social Criticism*. Newbury Park, Calif.: Sage, 1992.

Daniell, Rosemary. *Fatal Flowers: On Sin, Sex, and Suicide in the Deep South*. New York: Avon, 1980.

Denman, Rose Mary. *Let My People in: A Lesbian Minister Tells of Her Struggles to Live Openly and Maintain Her Ministry*. New York: Morrow, 1990.

Denzin, Norman K. *Interpretive Biography*. Newbury Park, Calif.: Sage, 1989.

Dillman, Caroline M., ed. *Southern Women*. New York: Hemisphere, 1988.

Doyle, Don H. *New Men, New Cities, New South*. Chapel Hill: University of North Carolina Press, 1990.

Edel, Leon. *Writing Lives: Principia Biographica*. New York: Norton, 1984.

Freud, Sigmund, and William C. Bullit. *Thomas Woodrow Wilson, Twenty-Eighth President of the United States*. Boston: Houghton Mifflin, 1967.

Fromm, Gloria G., ed. *Essaying Biography: A Celebration for Leon Edel*. Honolulu: Published for Biographical Research Center by University of Hawaii Press, 1986.

Gaventa, John. *Power and Powerlessness: Quiescence and Rebellion in an Appalachian Valley*. Urbana: University of Illinois Press, 1980.

George, Alexander and Julliette. *Woodrow Wilson and Colonel House: A Personal Study*. New York: John Day, 1956.

Gilligan, Carol. *In A Different Voice: Psychological Theory and Women's Development*. Cambridge: Harvard University Press, 1982.

Gillmore, Leigh. *Autobiographics: A Feminist Theory of Women's Self-Representation*. Ithaca, N.Y.: Cornell University Press, 1994.

Glaser, Chris. *Uncommon Calling: A Gay Man's Struggle to Serve the Church*. San Francisco: Harper and Row, 1988.

Greenstein, Fred I. *Personality and Politics: Problems of Evidence, Inference, and Conceptualization*. Chicago: Markham, 1969.

Hartnett, Koula Svokos. *Zelda Fitzgerald and the Failure of the American Dream for Women*. New York: Peter Lang, 1991.

Hawks, Joanne V., and Sheila L. Skemp, eds. *Sex, Race, and the Role of Women in the South*. Jackson: University Press of Mississippi, 1983.

Hollinger, Robert. *Postmodernism and the Social Sciences*. Thousand Oaks, Calif.: Sage, 1994.

Holmes, Richard. *Footsteps: Adventures of a Romantic Biographer*. New York: Viking, 1985.

Homberger, Eric, and John Charmley. *The Troubled Face of Biography*. New York: St. Martin's, 1988.

Jelinek, Estelle C. *The Tradition of Women's Autobiography: From Antiquity to the Present*. Boston: Twayne Publishers, 1986.

Langness, L. L. and Gelya Frank, *Lives: An Anthropological Approach to Biography*. Navato, Calif.: Chandler and Sharp, 1981.

Lasswell, Harold D. *Psychopathology and Politics*. Chicago: University of Chicago Press, 1930; reprinted in *The Political Writings of Harold D. Lasswell*. Glencoe, Ill.: Free Press, 1951.

Lomask, Milton. *The Biographer's Craft*. New York: Harper and Row, 1986.

Manning, Carol, ed. *The Female Tradition in Southern Literature*. Urbana: University of Illinois Press, 1993.

Matthews, Holly F., ed. *Women in the South: An Anthropological Perspective*. Athens: University of Georgia Press, 1989.

May, Rollo. *The Cry for Myth*. New York: Norton, 1991.

Mellow, James R. *Invented Lives: F. Scott and Zelda Fitzgerald*. Boston: Houghton Mifflin Company, 1984.

Meyers, Jeffrey, ed. *The Craft of Literary Biography*. New York: Schocken Books, 1985.

———, ed. *The Biographer's Art: New Essays*. New York: Macmillan Press, 1989.

Moraitis, George, and George H. Pollack, eds. *Psychoanalytic Studies of Biography*. Madison: International Universities Press, 1987.

Mumford, Michael, Garnett S. Stokes, and William A. Owens. *Patterns of Life History: The Ecology of Human Individuality*. Hillsdale, N.J.: Lawrence Erlbaum and Associates, 1990.

Nadel, Ira Bruce. *Biography: Fiction, Fact and Form*. New York: St. Martin's, 1984.

Noun, Louise R., ed. *More Strong-minded Women: Iowa Feminists Tell Their Stories*. Ames: Iowa State University Press, 1992.

Novarr, David. *The Lines of Life: Theories of Biography*. West Lafayette: Purdue University Press, 1986.

Oates, Stephen B., ed. *Biography As High Adventure: Life-Writers Speak on Their Craft*. Amherst: University of Massachusetts Press, 1986.

Olney, James, ed. *Studies in Autobiography*. New York: Oxford University Press, 1988.

Plummer, Ken. *Documents of Life: An Introduction to the Problems and Literature of a Humanistic Method*. London: George Allen and Unwin, 1983.

Reynolds, Larry. *Interactionism: Exposition and Critique*. 2d ed. Dix Hills, N.Y.: General Hall, 1993.

Riley, Glenda. *Inventing the American Woman: A Perspective on Women's History, 1865 to the Present*. Arlington Heights, Ill.: Harlan Davidson, 1986.

Rodgers, Harrell R., Jr., and Charles S. Bullock III. *Law and Social Change: Civil Rights Laws and Their Consequences*. New York: McGraw-Hill, 1972.

Scott, Anne Firor. *Making the Invisible Woman Visible*. Urbana: University of Illinois Press, 1984.

———. *The Southern Lady: From Pedestal to Politics, 1830–1930*. Chicago: University of Chicago Press, 1970.

———, ed. *What Is Happening To American Women*. Atlanta: Southern Newspaper Publishers Association, 1970.

Sims, Anastatia. *Feminism and Femininity in the New South: White Women's Organizations in North Carolina, 1883–1930*. Ann Arbor, Mich.: University Microfilms, 1985.

Steffan, Joseph. *Honor Bound: A Gay American Fights for the Right to Serve His Country*. New York: Villard, 1992.

Strachey, Lytton. *Eminent Victorians*. Garden City, N.Y.: Garden City, 1918.

Thomas, W. I. and Florian Znaniecki. *The Polish Peasant in Europe and America: Monograph of an Immigrant Group*. 4 vols. Chicago: University of Chicago Press, 1918–20.

Veninga, James F., ed. *The Biographer's Gift: Life Histories and Humanism*. College Station: Texas A & M Press, 1983.

Wagner-Martin, Linda. *Telling Women's Lives: The New Biography*. New Brunswick: Rutgers University Press, 1994.

Wedell, Marsha. *Elite Women and the Reform Impulse in Memphis, 1875–1915*. Knoxville: University of Tennessee Press, 1991.

Whittemore, Reed. *Whole Lives: Shapers of Modern Biography*. Baltimore: Johns Hopkins University Press, 1989.

Zinsser, William, ed. *Extraordinary Lives: The Art and Craft of American Biography*. New York: American Heritage, 1986.

Index

INDEX

INDEX

INDEX

THE CONFESSION OF DOROTHY DANNER

was composed electronically using
Weiss Roman types, designed by Emil Weiss
and originally cut by the Bauer Type Foundry in 1928.
The book was printed on Glatfelter Natural paper,
an acid-free recycled sheet, Smyth-sewn and
bound in Holliston Kingston cloth by Thompson-Shore, Inc.
Book and jacket designs are the work of Gary Gore.
Published by Vanderbilt University Press
Nashville, Tennessee 37235